The Treasure of

RENNES-LE-CHATEAU

A Mystery Solved

BILL PUTNAM & JOHN EDWIN WOOD

SUTTON PUBLISHING

To Janet and Maureen, without
whom this book would never have
been written.

First published in the United Kingdom in 2003 by
Sutton Publishing Limited · Phoenix Mill
Thrupp · Stroud · Gloucestershire · GL5 2BU

This new revised paperback edition first published in 2005

British Library Cataloguing in Publication Data
A catalogue record for this book is available from the British Library.

ISBN 0 7509 4216 9

Typeset in 10/14 pt Times.
Typesetting and origination by
Sutton Publishing Limited.
Printed and bound in England by
J.H. Haynes & Co. Ltd, Sparkford.

Contents

Figures in text

List of Plates

Preface to the Paperback Edition

The Da Vinci Code and Rennes-le-Château

A few months after the publication of the first edition of this book, Dan Brown's novel, *The Da Vinci Code*, appeared on the bookshelves. Its sales have been sensational, and it has created much interest and controversy, for the novel proposes that the whole of the Christian tradition is founded on a myth: Christ did not die on the cross, but survived, married Mary Magdalene and had descendants, some of whom may be living and walking among us even today.

Central to the plot of the novel is the idea that the truth about Jesus and Mary was known to a small group of initiates known as the Priory of Sion, who had kept the secret in existence, yet hidden from public knowledge, for many centuries. The Grand Masters of the Priory of Sion were an illustrious group which includes some of the most famous men who have ever lived, including Sir Isaac Newton, Sandro Botticelli, Victor Hugo and Leonardo da Vinci.

If this novel had been received simply as a work of fiction, it may have been widely read, but it would not have attracted the same degree of critical attention. Dan Brown gave his book an authority which novelists do not normally claim, by asserting right at the beginning of the book that it is based on facts. 'The Priory of Sion – a European secret society founded in 1099 – is a real organisation.' 'All descriptions of artwork, architecture, documents and secret rituals in this novel are accurate.' The characters are obviously not real people, but the reader who has not made a particular study of such matters as medieval history or the origins of Christianity is left in doubt as to what, in the mass of historical information presented by the author, is fact and what is fiction. The didactic way in which this is presented and the firm assertions at the beginning of the book would lead one to suppose that the book is soundly based on fact.

Little wonder then that the novel has become a best seller, or that it has resulted in a flood of reviews, articles and features in the glossy magazines. Already there are books which discuss seriously the historical and theological background to the story and several films, both documentary and entertainment, are in the schedules. Various places mentioned in the novel, such as the Louvre and the church of Saint-Sulpice in Paris, have attracted visitors who want to see where dramatic incidents were located and travel agents have not been slow in organising 'Da Vinci Code Tours'.

But to anyone who has read almost any book about Rennes-le-Château, the sources for *The Da Vinci Code* are familiar. Although Dan Brown nowhere mentions the little village in the south of France, he nevertheless reminds us of it in the very first chapter. His museum curator is called Saunière, the same name as the parish priest. Much of the inspiration from the book is clearly derived from *The Holy Blood and the Holy Grail* (published in USA under the title *Holy Blood, Holy Grail*) by Baigent, Leigh and Lincoln and this is tacitly acknowledged in the name of the English historian who figures so prominently in the novel. Leigh Teabing is a combination of the name of the second author together with an anagram of the name of the first. More obscurely, the Police Captain is called Bezu Fache, and Bézu is a place near Rennes-le-Château associated with the Templars.

The supposed discovery of the treasure at Rennes-le-Château and the strange events that followed have caused many books to be written which have greatly enlarged the scope of the story. It is this second wave of fantasy that Brown has enthusiastically adopted. He has made use of many of the accretions and ramifications to the original tale, bringing in Saint-Sulpice and its meridian line, the *Bibliothèque nationale* and the *Dossiers secrets*, the Golden Mean and Fibonacci numbers. The Priory of Sion figures prominently; it and its list of Grand Masters is central to the plot. All these topics are covered in later pages of the book you are about to read.

When we wrote this book there was considerable interest in the mystery of Rennes-le-Château, and a steady stream of books, articles and web sites perpetuating the myth. In comparison there was very little available, in English especially, which attempted to set the record straight and give a fair critical account of the historical events. The huge success of *The Da Vinci Code* has stimulated even more interest than existed before. Some of the older books have been re-issued and because of the exposure on television a new generation has become aware of this amazing historical mystery. Although some newspaper articles, and one television programme (*The Real Da Vinci Code*, broadcast in the United Kingdom by Channel 4 on 3 February 2005) have been analytical and factual, it seems that the myth of Rennes-le-Château, Saunière's treasure and all the rest of it will continue much as before. There is still a need for books like this one to expose the falsehood and deception.

In this edition we have taken the opportunity to correct a few errors (for which we apologise) and update the account where new information has come to light.

Preface

It is said that nearly three hundred books have been written about the mystery of Rennes-le-Château. In addition several television programmes have appeared; there have been conferences in academic institutions and now there are many web sites. Surely everything that could be said about the supposed discovery of treasure by an obscure priest in a tiny village in a remote part of France must, by now, have been said several times over. So why do we think we ought to add another book to the pile?

Well, primarily because of the nature of the books that have been written. The first book, *L'Or de Rennes* by Gérard de Sède, published in October 1967, caught the interest of the public, mainly in France, and then the television programme for the BBC's *Chronicle* series, *The Lost Treasure of Jerusalem,* researched by Henry Lincoln and transmitted in 1972, introduced Rennes-le-Château to English speakers. The story is fascinating, with the discovery of treasure, hints of secret societies, conspiracies and cover-up, ancient religions and the foundations of Christianity. No wonder that numerous people were inspired to join the hunt for more to add to the story. And indeed, they did add more and more.

Naturally, authors based their interpretations and hypotheses on the published works that had preceded theirs. Some acknowledged that perhaps hard evidence was lacking for a few of the basic facts; but the strange story of Rennes-le-Château, its priest Bérenger Saunière and his undoubted lavish spending, had been presented with quoted sources, seemed plausible and was credibly received. A few books, published in France, did question the basis of the accepted account, but in England there has been no book written with the aim of critically examining the source of the mystery and asking what facts are supported by hard evidence and what is supposition.

The claims for historical interpretation and reinterpretation (especially by recent authors) which are derived from the story of Rennes are so astounding that it is essential to test the strength of their foundations. This is what we have attempted to do. One of us (W.G.P.) is a professional archaeologist, the other (J.E.W.) studied physics. We have tried to look at the evidence in the same way that we would approach a problem in our own specialist fields, not with the intention of supporting or rebutting any particular theory, but asking what information is reliable and what seems suspect. We do come to some conclusions about the source of the story and although our findings are less sensational than some others that have been published, they are quite surprising nevertheless.

Acknowledgements

We are grateful to many friends and experts who have helped us with research for this book, especially Dom Cuthbert Brogan, OSB, Prior of Farnborough Abbey, for giving us access to rare books in the Abbey Library; Sylvie Caucanas, Director of the Departmental Archives at Carcassonne, who has supplied us with copies of material from the archives; Michael Costen, Centre for the Historical Environment at the University of Bristol, who helped us with research into the Cathars; Henry Lincoln, who brought Rennes-le-Château to the notice of the British public, and kindly discussed his findings with us; Sandrine Metgé, of Angers, who has helped us in several ways; Hector Parr, for valuable advice relating to the mathematics of ley lines and for the computer program in Appendix F; and Catherine Verdier-Stott, for help with some tricky aspects of French translation. We also thank Paul Smith for his useful comments on the first edition of this book, and Wieland Willker for the source of the text of Manuscript 2.

We also acknowledge the help of Michael Butler of Maiden Newton, Dorset, Celia Brook-Captier of Rennes-le-Château, Bill Cran of Invision Productions, Jim Davies of Weymouth, Dorset, Professor Charles Thomas of the Cornish Institute, Marilyn Richardson of Hatfield, Ian and Katherine Vibert-Stokes of Perruche du Buis and Lionel French, who first introduced us to the story of Rennes-le-Château.

We would like to thank the following authors and publishers who have kindly allowed us to reproduce extracts and/or illustrations from their books or films: The BBC and Bill Cran for extracts from his film *The History of a Mystery*; the BBC for extracts from the *Chronicle* programme *Shadow of the Templars*; Cassell & Co. for a passage from *Secret Societies* by David D. Barrett; Bibliothèque nationale de France for extracts from *Généalogie des Rois mérovingiens* and *Dossiers secrets* by Henri Lobineau, extracts from *Un Trésor mérovingien à Rennes-le-Château* by Antoine L'Ermite, and for figure 7.3; Bill Kersey of DEK Publishing for extracts from *L'Or de Rennes* by Gérard de Sède; *La Dépêche du Midi*, for extracts from issues of 12, 13 and 14 January 1956; Philippe Contal (www.cathares.org) for Plate 4 and the cover; and the Musée du Louvre for Plate 34.

All photographs not otherwise acknowledged are by the authors.

1

The Mystery

This book is about a hoard of treasure – or maybe it is not. We don't know, but one thing we are sure about is that in the last decade of the nineteenth century a poor priest of a remote village in the south of France suddenly began to spend huge sums of money. There is no doubt about this – what he spent it on can be seen to this day in the village where he lived: his house, his library, his garden and the lavish decor of the interior of his church. It has always been a mystery where the money came from. Many people think that he found a treasure, but even now no one knows exactly what the treasure was, where it is, or even if it ever existed.

Yet inside the church, everywhere you look, there are strange and unexpected little details in the numerous paintings and statues. Perhaps the priest, not wanting his secret to die with him, had them included to give clues to the source of his wealth. But are they really clues? A lot of people have thought so and have tried to interpret them. For the last half-century they have descended on this tiny village with plans and spades and picks and even dynamite. Signs of their excavations are still visible as gaping holes in the grounds of the presbytery. Eventually the authorities were obliged to erect a large notice warning the visitors *Les FOUILLES sont INTERDITES* . . . EXCAVATIONS are FORBIDDEN (Pl. 2). Treasure-hunting was banned. No hoards of treasure have ever been found, so if it really existed some of it may still be there.

The village is called Rennes-le-Château (Pl. 3). It is in the Department of Aude, in part of southern France known as the Languedoc. Deep valleys and forest-clad hilltops are set against the distant view of the snow-clad mountains of the Pyrenees. The capital of the Department is the ancient walled city of Carcassonne. Aude is an area that has seen much history, turbulent and tragic. The Romans left their imprint here, and after the fall of Rome came the Visigoths. In the twelfth century it was a stronghold of the Cathars, an ascetic Christian sect who were suppressed by the king of France with awful cruelty, leaving the ruins of their fortresses crowning the precipitous peaks. The Knights Templar also built castles in the area, and less than a century after the end of the Cathars met a similarly ruthless fate at the hands of the Church of Rome.

It is to the Church that we turn now, for the first major character in our story is the priest. The following is an outline of the story as told by many books.

Bérenger Saunière (Pl. 6) was born at Montazels on 11 April 1852, one of eight children of Joseph and Marguerite Saunière. Bérenger had a brother Alfred, three years

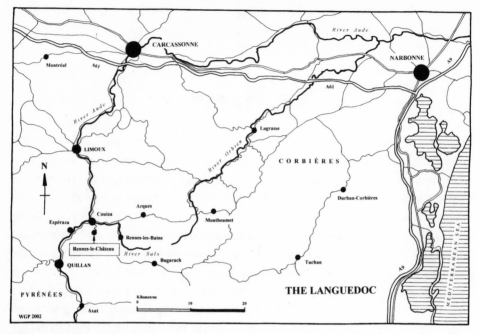

1.1 Map of the Languedoc.

his junior, and the two men were particularly close, perhaps because Alfred also trained for the priesthood, perhaps because they shared secrets that were known to very few.

The young Bérenger went to the school of St Louis at Limoux, a small market town only a few miles from Rennes-le-Château, then on to study at the Seminary in Carcassonne, where he was ordained in 1879. His first appointment was as *vicaire* (curate) at Alet-les-Bains, another nearby town. Three years after that, in 1882, he was promoted to *curé desservant* (priest-in-charge) at Le Clat, a hamlet less than 10 miles to the south. This was almost his final move. He lived the whole of his life in the same small area around the place of his birth, in the valleys of the Aude and the Sals, and among the wooded hills which surround them.

On 1 June 1885, Bérenger Saunière was appointed to be *curé* (parish priest) of Rennes-le-Château, a little village of 298 inhabitants. It is at this point that we have the first indication of troubles to come. Bérenger had royalist leanings and was not favourably disposed to the government who at that time paid the salaries of priests. Unwisely, he made critical speeches from the pulpit. He was reprimanded by his bishop and temporarily suspended, making him unable to take up his appointment for a whole year.

When he finally arrived at Rennes, Bérenger Saunière found that his new parish was very poor. The houses were ruinous, there was no reliable water supply and the village was only accessible with pack animals. His own salary was extremely low and he was forced into supplementing his diet with fish and game, which he caught himself.

The church, like the houses in the village, was in a terrible state of decay. Bérenger immediately set to work on restoration, using the limited funds that could be raised in such a poor community. In the church he began work on the dilapidated altar. It is said that during the demolition he found some parchments concealed in a hollow pillar, which had been made out of part of an ancient Visigothic column and reused as an altar support. Another version of this story says that the parchments were in a glass phial, which he found in a hollow pillar at the foot of the tower staircase.

Whichever way it may have happened, the discovery of the parchments had startling results. Copies of two of them survive. They were in Latin, and contained passages from the New Testament. Careful scrutiny showed that they concealed secret messages, in one case by the addition of extra letters to the Latin text, in the other by the displacement of certain letters in the text itself.

The hidden message in the second parchment could be easily read. It spoke of treasure belonging to King Dagobert II, a Merovingian King of the seventh century. But the extra letters of the first parchment were in a code which has proved very hard to break. While Saunière might well have understood the message about the treasure, he would have needed help decoding the message the first parchment contained.

Some versions of the story relate that Saunière took these parchments to his bishop in Carcassonne, and then went to Paris to obtain advice on their meaning. He is said to have consulted Emile Hoffet, the nephew of the Director of the Seminary at the Church of Saint-Sulpice, and an expert in linguistic studies. While Hoffet was busy with the parchments, Saunière managed to get himself introduced into Parisian society and met some of the most glittering people of the time, including the composer Debussy and the renowned opera singer Emma Calvé.

It is said that he also visited the Louvre, and purchased copies of three paintings, including one by Nicolas Poussin, *Les Bergers d'Arcadie* (The Shepherds of Arcady). This painting shows a tomb in an idyllic landscape with shepherds pointing at an inscription on its side – *Et in Arcadia Ego* (Even I, Death, am in Arcady). The tomb in the painting resembles a tomb by the roadside near Arques (Pl. 5), a village a few miles east of Rennes-le-Château. The background of the painting resembles the actual landscape south of Arques. Was it possible that in the seventeenth century Poussin was aware of some important secret and had left this painting as a clue? The parchments hinted at this, because when the difficult one was deciphered, part of the message read 'Poussin holds the key'.

3

On his return to Rennes-le-Château, Saunière resumed his restorations, dismissing his workmen and carrying out much of the work himself. The workmen reported seeing the glint of metal in the excavations before they left. At about this time he found the entrance to a tomb, a discovery which he recorded in his diary.

In the summer of 1891, Saunière set up a new statue of the Virgin Mary just outside the church door. For the plinth he took the altar pillar from which the parchments may have come, placing it upside down. On it he had the inscription MISSION 1891 carved.

Saunière proceeded to clear much of the old churchyard, and laid it out anew, to the great annoyance of the people of the village. They saw the tombs of their ancestors swept away, and made formal complaints. Among the old tombs was that of Marie de Nègre d'Ables, an eighteenth-century Countess of Hautpoul (or Haupoul) who had lived in the Château Hautpoul in Rennes-le-Château. It is said that he carefully obliterated the inscription on her tombstone – an inscription now known to be essential to decoding the first parchment. However, the wording had already been recorded by members of the Aude Society for Scientific Studies when they paid a visit to Rennes-le-Château, and they later published it in their proceedings.

Apparently there were originally two parts to this tomb, an upright stone and a flat slab. The lower part, equally crucial to the decoding, had disappeared completely before Saunière's arrival. Later it turned out that a drawing of it existed in a rare book by a local author, Eugène Stüblein, *Pierres gravées du Languedoc* (Inscribed Stones of the Languedoc). A copy of part of this work can still be found in the Bibliothèque nationale in Paris.

Saunière began to behave very strangely. He was often observed taking long walks in the countryside, sometimes carrying a heavy suitcase. He is said to have visited some of the many mines which had been dug in the hills by German miners. Sometimes he disappeared for days on end. He frequently took the train from Couiza to Perpignan, close to the Spanish border. He had an enormous amount of mail. The postmistress in Couiza reported that he received as many as 150 letters a day.

By now Saunière had access to considerable funds. He renovated the church in its entirety, rebuilding and redecorating in the exotic style of Catholic churches of the late nineteenth century in France. The details of the paintings and sculptures he created are extraordinary. Over the door is the alarming message TERRIBILIS EST LOCUS ISTE (Terrible is that place). Immediately inside is a startling statue of a devil supporting the holy water stoup. The Stations of the Cross show many odd details, and the large painting of Jesus succouring the afflicted on the west wall shows a bag spilling gold coins onto the grass. Some people believe that these are among the visual clues deliberately included by Saunière to the great secret he had discovered.

Building work now began on a grand scale. Saunière had much of the village rebuilt, and provided it with a new water supply and a new access road which wound up the hill four kilometres from Couiza. He built a new villa alongside the church in a luxurious style, quite out of keeping with the humble village. The house had elaborate gardens with a belvedere running dramatically along the edge of the plateau. At one end was a steel framed orangery and at the other end he built the *Tour Magdala*, a tower which contained his new and extensive library. The door giving access to the tower was of steel.

Bérenger Saunière and his faithful housekeeper Marie Dénarnaud (Pl. 7) did not live in the new house, but stayed in the old presbytery. The new house, which he called *Villa Béthanie*, while supposedly built as a retirement home for elderly priests, was in fact used exclusively for entertaining distinguished guests to a lavish degree, including, it was rumoured, the *diva* Emma Calvé, the Secretary of State for Culture, and even the Archduke Johann von Habsburg. The amount he spent came to at least 190,000 francs, which in modern terms is the equivalent of several million pounds.

In 1902, a new bishop was appointed who found it impossible to accept Saunière's extraordinary lifestyle. The *curé* was hauled before an ecclesiastical court and asked to explain where he obtained the money. His explanation that his wealth was legitimate was not accepted, and he was forbidden to take services in future and commanded to hand over his personal possessions to the church.

Saunière defiantly refused to do any of this, and began a long battle with his bishop and the authorities in Rome. Excluded from the church at Rennes-le-Château, he set up an altar in the *Villa Béthanie* and continued for the remainder of his life to say mass there while finding excuses to avoid further punitive action by the church authorities.

Saunière died in 1917. On his deathbed he made his confession to a priest from a neighbouring parish. This priest is said to have emerged from his bedroom looking shocked, and explained that he had been unable to give the dying man absolution for his sins. Saunière was penniless on his death, but many supposed he had already transferred his secret wealth to his housekeeper, Marie Dénarnaud.

She lived in the *Villa Béthanie* for another thirty-six years, but as old age advanced she found it more and more difficult to maintain the property. In 1946 the villa was acquired by Noël Corbu, a man who had visited Rennes-le-Château and had been attracted by the house. Marie made over the villa to him in return for a home for life. Although she led a frugal life, she encouraged Noël Corbu to believe that untold treasure lay hidden and that the secret would be disclosed to him one day. But Marie Dénarnaud never revealed that secret. She had a stroke and from then on was unable to speak. Marie died in 1953, and Saunière's secret died with her.

Many people have speculated about this treasure. Was it gold and silver? Where did it come from? Could it perhaps have been from the Visigoths? When they sacked Rome in AD 410 they seized a vast hoard, including such items as the menorah or seven branched candlestick that Titus had plundered from the Temple in Jerusalem in AD 71. Much of this treasure has never been found.

The Visigoths established a kingdom in northern Spain and southern France in the fifth century. If the treasure was taken there, it might later have come into the hands of King Clovis, a king of the Merovingian dynasty. The second parchment said that King Dagobert II had the treasure. He was a Merovingian king and is said to have married a Visigothic princess who lived at Rhedae, the northern capital of the Visigoths and later to be called Rennes-le-Château. Thence it might have passed to the Cathars, whose strongholds abounded in the neighbourhood of Rennes-le-Château.

Was it this fabulous treasure that Saunière located from the clues in the parchments? Some think that the Cathars, although finally destroyed in 1244, passed their secrets to the Freemasons, who have known about the treasure ever since.

In the shadows lurks the mysterious Priory of Sion, a secret organization which is said to have been the force that really controlled the Knights Templar. It is reputed to exist to the present day. A secret file in the French National Library, the Bibliothèque nationale, contains the list of Grand Masters, who include Claude Debussy and Jean Cocteau. The lost part of the tomb of Marie de Nègre had the letters PS prominently carved; might they stand for the Priory of Sion?

Others think that what Saunière discovered was not gold, but a secret that was so startling and dangerous that he was paid generously to keep silent. Knowledge of this secret may be dangerous; several of the main participants in the story have died violent deaths, including Noël Corbu. In 1953 three bodies were found buried in the grounds of his villa, all had been shot.

There is also a story that Jesus Christ married Mary Magdalene and had a family by her, and that after the crucifixion she came to France with her children to spread the early Christian gospel. The Merovingian kings were said to have descended from her and are therefore descendants of Christ himself. Another version says that Jesus did not die on the cross, but somehow survived and came to southern France, and that his body is hidden in a tomb whose whereabouts has been made known to a very select few. Are these the real secrets behind the affair of Rennes-le-Château?

Other writers have claimed that visual proof of the secret of Rennes-le-Château can be seen to this day in the landscape around the village. Rennes-le-Château and four other prominent hilltops form a regular pentagon. This amazing natural geometry must have been noticed in earlier times, giving the area a special, mystical significance. This would explain why many of the sites seem to have been placed at special positions, equidistant and at important angles from others. Some believe that the positions of these sites give important clues to the mystery in the hills and valleys of Languedoc.

So there are the bare bones of an extraordinary tale. Many authors have been intrigued by it, and it has generated millions of words in books and articles, as well as many hours of radio and television. But how much of it really occurred? We set ourselves the task of trying to untangle the various threads of the story, to see if it is possible, more than a century after the events, to arrive at the truth.

2

The First Account of the Treasure

There are several kinds of evidence that one can use in investigating an event that occurred in the past. One of them, talking directly to the people concerned, is, alas, not possible. The events in this story happened too long ago.

We can however look at the evidence on the ground. In Rennes-le-Château there is plenty to see. The church, the presbytery, the *Villa Béthanie*, the *Tour Magdala* and the belvedere still exist and are visited by thousands of eager devotees every year. Saunière's domain and the old presbytery now form the Bérenger Saunière Centre. This contains things such as tombstones, the 'Visigothic' pillar that once supported the altar, and many of the *curé*'s possessions, including some of his diaries.

There is also the written word. The little bookshop at Rennes-le-Château has hundreds of titles in many languages – many, it must be said, fanciful elaborations and interpretations of the story. There are a few however that are particularly interesting – collections of reproductions of original documents relating to the Saunière affair,[1] letters, estimates, invoices, minutes of meetings, and official reports for example, written at the time the events occurred. All are in French and most are handwritten, and not very legible. But the original documents are the important documents, and it is on them that we have relied for much of our work.

Regrettably, those original documents are very scattered. Some are lost, some are in private hands, some can be found in the Bérenger Saunière Centre, and a few, such as the minute books of the local council, are in the *Mairie* (the Town Hall) in the village.[2] There is an important collection of documents in the Departmental Archives at Carcassonne, the administrative centre for the Aude Department. Included in their archives is a collection of old newspapers, and it is to them that we turn for the first mention in print of anything unusual going on at Rennes-le-Château.

The regional newspaper is *La Dépêche du Midi* (The South of France Despatch) and for three successive days in January 1956 it ran a sensational story of treasure, illustrated by dramatic drawings and photographs.[3] No reference to treasure, secret codes, or anything else of an extraordinary nature can be found before this publication.

The journalist, Albert Salamon, gave the story the full works. The headline screams 'The fabulous discovery of the *CURÉ* with BILLIONS'. There is a drawing of Bérenger Saunière, his gaze directed towards a metal chest with its lid open, flowing over with gleaming coins. Beside lie four rolled parchments. We are unable to resist giving a translation of the article (with gaps indicated by dots where the purple prose was not very relevant).

La Dépêche du Midi, 12 January 1956

With a blow of the pickaxe into a pillar of the high altar, the *Abbé* Saunière brought to light the treasure of Blanche de Castile

Dusk was advancing rapidly over the countryside of the Aude as my friend's cantankerous car was carrying me with steady rhythm along the steep winding road to the 'high place' of Rennes-le-Château . . .

Soon at the top of the hill the car was swallowed up among the centuries' old stones of an ancient queenly citadel, and then the 'tower' appeared like something from a scene by Edgar Allen Poe – a black shadow on the starry background.

The aim of the night-time excursion? To reply to an invitation to a meeting with M. Noël Corbu, founder and proprietor of the Tower Hotel at Rennes-le-Château. It was an invitation doubly acceptable; ahead was the lure of lively philosophical discussions, and also I, as a reporter from *La Dépêche,* was eager to make further acquaintance with the brother of the test pilot Pierre Corbu, who died in 1927 with his comrade Lacoste on the *Bluebird*, while he was trying for the third time to cross the Atlantic, a little after the tragic end of Nungesser and Coli . . .[4]

Mme Corbu served Salamon with a meal of chicken, accompanied by fine wines. In the dining room his curiosity was aroused by a portrait of a priest with a piercing gaze. 'A relation, M. Corbu?. . .'

A thick file was placed before me: 'Diary' of a *curé*, hundreds of letters, bills, plans, estimates . . . and the story begins.

On the 1st June 1885 the *Abbé* Bérenger Saunière, native of Montazels (near Couiza), the son of a modest family, was appointed *curé* of Rennes-le-Château. For seven years until 1892 this young priest led the obscure life of a fairly good country priest, dividing his time between reading the prayer book, visits to his flock, and conducting the church services.

Though he wore his heart on his sleeve, as his parishioners said, the worthy priest had the soul of a builder, and seeing that the high altar of his church was in ruins, he made it his responsibility to restore it with the aid of financial support of loans from various sources.

And so it was that a blow of the pickaxe against one of the old pillars of the altar providentially revealed a hole, from where slipped some tubes of hollow wood, containing parchments written in Latin. Nobody – it goes without saying – knew Latin at Rennes-le-Château (not even the mayor, M. Rivière, who lived outside the village in a house in Couiza). Nobody, except of course M. l'*Abbé* Saunière.

Here begins the mystery. The works were immediately stopped, to be restarted some time later by the *curé* in person.

The *Abbé* Saunière refurbished not only the high altar, but the whole of the church, stained glass, statues, low reliefs and all. Enthusiasm got the better of him. Nothing could stop him; reconstruction of the presbytery, church garden, building a cemetery wall, the calvary.

The crowning moment came just three years after the discovery of the precious parchments. Alongside the modest presbytery, he started the construction of an ostentatious residence, the *Villa Béthanie*, with covered walk, Magdala tower, terrace, greenhouse and so on. In all, a million gold francs were thus swallowed up in the space of a few years. . . .

About 1908 *Monseigneur* de Beauséjour, Bishop of Carcassonne, provoked by the extravagances of his priest, asked him – not without justification – for an accurate account of the origin of his resources. Time and time again he was summoned to the bishopric. *Abbé* Saunière turned a deaf ear. Exasperated by the insubordination of the priest (and perhaps for reasons that we do not know) *Monseigneur* de Beauséjour charged him with trafficking in the Mass and sentenced him in his absence to suspension from his duties.

Saunière refused to submit and appealed at once to the Papal Court in Rome against this sentence. After two years the Court ruled that the main charge had not been proved . . . Nevertheless continuing pressure was put on the *curé* of Rennes-le-Château to try to get him to indicate, under oath of secrecy, the source of his wealth. In vain, prayers, menaces, pleas, nothing succeeded in getting the priest, obstinately hanging onto his secret, to speak.

And I read in *La Semaine Religieuse*, a yellowing copy of 3rd July 1915, the second prohibition, this time definite: 'There is, for the diocesan administration of Carcassonne, a deep sadness, but also an urgent duty to inform the faithful that the *Abbé* Saunière, one time *curé* at Rennes-le-Château, at present living in the same place, has been, by official judgement dated 5th December 1911, deprived of his priestly powers; thus he must no longer celebrate the Holy Sacrifice and from this moment on, he will not be able to accept the fees for Mass that are entrusted to him.'

The article is illustrated by three photographs, the *Tour Magdala*, a view of the distant hills from the library window, and the *Villa Béthanie* taken from the tower.

Albert Salamon writes romantically about the atmosphere at Rennes-le-Château and dramatises his journey to the hilltop. There are three points to note especially: first that he was invited by Noël Corbu and praised the hospitality he received, second that he says nothing about the parchments, except that they are in Latin, and third, that he does not explain the connection between the parchments and the treasure, except to imply that they gave its location.

At the end of the article Salamon describes Saunière's fall from favour, and this time offers evidence in the form of a quotation from *La Semaine Religieuse* of 3 July 1915. However, the reader is left in suspense over the treasure, and it is not surprising that the story continues the following day.

The second article continues the story to 1917, the year of Saunière's death:

La Dépêche du Midi, 13 January 1956
From the height of his pulpit, the new pastor of Rennes-le-Château delivered his sermon before a sparse congregation; the majority of the parishioners, staying faithful to the old *curé*, at the same hour used to troop into the little chapel set up under the verandah of the *Villa Béthanie*. . . .

For a short period of time the *Abbé* Saunière put a brake on his excesses . . .

We then come to the stage of megalomania. On the 5th January 1917, via a registered letter addressed to an important building contractor in the area, Saunière ordered 8,000 cubic metres of masonry, equivalent at the time to 3 million francs worth of work.

And what work – construction of a tower 50 metres high which would have enabled the *abbé* to see Couiza; a library running the height of the spiral staircase, leading to the entrance to a flat roof; the total rebuilding of the Couiza–Rennes road; running water to the houses of all the inhabitants and so on. Then suddenly, 17 days later the *curé* met his end.

On 22 January 1917, after a long struggle for life, the *abbé* died in an armchair in the drawing room.

'Which armchair, M. Corbu?'

'Exactly the one you are sitting in now.'

And while a slight shiver ran through me from head to foot, I learned that the *abbé* died in my armchair at the age of sixty-five of cirrhosis of the liver, complicated by a heart attack, and because of this his wonderful works remained only in the planning stage.

Salamon then describes the gastronomic delights of life at the *Villa Béthanie* during the Saunière period, quoting as evidence some of the bills for wine and liqueurs which he has been shown.

This article ends with a description of Saunière's travels:

So passed the life of the ex-*curé* of Rennes-le-Château, comforted by the vigilant and devoted affection of his faithful housekeeper, Mlle Dénarnaud.

The *Abbé* Saunière would often disappear on distant and mysterious travels to Switzerland, Belgium and Spain. Letters, written out in advance (and all identical) tell us of the explanations conjured up by the priest to explain these multiple absences. And it was Mlle Dénarnaud, acting as secretary, who was responsible for sending to its destination a short note such as the one you see here:

'Rennes-le-Château, Aude
In a hurry to leave to go and pay a call on one of my colleagues. I am happy for the moment to acknowledge receipt of your remittance and I thank you.
Yours sincerely, B. Saunière, priest.'

What did the *abbé* do in the course of these trips?
M. Corbu: 'Anyone who has bent over the large file and has gone through it from A to Z is certain – dispose of the coins that he had melted down. A person from Carcassonne who is still alive assured me that he had seen at the priest's house chests full of golden ingots.'

This second article is also illustrated with three photographs. There is a picture of Noël Corbu: 'Today's proprietor of the one-time residence of the *Abbé* Saunière', a view of the apse end of the church, and finally a photo of the 'Visigothic' altar pillar, with two captions, suggesting that the parchments were found in a second, similar one, which has since disappeared.
Finally on the third day the story of Albert Salamon's visit is concluded:

La Dépêche du Midi, 14 January 1956
Does M. Corbu know the hiding place of the treasure of the *Abbé* Saunière, which amounts to 50 billion francs?
During the second crusade of St Louis, the French barons rose in revolt against the royal power. Blanche de Castile, who was living in Rennes-le-Château, reckoned Paris was not safe for the royal treasure and had it transported to her domain, where it was buried in an underground cave.
Having taken this precaution, the Queen left for Paris to fight against the revolt which in other places was rapidly suppressed. Some time later she died and was buried in the Abbey at Maubisson.
On returning to his kingdom, St Louis consolidated his royal position, then departed for the third crusade and died at Tunis in 1270, without having touched the treasure at Rennes-le-Château . . . .
'Then what happened, according to you . . .?'

M. Corbu resumed without hesitation.

'No doubt it is possible that, thanks to the parchments falling into his hands, Saunière had discovered the famous treasure of Blanche de Castile; a royal treasure equivalent now to a minimum of 50 billion francs, since it comprises in part 18,500,000 francs in gold pieces, which at the very least is worth at the present time, in view of its historic and archaeological value, more than 400 million francs.'

'Certainly, M. Corbu, the hundreds of letters in your possession throw strange glimmers of truth on the puzzle of Rennes-le-Château. However, the reader – like myself – would want to know more.'

And my enthusiastic and inexhaustible conversationalist, who possesses the gift of convincing even the incredulous, related to me how, in the course of a walk in the neighbourhood, he became acquainted with Mlle Dénarnaud, who after the death of her master was living as sole proprietor of the *Villa Béthanie*. This delightful building, with its admirable view over the valley of the Aude, persuaded him – accompanied by his wife and children – to come back many times to enjoy the charming hospitality of Mlle Dénarnaud.

And the old lady, who had become fond of her guests, invited them to come and set up home permanently at Rennes-le-Château, and, better still, offered to make Béthanie over to them. It was thus that the *curé*'s old house became the present Tower Hotel.

My curiosity is insatiable.

'Did Mlle Dénarnaud know the secret?'

'It is up to you to judge. One dreadful day, when I was conversing with the venerable lady about the loss of the major part of my fortune (60 million francs lost in an unfortunate business with Moroccan sugar) Mlle Dénarnaud took me by the arm, looked at me thoughtfully for a little while and at last said to me, shaking her head like an old fairy from a story in the Tales of Pérault;

'Smile, M. Corbu . . . 63 million is nothing. When I die you will be very rich, immensely rich, richer than you could ever imagine. . .'

'M. Corbu, tell me, is it within your power to discover this treasure?'

'Who knows?' . . . and in the speaker's enigmatic smile I believed that I read the answer with certainty.

'Has the work begun?'

'Those at the hotel will finish on Christmas Day. As for the others, we will inform you later. Elsewhere ground at Rennes-le-Château has already yielded, besides the treasure, some little bits of its incalculable archaeological riches. Look –'

And in a little display cabinet I fingered the skull of a dead ancestor of 10,000 years ago. I looked, I thought, then I started on the following list:

Palaeolithic period: skull, bones, jaws, teeth, flint arrowhead, pottery.

Neolithic period: flint axe and bones.

Gaulish period: pieces of amphora.

Gallo-Roman period: pottery, coins, medals.

Visigothic period: engagement ring of a princess, unique in the world.

Louis XIII period: coin of Gaston d'Orléans.

Louis XVI period and first year of the Republic: coin . . .

It is one o'clock in the morning. The ghosts that sat down at the host's table in the course of this thrilling story have kept secret right to the end the mysterious hiding place whose 'open sesame' the *abbé* accidentally stumbled upon . . .

And when the door of the Tower Hotel was opened on to the night, and I held out my hand to M. Corbu in 'au revoir', there seemed to me to be shining, where a moment ago there were stars, millions of golden pieces of the fabulous treasure of Blanche de Castile.

We learn from reliable sources that excavations connected with archaeology have been made at Rennes-le-Château and have already led to the discovery of certain pointers promising good results. Rennes having been a large Visigothic fortress with buried treasure, there is a strong chance that the Cathar treasure, including the famous Holy Grail, was taken there.

This final article has three further photographs. The first is of Pierre Corbu, test pilot and brother of Noël, the second picture is of the baptismal font of the 'Visigothic' period, and the third shows various objects in a display case captioned: 'The property of the *abbé* harboured numerous archaeological pieces'.

These original newspaper accounts are very revealing. Bérenger Saunière had died in 1917, and his housekeeper Marie Dénarnaud, in whose name all the property was registered, continued to live in the old presbytery. In 1946 she sold the property to Noël Corbu, and he allowed her to continue to live there until she died in 1953. She was buried alongside Saunière in the village churchyard.

From other sources we know a little of the history of Noël Corbu.[5] He was something of an entrepreneur, had started several small businesses and even written a detective novel. During the war he lived at Perpignan and got mixed up with the black market. In 1944 he and his wife and their two children moved to Bugarach, to be away from the unpleasant rumours which had become linked to his business affairs. He became friendly with the local schoolmaster, who is probably the person who first told him about Bérenger Saunière, his extravagant spending and the local rumour that he might have found some treasure. This appealed to Corbu; maybe he thought that there was a plot here for a new novel. The Corbus had a family excursion to Rennes-le-Château in 1945, met Marie and evidently got on together very well.

Corbu decided to turn the extensive premises into a hotel, and named it the *Hôtel de la Tour* (Tower Hotel) after the extraordinary tower that Saunière had built to house his library. Corbu ran the hotel until 1964, and sold it Henri Buthion in 1966. He had a considerable problem if he was to obtain a satisfactory return from the business. The village of Rennes-le-Château is situated at the end of a 4 km winding road from Couiza. The road leads nowhere except to the village itself. There was little prospect that casual visitors would reach the hotel.

It seems clear that the articles by Albert Salamon in *La Dépêche du Midi* are a device to make the hotel famous, and to attract visitors with the lure of treasure. Nevertheless it is equally clear that the story was not entirely invented by Corbu, but that he made skilful use of elements which were already in place. Bérenger Saunière was certainly a very unusual priest who did some unusual things and was very secretive about his business affairs.

For the present, it is enough to say that Saunière acquired by one means or another the money to restore his church and build the extraordinary estate that still attracts visitors today. It cost him perhaps 190,000 francs, the equivalent of more than a million pounds today. Where did he get the money? When Noël Corbu arrived in Rennes, there were already stories from people who claimed to be eyewitnesses, that Saunière had found something during his extensive building works, which included the destruction of all the existing graves in the cemetery.

Corbu found himself in possession of a substantial archive of documents which had belonged to Saunière, much of which survives today, though in a variety of locations. These included bills for the building works, bills for his purchases of food and drink and luxurious furnishings, correspondence with contractors, some of his diaries, some of his accounts, and the correspondence concerning his trial by the ecclesiastical court. (We shall return to these documents in chapter 14.)

It needed only a short leap of imagination to see that the apparently unexplained wealth of the priest could be presented to the public as the treasure story to end all treasure stories.

When the journalist arrived, Corbu made the story as exciting as he possibly could, inventing possible contexts for the discovery of treasure. There is no historical evidence for the existence of the treasure of Blanche de Castile, and its precise assessment as 18,500,000 francs in gold pieces gives a feeling of truth to an entirely imaginary tale.

The production of archaeological artefacts found on the hilltop is no surprise. There is little doubt that Rennes-le-Château has a long history. There has been no major modern excavation, but a defendable hill of this sort will have seen occupation at most periods in human history. The finds lend verisimilitude to the story of digging things up.

Add the tantalising suggestion that the digging is continuing and at any moment will produce the treasure and who would not want to be present (and staying in the hotel) when the discovery is made?

It remains unclear whether the reporter actually believed the tale, or whether he and Corbu hatched it for their mutual benefit. The result was the same – Rennes-le-Château became famous.

The climax of Noël Corbu's successful attempt to use the story of Bérenger Saunière to ensure the success of his hotel came early in May 1961. A team from the French television service ORTF – *l'Office de la radiodiffusion et télévision française* – descended on Rennes-le-Château to make a film of Bérenger Saunière discovering the treasure, installing the water supply and making all the other changes to the village.

Many local inhabitants took part as extras. It was Noël Corbu himself who played the part of Bérenger Saunière, dressed as a priest of 1900, and wearing the Roman hat and the cassock that Saunière was usually seen in. René Descadeillas, the head of the library at Carcassonne, was present and described the event.[6]

The programme, broadcast under the title *La rue tourne* (the wheel turns), had awful consequences in that it encouraged the amateur treasure hunters who did so much damage to the village.

In the hotel in the evenings many visitors discussed the nature and the location of the supposed treasure, maps were studied, and Blanche de Castile, the Cathars and the Templars entered the debate. The drama and excitement of the story was to attract many others, as we shall see.

In 1965 the Corbu family finally left Rennes-le-Château. One of the major sources of evidence for their stay is the account written by Noël's daughter Claire, together with her husband Antoine Captier, in *L'Héritage de l'Abbé Saunière*.

On 20 May 1968 Noël Corbu was killed in an horrific accident on the road from Carcassonne to Castelnaudry. While at the *Hôtel de la Tour* he had made a tape recording of his version of the history of Rennes-le-Château and Saunière's discovery of the treasure for the interest and enjoyment of his visitors. The text of the recording found its way into the Departmental Archives at Carcassonne. The text appears in the next chapter and we will see how that story has developed from the original newspaper articles in *La Dépêche du Midi*.

3

The Archives at Carcassonne

The Departmental Archives at Carcassonne include documents of all kinds, secular and ecclesiastical, minutes of meetings of the municipal and parish councils, old newspapers and many others. Some papers have been deposited there by their authors as a permanent record of their work.

In this chapter we are examining two documents, both by individuals. The first one has the title *L'histoire de Rennes-le-Château*[1] (The History of Rennes-le-Château). It was placed in the archives on 14 June 1962 (a year after the film made for television) by a Maurice Tous of Alet-les-Bains. Oddly this document does not bear the author's name, but there is no doubt that it was written by Noël Corbu. Firstly the document was actually typed on the same typewriter as Corbu used for his own personal correspondence. Secondly, there is a curious spelling mistake: Saunière is spelled with a final 's', and amazingly that is the way Corbu typed the *curé*'s name.[2] Also, at some time the text of this 'History of Rennes-le-Château' was retyped on another machine, and displayed in the Museum at Rennes-le-Château with a remark to the effect that this was what Corbu told his visitors to the *Hôtel de la Tour*.

The second document is an academic paper entitled *Notice sur Rennes-le-Château et l'Abbé Saunière* (Account of Rennes-le-Château and the *Abbé* Saunière) by René Descadeillas, the librarian at Carcassonne. It is dated 3 December 1962 and was archived by the author on the same day. Together these two documents give us a 'snapshot' of the story of Rennes-le-Château as it was at the end of 1962 and before the first of the many books based on the story of Bérenger Saunière was published. Strange as it is, it is nothing like as sensational as what was to come later.

Corbu's archived account is much more detailed than that in *La Dépêche du Midi*. It begins by giving us the origins of Rennes-le-Château.

The history of Rennes-le-Château is lost in the mists of time. It can be said with confidence that this plateau has always been populated. Some historians have attributed the foundation of Rennes-le-Château to the Visigoths, around about the fifth century AD. This is certainly contradicted by the quantity of more ancient remains that are found on the surface of the ground: prehistoric, palaeolithic or neolithic, Iberian, Gaulish, Roman and Gallo-Roman. Their abundance and diversity prove, without any doubt, that Rennes-le-Château was a large city even before the Visigoths.

19

Others think that Rennes-le-Château was the capital of the Socintes, a very strong Gaulish tribe who held Caesar in check for a long time . . . it is reasonable to suppose that Rennes-le-Château, before becoming the powerful Visigothic capital, had been a Gaulish capital, then a large Gallo-Roman city, and certainly before that time a large prehistoric habitation.

Later in his text he tells us that: 'In the 5th century Rennes-le-Château, then called Rhedae [or Aereda], was a great city. As capital of the Visigoths it had more than 30,000 inhabitants.'

The town, says Corbu, declined during the wars of religion, and was sacked in 1370, after which it never recovered, and would have remained obscure and unknown if it had not been for *Béranger Saunières* (*sic*) and the discovery of the treasure. As to the actual discovery, the account is much the same: in February 1892, in the course of repairs, wooden tubes containing parchments were found in one of the pillars supporting the old altar. What is new in this account is that, according to Corbu, the following day the *curé* set off for Paris, for reasons unknown. (There is no mention of taking the parchments to the Bishop, or meeting famous people in Paris, or purchasing pictures.)

Corbu's account of the building works carried out by Saunière is essentially what was in the newspaper articles, although he adds one fact which becomes of great significance in the later stages of the saga of Rennes-le-Château. Corbu writes: '[On his return from Paris] he had the work restarted but he did not have only the high altar done but all the church: he then set about the cemetery where he often worked alone. He even demolished the tomb of the Countess of Hautpoul-Blanchefort[3] and he himself obliterated the inscriptions which were on this stone. The Council got excited about this and forbade him to work in the cemetery, but the evil was done . . .'

Corbu goes on to describe the conflict with Bishop Beauséjour, Saunière's suspension and the hearing by the Church. And finally he makes a new estimate of the value of the treasure, arriving at the unbelievable figure of 4,000 billion (old) francs. 'Thus in this quiet village with its magnificent view and glorious past, there is one of the most fabulous treasures in the whole world.'

Now what would a professional historian or archaeologist think about all this? The town of Carcassonne was fortunate to have at that time a well-respected man of letters called René Descadeillas, whose contribution to the story of Rennes-le-Château is important because he is one of the few academic historians to comment on the mystery, and because he had no pecuniary interest in the story.

René Descadeillas was born at Moissac in 1909 but spent his childhood in Carcassonne. He went into journalism, and his first job was as secretary to the head of *La Dépêche du Midi*, Albert Sarrault. Later he was a correspondent for a publication called *La Démocratie*, during which time he became interested in historical matters. In 1938 he was elected a member of the Society of Arts at Carcassonne, and in 1950 he became Librarian at the Municipal Library there, a post he held until his retirement in 1974. He was President of the Society of Arts in 1957 and the Society's General Secretary from 1969 to 1980. He died in 1986.

As the authority on local historical matters, and familiar with the archives, it is not surprising that the fuss about treasure at Rennes-le-Château stimulated him to collect together all the known facts and set them out in a note, together with supporting documents. As we said earlier, he put the results of this work in the archives at Carcassonne in December 1962, just after Corbu's history was deposited. Perhaps he thought he had done enough to set the story straight; he made no attempt to give his findings wider circulation and in fact his *Notice sur Rennes-le-Château et l'Abbé Saunière* was not printed until after his death, and by then writing about Rennes-le-Château had become a minor industry.

Being a professional librarian, Descadeillas was usually careful to give the sources of his information. Attached to his note on Rennes-le-Château, and reproduced in the printed edition, are photocopies of sixteen documents that he consulted. They include some ecclesiastical reports on the state of the church, letters from Saunière and others, a page from one of Saunière's notebooks, even a letter from his wine merchant. But Descadeillas also talked to inhabitants of the village and in this, it must be admitted, he is less satisfactory in his account. He writes about witnesses, without giving their names or sufficient details for one to be able to judge their closeness to the events which occurred about seventy years before. His 'witnesses' could have only been children at the time.

In *Notice sur Rennes-le-Château*, Descadeillas recounts how Saunière was appointed *curé* at Rennes and how his installation was deferred because of political remarks that Saunière had made publicly during the election of 1885. Then we read about the poor state of the church fabric. A fund for repairs is set up, and Saunière lends it 518 francs (more than three thousand pounds in today's money).[4] Was he really as poor as he has been made out? His stipend was low, but it seems that even in 1885, he had money from somewhere.

Repairs began. Descadeillas writes:

The church at Rennes . . . possessed a crude altar, made of a stone slab, supported in front by two square pillars, one of which bore archaic carvings. It appeared – several witnesses are still living and they are categorical about this – that while pulling out the slab, a cavity full of dried ferns was discovered, in the middle of which one could make out two or three scrolls. These were the parchments which the *curé* grasped hold of. He stated – in the words of a witness – that he would read them and translate them if he could. The mayor, when told of this, requested a translation from the *curé*; a little later the latter passed over to him a translation written in his own hand. It seems the translated text related to the construction of the church and the altar. It is not known what became of this document.[5]

We are told what became of one of the stone pillars.

21st June 1891 there was great solemnity on the occasion of the first communion, the *curé* had had a statue of the Virgin set up and blessed on common ground in front of the door of the church. He called it 'Our Lady of Lourdes' and for a pedestal it had one of the two pillars which had formerly supported the high altar. As the carvings which covered the pillar were partly obliterated, the *curé* of Rennes had entrusted to a workman of Couiza the job of deepening them with a chisel. The result was not very happy, as one can judge.[6]

We learn from this that Saunière has little respect for antiquities. This extract also reveals one of the many inconsistencies that make it so hard to unravel what happened and when. Corbu dates the discovery of the parchments to February 1892, but Descadeillas points out that the pillar was reused in June 1891, and in fact 'Mission 1891' was inscribed on the stone. (He does not mention that the pillar was reused upside down.) Some of the confusion may be because there seems to have been more than one discovery in the church. Descadeillas again:

One of the foster sisters of the *curé*'s maid, who is still living, is adamant that while repairing the church the *curé* might have found a pot of gold pieces. This seems to me to be quite possible, because it is plausible that Saunière's unfortunate predecessor, the *Abbé* Antoine Bigou, an old man of seventy in September 1792 when he had to cross the Spanish frontier, had buried his savings at the same time as the religious objects that he wished to preserve for the future. This is obviously only a hypothesis, but my research on Rennes in the 18th century and during the revolutionary period allows me to put it forward. This was not a treasure in the usual sense of the word, but only a nest-egg.[7]

This account of the finding of the parchments and their probable content (a note about repairs to the church), and the discovery of gold pieces and their possible origin, seems to have an air of plausibility. The discoveries are not sensational but interesting enough to be remembered for a very long time in the village. No doubt they were discussed over and over again, and who would not have wished to add his own bit of speculation as to the message in the parchments and the origin of the gold?

More was to be found in the church. Descadeillas adds: 'The *curé* may also have pulled up the slab-stones which paved the church and excavated the ground. There are still witnesses to this, including a very old man who was then a child learning the catechism.'[8]

Indeed the *curé* did pull up the slab-stones. He records in his diary *découverte d'un tombeau* (discovery of a tomb), but that was on 21 September 1891, after the Mission, and hence had no connection with finding the parchments.

But the story is only just beginning. Descadeillas tells us about the protests made by the villagers when Saunière began to rearrange the cemetery, and to move the flowers that they had placed over the graves of their ancestors. One wrote

14 March 1895

Monsieur le Préfet,

We are not at all happy about how the cemetery is being worked on, particularly under the conditions that there have been up to now; if there are crosses they are uprooted, also stones from the tombs, and at the same time this said work involves neither compensation nor nothing.[9]

This letter was signed by (or marked with the cross of) several inhabitants. As Descadeillas admits, no one really knew what Saunière was doing in the cemetery, but by the time that they managed to stop him, he seems to have destroyed much of what was previously there. Saunière certainly had little respect for the past.

Having spent the last five years of the 1890s repairing the church, in 1900 Saunière set about even grander works. He bought property around the church (but not in his own name), and built the *Villa Béthanie*, beside which he laid out a garden. Then began the construction of the terrace with its water cisterns beneath, the Magdala Tower, the conservatory and more gardens in the space between the terrace and the house. Descadeillas says: 'At his home he held open house, and after 1900 there was not a week when he did not entertain sumptuously. People used to mention his relations with Emma Calvet, of the opera, born in Aveyron, who came to see him at Rennes; local men of politics, Dujardin-Beaumetz, born in 1852, consul-general of Limoux. . . . Others less known, local or regional heads of the radical-socialist party, already quite powerful in the Aude.'[10]

There is no doubt that he entertained well: his expenditure on wine alone attests to that. But as to whom he entertained, we are not so sure. Emma Calvé (or Calvet; she changed her name) may have been one of his guests if we believe the gossip. On the other hand, in her autobiography, *My Life*, she mentions neither Rennes-le-Château nor Bérenger Saunière, which seems odd if she had been a friend and a regular visitor.

Descadeillas confirms that Saunière made frequent and unexplained trips away from Rennes to undisclosed destinations and for unknown purposes. He prepared in advance letters to be sent in reply to correspondence received from important people, such as his superiors in the Church. Marie Dénarnaud would post them when required, thus giving the impression that he was not away at all. Here is an example:

> Sir,
>   I have read with the most humble respect the letter which you did me the honour to write to me, and to which I am giving the most earnest attention. Believe me, the importance of the matter that you have now brought up does not escape me, but it deserves consideration. Therefore allow me, at the moment occupied by an urgent matter, to send my reply in a few days.[11]

We have to admire the ingenuity of a man who could deal with potentially embarrassing situations like that. In the end even Saunière's luck ran out. The new bishop, *Monseigneur* Beauséjour, was appointed to the Diocese of Carcassonne in 1902, and unlike his predecessor he took an interest in Saunière's activities and sources of cash.

For the next ten years Saunière was put under increasing pressure. Descadeillas carefully documents the proceedings. He describes how Saunière was asked time and time again to give details of his finances, and how Saunière disregarded the Bishop's requests, at the same time continuing his lavish style of life. The Bishop nominated Saunière to another living. After all his work at Rennes, it was obvious Saunière would refuse to go. The Bishop lost patience, and in 1910 he had Saunière up before the Ecclesiastical Court. There was evidence that Saunière was collecting a large amount of fees from France, Italy and Switzerland for saying the Mass. Saunière refused to go before the Court and was found guilty in his absence. Eventually the case escalated to Rome.

On 5 December 1910, Saunière was suspended from the right to celebrate the Mass and this put him in a difficult position. He began to think of selling what he owned at Rennes, but he could not find a buyer. There is documentary evidence at this time, given by Descadeillas, that the *curé* had considerable financial difficulties. In 1913 he took out a loan from *Crédit Foncier*. His last few years were spent at Rennes, looked after by Marie, and when he died in 1917 he left all his possessions to her. Marie also inherited the loan from the bank and repaid in instalments for a while, until they realized that full repayment was unlikely and stopped pressing her for money. She had little income and was obliged to sell some of the contents of the Villa to make ends meet.

The documents collected by Descadeillas conflict with the widely-held belief that Saunière had found a fabulous treasure, for if he had, he would not have been in debt in his later years. But the mystery remains – how did he finance all the expensive works at Rennes-le-Château? Descadeillas examined the evidence.

To begin with, how much did Saunière actually spend? There was not a lot of information available to Descadeillas about the *curé*'s expenditure, but he did find one piece of paper, which is reproduced in the printed edition of his Notice. It is in Saunière's own hand, an untidy, hastily scribbled note that he wrote for the Ecclesiastical Court in 1911 when they were badgering him for a statement. It reads as follows:

1.	Purchase of land	1,550
2.	Restoring the church	16,200
	Calvary	11,200
3.	*Villa Béthanie*	90,000
	Magdala Tower	40,000
	Terrace and gardens	19,050
4.	Internal fitting out	5,000
	Furniture	10,000
	TOTAL	193,000

If we take one French franc as having the same purchasing power as £7 in today's money, this is equivalent to almost £1½ million. The scrap of paper was not supported by builders' receipts, and (as we shall see later in chapter 14) there are reasons for doubting the accuracy of this amount. It does not include any of his housekeeping expenses, and it is known for certain that the household's wine and spirit consumption was large. In total, Saunière must have spent, if not the billions implied in the newspaper report, a considerable sum of money.

Where it came from was not made clear. Saunière's one explanation to the Court was ridiculous. He said (presumably referring to the family of Marie Dénarnaud) that he took into his home a father and mother and two children. They combined their resources, and out of the family's income of 300 francs a month, in twenty years they saved 52,000 francs (i.e. 216 francs a month). Selling picture postcards, and dealing in postage stamps and second-hand furniture also brought in money.

Descadeillas is certain that Saunière had organized large-scale selling of the Mass. He wrote:

Moreover, at certain periods the *curé* of Rennes received each day a large quantity of money orders – up to 100 to 150 francs a day – in little sums of 5 to 40 francs. These orders were paid to him at his home in Rennes. Many others were addressed to him, poste restante, at Couiza, where he used to go to cash money. One of the post-mistresses who used to pay him is still alive[12] . . . The traffic in the Mass? He admitted it. There is no question on this matter. But this traffic, although it was significant, did not produce amounts sufficient to allow him to erect such buildings, and at the same time to live so grandly. Therefore there was something else.[13]

The other source of income, according to Descadeillas, was gifts from benefactors. He thinks that Saunière was in league with his younger brother Alfred. Alfred Saunière had also studied as a priest, and in 1878 he was appointed to the parish of Alzonne, near Carcassonne. He was keen on travel and had an interest in business deals. Alfred was reputed to have led an immoral life and he became an alcoholic. He died at Montazels on 9 September 1905. Descadeillas quotes a letter from Saunière to his lawyer: 'My brother, being a preacher, had numerous contacts. He acted as middle-man for these generous deeds.'[14]

Steadfastly Saunière refused to say who these benefactors were: 'for to reveal them without permission would be to put oneself in the position of bringing trouble to certain families or households, whose members have supported me, some in secrecy from their husband, the others from their children or their heirs.'[15]

Without any further information Descadeillas can only speculate. He wonders if somehow Saunière was helping people who had become mixed up in criminal activities or political intrigue. He has to leave the question open. He concludes his paper: 'The treasure of Rennes does not exist. But the secret of the *curé* of Rennes is real. And it is in him that the mystery resides.'[16]

We are left to wonder if Descadeillas's low-key investigation had been published earlier whether there would have been the great interest in Rennes-le-Château that there was in subsequent years. But his report lay in the archives at Carcassonne, known only to a few, and five years later in 1967, a book appeared that hinted at darker happenings and sparked off chains of investigation which led to mysteries and conspiracies far from the little village in the south of France.

4

The Gold of Rennes

The first book about Rennes-le-Château which came out in 1967 was entitled *L'Or de Rennes, ou la vie insolite de Bérenger Saunière* (The Gold of Rennes, or the Strange Life of Bérenger Saunière). It was in great demand and soon after was published with an even more dramatic title: *Le Trésor maudit de Rennes-le-Château* (The Accursed Treasure of Rennes-le-Château).[1] The author, Gérard de Sède, was a journalist with a keen interest in history, particularly the more sensational aspects of the history of the Middle Ages. He had previously written books about the Knights Templar, *Les Templiers sont parmi nous* (The Templars are among us), published in 1962, and the Cathars. He was born in 1921 and had had a varied life. During the war he was in the Resistance, was captured by the Germans and escaped.

After the publication of *L'Or de Rennes*, the mystery, which previously had attracted only moderate attention from the general public (although it had greatly interested enthusiastic treasure hunters), was suddenly known to all France. And what a story now emerged! No longer was the tale confined to the strange activities of a local *curé*, spending large sums of money acquired by dubious means: we are now introduced to a wider setting, in which Saunière appears as one participant in a shadowy world of secret societies, conspiracies and unexplained deaths. Furthermore, a glance at the book shows an impressive list of references. Research has been carried out and archives have been consulted. Surely we have here a work which all serious historians ought to take into account?

Of all the books written about Rennes-le-Château, this can make a claim to be the most influential. In our investigation of the true story of Rennes it demands close study to find what new aspects have been brought to light and then, if possible, we have to uncover the evidence on which they are based.

Part 1

The Devil in the Stoup

The book is divided into four parts. In the first, *Le diable dans le bénitier* (the devil in the Stoup, or basin for holy water), de Sède introduces us to Saunière, the poor priest with the dilapidated church. He then describes how, 'at the end of 1891' (an incorrect date because the altar support had already been reused by then), work began on renovation, and some interesting details are given:

The high altar is the finest monument in the church; it stands on two antique Visigothic pillars, on which crosses and hieroglyphs are finely carved. But the stone table is in a pitiful state; it spoils the general effect and has to be replaced. Saunière undertakes the work, helped by two masons, Rousset and Babou. They take off the heavy slab. A surprise, one of the pillars is hollow and stuffed with dried ferns. In this nest of leaves they find three wooden tubes sealed with wax. They open them: they contain parchments.

Because witnesses were present the discovery soon got around.

'Let's keep these old documents in the public archives,' suggests the mayor, who delights in accumulating papers.

But the *Abbé* Saunière has another idea.

'These parchments', he said, 'will go mouldy in the town hall to nobody's advantage. Well, in large towns there are collectors of antiquities who will surely give a good price for them. Better to sell them: I'll see to it.'[2]

However, the mayor demanded exact copies to keep. 'Of course only the *curé* was capable of completing this scribe's work. We have had two of these tracings in our hands and are going to discuss them later.'

But according to de Sède, Saunière did not sell them immediately. Early in 1893 he took them to Bishop Billard at Carcassonne, who examined the four parchments with great care.[3] In spite of the fact that the conversation took place in private between two men who are long since dead and who made no notes, de Sède recounts it word for word – here is a brief summary.

The Bishop asks if Saunière is going to get rid of them, but he denies this and adds that they are difficult to decipher – he has been trying for more than a year – at which point the Bishop suggests he should go to Paris to consult specialists in palaeography. The Bishop offers to pay for the trip and give the *curé* a letter of introduction. Saunière then says that the mayor wants the parchments to be sold so that he can be repaid the loan of 1,400 francs, which was borrowed for church repairs. The Bishop says that the Church will settle the debt and Saunière sets off for Paris.

De Sède describes how Saunière, on his arrival in Paris, went directly to the house of *Abbé* Bueil (de Sède spells him Bieil), of the church of Saint-Sulpice. He stayed three weeks in Paris, while the parchments were examined by experts, including Bueil's nephew Emile Hoffet who at the age of twenty already spoke several languages, was interested in ancient writing and studied it with the learned *Abbé* Baguès. As to the result of the examination of the parchments, de Sède is very vague: 'On the agreed day he went back to *Abbé* Bieil's house. We have not been able to establish with certainty what was said and what happened between the two men. It seems that they did not give the manuscripts back to Saunière, or else they gave back only some of them. . . . Had there been a bit of trading, the *curé* giving up these precious documents for some interpretation just as valuable?'[4]

While waiting for the parchments to be deciphered, de Sède reckons that Saunière took full advantage of the art collections in the capital. He went to the Louvre and there he purchased copies of three paintings: *The Shepherds of Arcady*, by Nicolas Poussin (1593–1665); *Saint Anthony the Hermit* by David Teniers (1610–90); and a portrait by an unspecified artist of Pope St Celestine V. These he hung on the walls of the presbytery at Rennes on his return. (We are not told where the money came from for these pictures.) Saunière also discovered music. He was said to have visited the house of Emma Calvé, at that time at the peak of her fame as an opera singer. De Sède suggests that Hoffet had introduced them.

There are several new details in this account. Neither Corbu nor Descadeillas had mentioned any meeting with the bishop, let alone any record of their private conversation. Corbu said Saunière had gone to Paris for reasons unknown, but neither he nor Descadeillas included the purchase of copies of paintings. Neither of these two had brought in Emile Hoffet, or Saint-Sulpice or a social call on Emma Calvé, though Descadeillas had related gossip that she came to Rennes. Without some strong evidence in support, which alas is not given, we are left with the thought that a few bare facts have been elaborated to make a more exciting story.

De Sède relates how, on his return to his parish, Saunière continued with the renovations, discovering a tombstone with a carving of horsemen. In fact this stone had already been uncovered some years earlier in 1886 and, after a period in Carcassonne, has now been put on display at Rennes-le-Château. Saunière did discover a tomb and he made a note of it in his diary on 21 September 1891. Also de Sède tells us that Saunière dug up the tombstones around the church including two from the grave of Marie de Nègre d'Ables: 'he patiently polished one of them to erase the inscription and soon afterwards got rid of the other one.'

The implication is that Saunière needed to obliterate the inscription because of what it revealed: 'What Saunière did not know was that he had taken trouble – or a precaution – that was useless. In fact before he had got rid of them, the inscriptions carved on the tomb of the Marchioness of Blanchefort had been copied during an excursion by local archaeologists. One had been reproduced in the *Bulletin of the Aude Society for Scientific Studies*; the other is reproduced in a work by Eugène Stüblein that is today very rare, *Engraved Stones of the Languedoc*.'[5]

These two stones (Figures 7.1 and 7.3) are very significant in the Rennes story, because their inscriptions are used in the deciphering of the message hidden in one of the parchments. Neither stone now exists, but the one illustrated by the Society certainly did. The members visited Rennes-le-Château on 25 June 1905,[6] and after noting the statue of the virgin standing on its ancient plinth, they saw the tombstone and recorded its size (1.3 m by 0.65 m) and its inscription, which they later published in the Society's *Proceedings*.

The words on the stone translate as follows: 'Here lies the noble Marie de Nègre of Arles, Dame of Haupoul of Blanchefort, aged sixty-seven years, died 27th January 1781, may she rest in peace.'

There are three points to note. First, the illustration given in the *Bulletin* is not a copy of a drawing. (It is not even in the right proportions.) It has the inscription set up in printers' type in a box. We cannot be certain of how it looked in reality. Second, the stonemason, presumably not very literate, made several mistakes (including Marie's name, Arles instead of Ables), which he attempted to correct by inserting small letters where needed. Third, is the date of the visit. Though the stone had been removed from the grave, the inscription was still visible, unhidden in the churchyard, more than ten years after the parchments came to light and ten years after the letter of complaint cited by Descadeillas. Does this look like a hasty and deliberate attempt to hide evidence which would lead someone to a vital secret?

Evidence that the other stone even existed is quite a different matter. No copy of Stüblein's book has ever been found, although reproductions of a few pages are said to have been lodged in the Bibliothèque nationale in Paris. We shall follow this trail in chapter 10.

De Sède next tells us about Saunière's renovation of the church, building the *Villa Béthanie*, the terrace and the *Tour Magdala*, his collection of ten thousand postcards and one hundred thousand stamps. To illustrate the high living, he quotes the same wine bills as had been in *La Dépêche du Midi*. Finally, in the first part of his book, he tells us about the later years when the *curé* was in conflict with Bishop Beauséjour, following much the same thread as Descadeillas, except that de Sède gives us verbatim accounts of conversations.

On his deathbed Saunière called an old friend, the *Abbé* Rivière, a priest from the nearby parish of Esperaza, to hear his confession: 'What passed between the two men? We shall never know. But when Rivière left his dying friend he was pale and distressed. His distress lasted a long time: he became withdrawn, taciturn, quiet. Until his death he was never seen to laugh again. What terrible secret had he received in confidence?'[7]

Part 2

The Gold of Rennes

In the second part of his book, entitled *L'Or de Rennes*, de Sède reminds us of the large sums of money spent by Saunière, deducing that between 1891 and 1917 he got through between 15 and 24 million gold francs, a sum far too large to be accounted for by traffic in the Mass. Nor does he think that it could be accounted for by gifts: 'Bérenger

Saunière had discovered a treasure, a treasure so fabulous that it was far from exhausted when he was overtaken by death.' So what could be the source of this wealth?

This question leads de Sède to a review of the history of Rennes-le-Château and some of the legends about treasure, including the one about the shepherd boy Ignace Paris, who in 1645 was looking for a lost lamb which had fallen into a hole. On going down to retrieve the lamb, he found a cave where there were skeletons and heaps of gold. He filled his hat with pieces of the precious metal, but on returning to the village refused to say exactly where he had found them. The villagers assumed that he had stolen them and stoned him to death.

De Sède recounts another tale passed down through the ages concerning the Visigoths, who sacked Rome in 410 and took away a lot of booty, including the spoils from the temple of Jerusalem which the Roman Emperor Titus had seized in AD 70. This treasure is said to have been taken by the Visigoths to the Languedoc in the fifth century and lodged by Alaric II at Carcassonne. When Clovis took Toulouse in 507, it is supposed to have been moved to Spain for safer keeping, and some eventually fell into the hands of the Arabs. But, says de Sède: 'The part of the sacred treasure of the Visigoths which does not seem to have been discovered by either the Francs or the Arabs, could it not have been entrusted to the deeply gullied land of Razès?' (Razès is an old name for the region in which Rennes-le-Château is situated.)

De Sède continues his review of the history of the area, bringing in the Knights Templar, Blanche of Castile and the Albigensian Crusade. He summarizes his findings as follows:

1. Since the Middle Ages there has been a tradition that treasure has been hidden in the district around Rennes.
2. This is not an absurd idea, because it is supported by some well-established facts and probabilities: the (probable) presence of a Visigothic treasure at Carcassonne, the existence of a gold mine at Blanchefort, the exploitation of this mine in the Middle Ages . . . , money counterfeited at Bézu, and nineteenth-century discoveries of significant quantities of cast gold.
3. However, no authentic ancient document exists which allows us to accept these hypotheses with certainty.[8]

There is another, important matter to be included. De Sède consulted two files in the Bibliothèque nationale:

But we still have not finished with the mythology of Rennes. Because we are unable to resolve the uncertainties which surround their origin and purpose, it is under the heading of mythology that we classify two very strange works, published recently at

Geneva. There were only a small number of copies and the authors used pseudonyms which were clearly symbolic. The first appeared in 1956 under the name of Henri Lobineau, entitled *Genealogy of the Merovingian Kings and the origins of various French and foreign families of the Merovingian line, after Abbé Pichon, Doctor Hervé and the parchments of Abbé Saunière of Rennes-le-Château*. The second, from 1963, is entitled *The Merovingian descendants or the enigma of Visigothic Razès*, by Madeleine Blancasall, translated from the German by Walter Celse-Nazaire.[9]

In the course of our researches for original documents, we obtained copies of these files from the Bibliothèque nationale. They are indeed very strange. The file dated 1956 (but not deposited in the Bibliothèque nationale until 1964) is a collection of genealogical tables, hand-drawn, using a template for the letters. One of these, Table 8, has an additional text, *L'Enigme de Rhédéa et L'Abbé Béranger* (sic) *Saunière* (The Enigma of Rennes and the *Abbé* Bérenger Saunière) which begins as follows: 'One day in February 1892[10] the young *Abbé* Hoffet received an unusual visitor, the *Abbé* Saunière *curé* of Rennes-le-Château from 1885, who came to him to ask this learned young linguist to translate some mysterious parchments which had been found in the pillars of the Visigothic high altar of his church. . . .'

Though he does not refer to it in the main text, de Sède includes another document in his list of references, *Les Dossiers secrets d'Henri Lobineau* (The Secret Files of Henri Lobineau). This file of 1967 also contains genealogical tables, as well as letters (including the one mentioned in chapter 3, with Corbu's signature) and various drawings. One of them is a copy of page 101 of the *Bulletin of the Aude Society,* which has the illustration of the tombstone of Marie de Nègre, but it is not a photocopy; every letter is laboriously drawn by hand, to be as near as one could achieve to pass for the page of the Society's report. And that is not all – amazingly they contain an illustration of the missing stone from Marie de Nègre's grave, supposedly published originally by Eugène Stüblein. It too is drawn by hand. Both illustrations have typewritten notes, typed on the same machine.

Although de Sède was a little cautious about the origin of these files, they were obviously one of his main sources. So they are very important and we need to know who the authors were and if we can rely on the information given. We will be coming back to them and will discuss them in detail in chapter 10.

Part 3

The Barbers of Midas

The third part of his book de Sède entitled *Les barbiers de Midas* (The Barbers of Midas).

He retells the legend that Midas' barber discovered that the king had donkey's ears hidden under his hat. He dared not mention this to any one, but he felt a great need to pass on the secret. So he dug a hole, whispered the secret into the ground and then filled the hole in again. But before long grasses grew over the hole and when the wind blew it whispered the secret to all the world.

The legend is introduced to provide some sort of explanation for the contents of this part of de Sède's book, which is all about clues to the location of the treasure. The implication is that Saunière, or someone, knew where the treasure was, was afraid to reveal where and yet was unable not to try to impart the secret. Thus clues are left everywhere, and the most important clues are the first ever illustrations of two of the parchments which Saunière was alleged to have discovered in the high altar.

The longer of the two, which we shall call Manuscript 1 (Fig. 6.1), is from John, chapter 12: 1 to 12. It relates, in Latin, the well-known story of Christ visiting the house of Lazarus and his two sisters, Martha and Mary, in Bethany. Mary anoints Jesus' feet with expensive oil and Judas reproves her, saying that the oil could have been sold and the money given to the poor. Jesus tells him to leave her alone, she has saved this oil and adds 'For the poor always ye have with you: but me ye have not always.'

The second parchment, Manuscript 2 (Fig. 6.2) also in Latin, is much shorter and is an unusual version (see Appendix A) of the story told in Matthew 12: 1–8 about the disciples picking ears of corn to eat on the Sabbath day. The Pharisees object to this action on the grounds it was unlawful, but Jesus reminds them that David had entered the temple on the Sabbath and eaten the bread reserved for the priests.

De Sède says: 'I immediately noticed two things: first in spite of their archaic style, these documents did not appear to be very old; both seemed to be in code; 128 extra letters had been inserted in the clear text of the first manuscript, without making any apparent sense; in the second manuscript you can see some letters displaced, others underlined with a dot, lines of unequal length; finally in both are drawn kinds of hieroglyphs which could be keys to reading them.'[11]

De Sède consulted M. Debant, the current Director of the Archives of Aude Department, who thought they were not old, but could not date them any more accurately than saying they were not earlier than the Renaissance. De Sède took them to an expert in encryption who gave no solution but made an observation that is so remarkable that we will have to look at it again in chapter 6. He said that the texts had been encrypted by a double key cipher, followed by a transposition using a chessboard.

One might think that a discovery as important as this – after all the parchments had been missing for at least seventy years – would be documented in every detail, but not so. De Sède simply says that after a lot of prevarication, they were given to him in Paris on a day in February 1964. Not the slightest hint of who handed them over, or where they had been for so many years.

So who did write them? According to an expert de Sède consulted, they were by a churchman brought up on religious texts, someone who loved mystery and fantasy. On the shorter parchment there is a sort of hieroglyph, the letters PS enclosed in a curly line. Exactly the same hieroglyph occurs on one of the two stones from the tomb of Marie de Nègre. This seems to lead us to Antoine Bigou, *curé* of Rennes-le-Château at the time of Marie's death, who was probably responsible for setting up her tomb. He was the man whom Descadeillas had suspected of burying his savings in the church. But Bigou was not known for expertise in cryptography; de Sède thinks it was more likely to have been a man called Henri Boudet, born in 1837 and at one time *curé* of Rennes-les-Bains.

By any standards Boudet was an extraordinary man. He had an obsessive love of words as well as an interest in antiquity. In 1886 he had published a strange book with the title *The True Celtic Language and the Cromlech of Rennes-les-Bains* (see Appendix H). In this book Boudet sets out his theories of etymology. They are totally contrary to all modern understanding of the subject. He derives words in ancient languages from modern English, simply on the grounds that they sound similar. It is tempting to believe the book is all an elaborate hoax. For example, Boudet derives the Basque names of the months like this: January, Urtharilla, from hurt and harrow, i.e. a bad month when it will hurt to harrow the fields; February Otsaïla, from hot and sail, i.e. it is now warm enough to put to sea. These examples are not relevant to the story of Rennes-le-Château; they simply illustrate that if anyone could do strange things with words, that man was the *Abbé* Boudet.

Next de Sède turns his attention to Henri Boudet's church at Rennes-les-Bains. In the churchyard there are several monuments with, according to him, unusual inscriptions. De Sède interprets these as instructions to stand at the calvary outside the west door of the church and look in various directions. One of his alignments directs him to Rennes-le-Château.

He goes on to describe the church at Rennes-le-Château in detail. He maintains that there are hidden messages and symbolism everywhere. For an example of his method we can take the prayer at the foot of Parchment 1, which was at one time also displayed on a board attached to the base of Saunière's new altar in the church at Rennes-le-Château.

JÉSU.MEDÈLA.VULNÉRUM+SPES.UNA.POENÌTENTIUM
PER.MAGDALANAE.LACRYMAS+PECCATA.NOSTRA.DILUAS
(Jesus, healer of wounds, the one hope of penitence through the tears of Magdalene, wash away our sins.)

Note that some letters are accented: this is not done in Latin and might be to attract our attention. De Sède now plays a verbal game worthy of the *Abbé* Boudet himself. If we pick out the pairs of letters which end with an accented letter we have the syllables JÉ, DÈ, NÉ. De Sède also adds NI, saying that the first I in POENITENTIUM had a dot over it. These syllables have the same sounds in French as the words *jais* (the mineral, jet), *dé* (a die), *nez* (nose) and *nid* (nest). In turn de Sède links them to a jet mine whose entrance is marked by a dolmen near the village of Sougraignes, a stone in the shape of a cube near Serbaïrou, a rock looking like a nose near Peyrolles and the 'eagle's nest of Cardou', a high point in the area. Thus four points in the topography are identified which we are asked to believe are significant. There is much arbitrary association of words, places and pictures.

The stations of the cross come in for similar scrutiny. In each picture de Sède looks for unusual details, his idea being that within them are subtle clues to some place of significance near Rennes-le-Château.

'Signs of the same sort are read at the sixth station (Pl. 17). There, a soldier holds his shield high; you see a tower half hidden and a dome; Veronica holds out to Jesus a linen shroud, while Simon Peter looks on. Together they show us precisely how to orientate ourselves on the ground, using a sort of puzzle which we shall leave you to work out for yourself.'[12]

At other stations of the cross and in other paintings in the church de Sède finds strange details in profusion. He believes there was a group of people in the background who were inspiring Bérenger Saunière. He points out that there are roses and crosses in the decoration of the porch of the church and suggests it was probably the work of a Rosicrucian sect.[13]

Part 4
Some Danger

In the fourth and final part of de Sède's book, *Un certain danger*, he turns to more sinister matters, with an account of crimes and sudden death. Bernard Mongé, the tutor of Marie de Nègre before her marriage, was murdered in 1732. *Abbé* Antoine Gélis, *curé* of Coustaussa near Rennes, and a friend of Saunière, was found dead in his presbytery in 1897 with serious head wounds. No money was missing and no one was ever brought to justice for the crime.

Other strange and macabre events were told to de Sède in 1963 by *Abbé* Joseph Courtauly, *curé* of Villarzel-du-Razès. Courtauly met Saunière in 1908, when the former was eighteen years old. He told de Sède that *Abbé* Rescanières, who was successor to *Abbé* Boudet, at Rennes-les-Bains, was found dead in 1915, fully clothed on the floor, and that the cause of his death was never established.

Much later in 1956, de Sède says that a small group of excavators, including Descadeillas, carried out an excavation in the floor of the church at Rennes-le-Château, near where Saunière had uncovered the stone carved with the figure of a horseman and found a human skull with a gash in it. Then in the garden of the presbytery they found the decomposing remains of three bodies, still with fragments of clothing on them.

No connection is drawn between these deaths but to de Sède they add to the mysteries of Rennes-le-Château. He concludes his work darkly with a quote from *Abbé* Mazières, *curé* of a parish near Carcassonne, who says to him: 'I know that you are quite interested in this affair; it excites me too. But I have to warn you: it involves some danger.'

Conclusions

When we come to comparing the accounts given by de Sède with those of Corbu and Descadeillas, we note that although the essentials of the story of Saunière's finding the parchments are much the same, there are several new details given. If we were to pick out just four points which seem to be the most significant they would have to be these:

1. We are told about Saunière's trip to Paris, where he stayed, whom he met there and that he bought copies of three paintings.
2. We learn that the grave of Marie de Nègre had two stones, one of them only recorded in an obscure book of which no copies are now known (though by chance a drawing of this particular stone was made and deposited in the Bibliothèque nationale).
3. We are given the text of the two manuscripts, said to have been found by Saunière in the high altar. After having been missing for many years, they turn up in Paris (but de Sède does not say who gave them to him).
4. We see that the manuscripts contain encrypted messages. We are told how one of the ciphers was composed, although no solution is given.

All these points we shall follow up in later chapters.

De Sède has introduced new dimensions to the story. In his book the village tale of a country *curé* who may have found treasure is just the beginning. There are suggestions of further and deeper mysteries. The cipher messages in the manuscripts are only part of the puzzle. There are hints and allusions and coincidences. There are unexpected and presumably significant details in paintings and inscriptions – if we could understand them, what would they tell us? The site of hidden treasure or something more? In the shadowy background there may be a secret society, possibly the Rosicrucians, exerting their influence in mysterious ways. The book was cleverly targeted to a readership who liked their history served up with a dash of the unexplained and the inexplicable.

5

The Chronicle Programmes

The affair of Rennes-le-Château might never have become known to the English-speaking world if it had not been for the author and broadcaster, Henry Lincoln, a fluent French speaker, who came across an edition of de Sède's book while on holiday in the Cevennes in August 1969.[1]

Henry Lincoln, original name Henry Soskin, began his career in the theatre. During the 1960s he acted in television series such as *The Avengers* and *Man in a Suitcase*, and wrote many scripts, including episodes of the popular *Emergency Ward 10* and *Dr Who*. He was thus well experienced in the techniques of television production. Intrigued by de Sède's story of Rennes-le-Château, he approached Paul Johnstone, the editor of the *Chronicle* series, and this led to the making of the first of the three programmes which introduced the subject to British audiences. Since then Lincoln has written extensively about Rennes-le-Château and its ramifications, notably as co-author of the best-seller *The Holy Blood and the Holy Grail* (1982), a book which sets out in print much of the material first dealt with in the television programmes.

The three programmes and their dates of transmission were: *The Lost Treasure of Jerusalem?*, 12 February 1972; *The Priest, the Painter and the Devil*, 30 October 1974; and *The Shadow of the Templars*, 27 November 1979.

The Lost Treasure of Jerusalem?

Synopsis

The story, told through the voice of the narrator, begins with the village of Rennes-le-Château, the impoverished priest and the discovery of the parchments. We hear of Saunière's trip to Paris, his consultation with experts at the Seminary of Saint-Sulpice, his association with Emma Calvé and his purchases of paintings, including Poussin's *Les Bergers d'Arcadie*, at the Louvre. On his return he works in the churchyard, obliterates inscriptions and constructs a grotto. Then follows Saunière's considerable expenditure on the church, the *Villa Béthanie* and the village. We are led to believe that his newly-found wealth is due to the discovery of a treasure, and that the clues to the location of the treasure are in the decoded parchments, which could only be understood because Saunière had a detailed knowledge of the landscape around the village.

Next a hypothesis is constructed around the possibility that Solomon's treasure, seized from the Temple at Jerusalem by the Emperor Titus in AD 70, and captured from Rome by the Visigoths in AD 410 was brought back to the kingdom of the Visigoths, which in the fifth century covered much of what is now southern France and eastern Spain. Some of the treasure was kept at Toulouse and some at Carcassonne, but could the treasure have been taken to Aereda, or Rennes-le-Château, which the film claims was a large city at this time?

Connections are now drawn between Rennes-le-Château and the Merovingian king Dagobert II, who was assassinated in AD 679. It is suggested that his infant son Sigebert was taken to Rennes and later became Count of Razès. A carved stone found by Saunière in the church may depict the rescue of the young king.[2]

The next part brings in the idea that Bérenger Saunière hid clues to the whereabouts of the supposed treasure in the design of the works of art in the new church. We are given the convoluted interpretation of the picture at the sixth Station of the Cross (see footnote 12 in chapter 4). Other clues are supposedly hidden in the picture beneath the new altar. The trail is said to lead towards the castle of Blanchefort, the hill of Pech Cardou and the village of Arques.

Now we are introduced to something that is entirely new in the story of Rennes-le-Château. It is claimed that Nicolas Poussin's painting *Les Bergers d'Arcadie* was not a scene in an imaginary landscape, but a painting of an actual tomb not far from Rennes, by the road to the village of Arques. The skyline, it is said, bears a strong resemblance to the actual horizon, and on the right of the painting one can see the hill on which Rennes-le-Château is built. Further connections are made – between the motto on the tomb, the inscription on one of the stones on the grave of Marie de Nègre: all are said to be clues as to the whereabouts of the treasure. Finally Henry Lincoln himself appears, to assure the viewer that much more remains to be discovered about Rennes-le-Château.

The Lost Treasure of Jerusalem?
Observations

This programme was not typical of the majority of those in the *Chronicle* series, which aimed for the most part to present history in a serious and academic style. Here we had a dramatic presentation, with little attempt to present evidence to support the claims. Many statements are made without the slightest clue as to their origin or degree of reliability. Saunière's trip to Paris, his visit to Saint-Sulpice, his deathbed confession, the visit of the painter Poussin to Rennes-le-Château (essential to the story), the identification of the tomb in the church with Dagobert, the nature of inscriptions supposed to have been erased from tombstones – all these are presented with no explanation of where the information comes from nor any assessment of its value.

In retrospect it is very obvious that the programme was based on the book by Gérard de Sède, but surprisingly there was no reference to his work, nor did he figure in the programme, except that his name was included in the list of credits at the end, as a 'consultant', along with the producer, cameramen and others.

This seems strange, but there were several strange things that happened during the making of the programme. Lincoln himself gives us an account of them in his book *Key to the Sacred Pattern*, published much later, in 1997. He describes how, when looking carefully at the illustration of the shorter of the two manuscripts in de Sède's book, he noticed that some of the letters were raised slightly above the line of text. Extracting these letters gave a short message in French, which when translated into English reads either 'This treasure belongs to King Dagobert II and to Sion and it is death', or possibly 'This treasure belongs to King Dagobert II and to Sion and he is there dead'. Lincoln was surprised to find that there was no mention of this message in de Sède's book, and it was this discovery that interested Paul Johnstone and initiated the making of the film.[3]

Lincoln and Johnstone went to Paris just before Christmas 1970 to meet Gérard de Sède. At this meeting Lincoln asked de Sède why he had not published the hidden message in his book, only to receive the initial response 'What message?' After some verbal sparring Lincoln concluded that perhaps de Sède was indeed aware of the message. He eventually gave the unconvincing answer 'Because we thought it might interest someone like you to find it for yourself.'[4] De Sède did not explain whom he meant by 'we'.

In February 1971 Lincoln visited Rennes-le-Château for the first time on a reconnaissance trip. Though Noël Corbu was no longer there, the *Villa Béthanie* was still in business as the *Hôtel de la Tour*, under the proprietorship of Henri Buthion, who was delighted by the idea of filming in the village.

The following month they were back again, this time to make a short film for a magazine article in the *Chronicle* series. On this occasion Gérard de Sède arrived at the village and deliberately drew Lincoln's attention to the passage in his book saying that Saunière had bought a copy of Poussin's painting of *Les Bergers d'Arcadie* on his trip to Paris. Lincoln comments that he had not given much attention to this statement, since it seemed to be irrelevant to the rest of the story. But now came a surprise – according to de Sède someone had discovered the actual tomb painted by Poussin and it was not far from Rennes-le-Château![5]

After his return to England there came another surprise for Henry Lincoln. In his book de Sède had said that the longer parchment had 128 interpolated letters making up a hidden message, which was encrypted by means of a double key cipher and a transposition of letters. The solution was not given in the book, but now de Sède said that the cipher had been broken by French Army experts using computers, and he gave the text. We give the full message in the next chapter, but for the moment it is sufficient to know the English translation of a few words: 'Poussin holds the key'. Lincoln was told by a British expert that without the key, this cipher was unbreakable.[6] These events convinced Lincoln and the producer that the subject was now worth more than a short film, and plans began to make a full 40-minute item for transmission in the following year.

In September the team returned to France and located the tomb. Lincoln was convinced that this really was the tomb painted by Poussin and he found similarities between the actual landscape and the background in the painting. Research in the area failed to provide much history of the tomb. There was no record of it in the Departmental Archives at Carcassonne. René Descadeillas, whom Lincoln met, knew nothing about it. However Lincoln came across a local photographer, Georges Basset, who told him that two American ladies, by the name of Lawrence, had been buried there in the 1920s. When the tomb was opened for the interment of the elder lady in 1920, it was definitely empty.[7] When it was constructed, no one could say.

Some incidents that occurred during the making of the film led Lincoln to the conclusion that he was being watched. The first occurred during the initial reconnaissance trip. Lincoln visited a place called *La Fontaine des Amours*, the Lovers' Fountain. Here he found an inscription on a rock. In a heart transfixed by an arrow was the name Calvet (the birth name of Emma Calvé with whom Bérenger Saunière supposedly had an association on his trip to Paris) and the date 1891. This is illustrated with a photograph.[8] It is quite clear that the inscription was not on the rock itself, but on a smear of clay or cement, which had been recently applied to the rock. The following day Lincoln found that it had been erased. It is difficult to avoid the conclusion that someone, whether from his own party or the local community, was teasing him.

There were more serious incidents too. During the filming of the tomb, when the crew was not present, someone had broken into it and severely damaged it. Further damage occurred in the churchyard. Lincoln had identified a slab with one of the gravestones of Marie de Nègre. Someone had broken this into three pieces.[9]

Whether Lincoln's team was being watched it is impossible to say, but there is no doubt that he – and de Sède – were being manipulated by a person or persons unknown. Someone had produced the solution to the unbreakable cipher, and that could only be someone who knew the key. And someone had told de Sède to include a reference to Poussin's painting in his book; they must have known about the tomb many years before. It was several years before Lincoln found out who was pulling the strings.

The Priest, the Painter and the Devil

Synopsis

The first quarter of this film recapitulates the story told in *The Lost Treasure of Jerusalem?* The new material begins with the letters PS found on the shorter of the two parchments. Lincoln suggests that they stand for the Priory of Sion, which he asserts is a secret organisation connected with the Knights Templar. The Knights Templar were founded in 1118 and their original purpose was to protect pilgrims visiting the Holy Land. They fought bravely against the Saracens and became very wealthy and powerful. One of their castles was near the village of Bézu, only about 6 km to the south-east of Rennes-le-Château. Because they acknowledged allegiance only to the Pope, they also became a threat to the king of France, Philippe le Bel, who suppressed them with great cruelty in 1307. Only one Templar castle in the region was spared – that at Bézu.

Next we are told about the Albigensians, or Cathars, a group who believed that there were two gods, the God of the spirit who was incapable of creating physical matter, and Rex Mundi, the ruler of the earth who created all physical things. There was a long campaign against this doctrine which was seen as a heresy. The Albigensians' last stronghold was at Montségur. There in 1244 two hundred men and women were burned for their beliefs. But three men escaped the besieging army, supposedly taking with them the treasures of their faith.

So Lincoln leaves us with a selection of possible sources for the treasure that might have been concealed at Rennes-le-Château – from Jerusalem, the Visigoths, the Templars and the Cathars.

The film now takes a different topic, the hidden message in the longer parchment and gives a detailed explanation of how it was encrypted. From the clear message Lincoln once again pays most attention to the words 'Poussin holds the key', which leads him to further study of the painting *Les Bergers d'Arcadie*. He has its geometry analysed by Professor Cornford of the Royal College of Art. Cornford notes that the proportions of the canvas are in the ratio of the Golden Section and finds that the composition is based on a pentagon, a figure of importance to those who practised magic.[10]

Lincoln also finds a five-pointed figure in the layout of the shorter of the two manuscripts, though it is not in this case regular: the sides are of different lengths.

Lincoln's final conclusion is that Saunière's secret was that he too worshipped the Devil. Indeed his church has a statue of the Devil and symbols of the occult. The priest's source of money was, according to Lincoln, from benefactors who were his fellows in a secret society who practised the black arts. Little wonder then that Saunière's deathbed confession had such an effect on the priest who heard it.

The Priest, the Painter and the Devil
Observations

The origins of the second *Chronicle* film were very unusual. The BBC itself had already been enticed into filming the uncovering of the treasure by an unnamed person who claimed to have discovered its whereabouts, and would allow the cameras in, providing Henry Lincoln was kept out of it. Unbelievably the BBC was taken in by this claim and despatched a team to Rennes-le-Château in the spring of 1973.

The villagers, more sceptical than the BBC, had demanded the presence of Henry Lincoln, someone they knew and trusted. Lincoln responded to the request to sort things out. In spite of the apparent craziness of the treasure hunter's ideas, the preparations were made to film the great discovery. Lincoln had the courage of his convictions, said there would be nothing there, and retreated to the village for a drink.

Of course, there was nothing there. But the result was that Roy Davies, the director, was only too eager for Henry Lincoln to write an updated film on his own continuing researches into Rennes-le-Château. The film crew were already on site, and Henry Lincoln found himself having to produce a shooting script in just two days.

Shortly after this filming, Gérard de Sède (who was somewhat put out that he had not appeared in the first film) wrote to Henry Lincoln declaring that he had found the treasure of Bérenger Saunière. He was willing to sell the BBC a ten-minute film of its discovery. Lincoln was immediately suspicious, and as it turned out, with good reason. The story of this treasure was published in an edition of a quarterly magazine in Paris called *Charivari*, by a journalist called Jean-Luc Chaumeil. It claimed to be from Rennes-le-Château, but the pieces illustrated came from Petroassa in Romania.[11] It is difficult to imagine the point of this charade, certain to be detected by any competent investigator.

Shadow of the Templars
Synopsis

After introductory shots the film relates the history of the Knights Templar in rather more detail than was given in the previous programme. Lincoln tells us that when the Templars were founded by Hugues de Payen, they were given accommodation in part of the royal palace in Jerusalem, on the site of the ancient temple of Solomon. There were only nine knights and they remained at that number for nine years, during which time they appear to have cleared out Solomon's stables. Lincoln hints that they might have found something valuable there.

In 1128 the Knights Templar were recognized as a military order and began to recruit and to acquire wealth. In 1147 they embarked on the Second Crusade. Under their fourth Grand Master, Bertrand de Blanchefort, they flourished, establishing markets and receiving huge gifts of money and lands. They created a network of castles throughout Christendom.

At the beginning of the fourteenth century, the Knights Templar fell foul of the king of France, Philippe le Bel, who owed them a lot of money and wished to get rid of them. With considerable scheming he managed to get his candidate, Bertrand de Goth, Archbishop of Bordeaux, who was related to the Blanchefort family, installed as Pope in Avignon as Clement V. Papal opposition now out of the way, Philippe organized a co-ordinated attack on the Templars' fortresses on 13 October 1307. The Order of Knights Templar was finally dissolved in 1312.

The film now moves on to a brief account of Dagobert II and his son Sigebert, whose descendants, it was claimed, included Godefroy de Bouillon who recaptured Jerusalem from the Saracens in 1090. In recognition of this success, Godefroy was offered the kingship of Jerusalem by a powerful group of men whose names are no longer known. Lincoln argues that this group were the members of a religious order, the Order of Our Lady of Sion, and in support he cites documents which he has come across in the French National Library. He links this order with the group who founded the Templars twenty-eight years later.

A century after this, in 1187, Jerusalem was again lost to the Saracens in a disastrous campaign. The Order accused the Templars of treachery, severed its connections with them and renamed itself the Priory of Sion.

Lincoln says that he has also found documents giving genealogies of the line of Dagobert, and that one of his descendants is someone called Pierre Plantard, who lives in Paris. In the film he interviews Plantard, who assures him that the Priory of Sion still exists.

Another theme developed in the programme is the geometry of Poussin's painting. Having found a pentangle, or five-pointed star, hidden in the composition, Professor Cornford suggested to Lincoln that there might be a geometrical connection with Rennes-le-Château. Lincoln discovered that the three peaks, Rennes-le-Château, Blanchefort and the Templar castle at Bézu made a triangle whose angles were 72°, 72° and 36°; angles which one can find in a pentangle. Further investigations revealed that two other hilltops completed a regular pentagon of peaks, which, argues Lincoln, must be an especially unusual occurrence.[12]

He links these discoveries with the planet Venus, whose movements make a five-pointed figure in the sky, Mary Magdelene, after whom Saunière named his tower and the five-pointed figure that he claimed to find in the parchment. To those who practised magic – and this Lincoln asserts included the Templars – the pentacle, which is a pentangle with a surrounding circle, was of immense significance. Lincoln puts forward the hypothesis that because of its unusual natural geometry, Rennes-le-Château was especially important as a place, and that Saunière was in fact its custodian financed by the Priory of Sion. He concludes that 'the real treasure of Rennes-le-Château is not one of gold and jewels, the real treasure is a secret – the pentacle.'

Shadow of the Templars
Observations

While preparing for this film, Lincoln met Richard Leigh, a student of Templar history, and Michael Baigent, a photo-journalist from New Zealand with a similar interest. They collaborated with Lincoln in the making of the programme, and together went on to write two books, *The Holy Blood and the Holy Grail* (1982) and *The Messianic Legacy* (1986).

The most dramatic event during the period of research for the film was the BBC's success in finding and meeting the shadowy characters (the mysterious 'we') who had fed Gérard de Sède information to pass on to Lincoln. At last, as a result of a search for the Priory of Sion, the BBC researcher tracked down a man called Pierre Plantard de St Clair, who according to Lincoln was its Grand Master.[13] A meeting was arranged in Paris with Lincoln and a BBC team on the one hand, and Plantard, his friend Philippe de Chérisey and a small number of members of the Priory of Sion on the other. Gérard de Sède was not with them. At this meeting they screened *The Priest, the Painter and the Devil*. Lincoln observes that when Plantard and de Chérisey saw the picture of the pentacle overlaid on the parchment, they seemed surprised. Plantard said that the parchments had been concocted by his friend de Chérisey, but Lincoln could not bring himself to believe this, which is understandable in view of the hypotheses he had constructed on the basis of the geometry.

Plantard agreed to cooperate in the making of the third film by letting Jean-Luc Chaumeil, a journalist, be the spokesman. The interview was arranged to take place above an art gallery owned by Mme Chaumeil, Jean-Luc's mother. At the last moment Plantard himself took over.[14] Chaumeil and his mother were both upset. Lincoln asked Plantard about the geometry in the parchment. He responded by saying that he could not give a reply. Lincoln took this to be confirmation that the geometry was intentional and significant.

Lincoln had been very keen to see the parchments, and was promised that they would be produced for his inspection. He was disappointed: de Chérisey produced only black and white photographs. Lincoln makes a very significant observation: 'The parchments, as reproduced in de Sède's book . . . have many dots, strokes and accents inserted into the spaces between the lines of text. Many researchers have spent much time in trying to wrest some sort of sense from these marks. The photographs I am shown demonstrate that these are not present in the originals. They have been added in blue ink, clearly visible on the glossy surface of the prints.'

Between them these three films greatly extend the story of Rennes-le-Château from the original tale of a poor priest finding treasure and using the money to renovate his church. Henry Lincoln has introduced the Cathars, the Templars, the Priory of Sion, and geometry of the hills. Not everything can be checked, but now we have looked at the first accounts of the discovery of the treasure and the way the story has been developed, firstly by Gérard de Sède and then by Henry Lincoln, it is time to take a close look at the evidence on which their work is based.

6

The Parchments

The two parchments, which were reputedly found in the church at Rennes-le-Château by Bérenger Saunière, are central to the mystery. Without them there would have been no hidden messages; without cracking the codes, there would have been no discovery of a treasure. Without a treasure, Rennes-le-Château would have remained obscure in a remote part of France. Instead, Rennes-le-Château is now claimed by some authors to be a place of great significance, the location of the lost treasure of Jerusalem, even, as we shall see, the burial place of Christ himself.

It might be thought that documents of such importance would be made available to academic historians for careful analysis and scrutiny. Using modern scientific and forensic techniques there is much that can be done. Chemical analysis and microscopic examination of the vellum or paper could perhaps reveal its source. Certainly boundaries could be put on its date of manufacture. The ink similarly can be tested, and possibly be dated independently; this is a useful test for genuineness. Unfortunately the parchments have not been made available. Their whereabouts since their discovery have been a mystery. We have not seen them and the only illustrations are those first given in Gérard de Sède's *L'Or de Rennes*, endlessly copied since.

It is interesting that de Sède does not claim to have seen the original parchments. Recapping from chapter 4, he says that he had copies of two of the documents which Bérenger Saunière had found under the high altar of his church. And then he says 'despite their archaic appearance they do not appear to be very old'.

Clearly, de Sède was not given photographs of the parchments; if that had been the case, the statement that they did not appear to be very old would have been meaningless. Nor in 1967 could they have been dry photocopies such as we commonly use at the present time. The remaining possibility is ink on paper. If they were copies they must have been based on meticulously accurate tracings, since even minute displacements of the letters were reproduced, and as we shall see were quite important, especially for the shorter of the two documents. It is hard to imagine anyone copying these documents with such precision, patience and labour unless they were aware of the significance of the accurate position of the individual letters and, by implication, the messages hidden in the texts. We think that de Sède was mistaken (or misled) when he said he had been shown copies of the parchments – it is more likely that he saw the only ones that existed.

Though described as parchments, which are strictly speaking produced from animal skin, we cannot be sure of what they were made. They were obviously hand-written and more appropriately should be called manuscripts.

Even without the manuscripts, either original or copied, with the published pictures there are four aspects that can still be discussed: the style of the lettering, the Latin texts, the layout of the manuscripts, and the cipher in Manuscript 1 (Fig. 6.1).

The Style of the Lettering

The manuscripts seem to be written by the same hand and are in an apparently old-fashioned script. In fact the letters are in a style similar to uncials, a script which originated in the second century AD and continued in use for about another 500 years, including the Merovingian period. The choice of lettering is rather curious, because there is no possibility that the manuscripts date back to the period when this script was in use. They must be more recent than the death of Marie de Nègre d'Ables who died in 1781, because, as we shall see shortly, their author was aware of the inscription on her tomb. The only rational deduction is that they were written in the uncial script in order to make them seem ancient. This should make us suspicious of the manuscripts from the start.

The Latin Texts

Both manuscripts are in Latin, and appear to be extracts from the Bible. We thought it important to establish, if possible, which edition of the Bible they were taken from, because this fact would add another boundary to their date. Latin versions, like English ones, differ in detail in their texts. One of us did a study of all Latin New Testament texts (see Appendix A) and found that Manuscript 1, the account of Jesus visiting the house of Lazarus, was taken from a version of the Bible published in 1889.[1] Not only does this conclusively eliminate Antoine Bigou as the author – he died about the end of the eighteenth century – but it makes it difficult to see how Henri Boudet, *curé* of Rennes-les-Bains from 1872 to 1914, could have been responsible, as Gérard de Sède supposed.

Saunière was appointed to Rennes-le-Château in 1885. Is it likely that Boudet, or anyone else for that matter, could have obtained a copy of a new edition of the Bible in 1889, devised the encryption and managed to secrete parchments in the altar pillar under Saunière's nose only a few months before they were allegedly discovered by the *curé*? The date of the text throws a lot of doubt on whether the parchments shown to de Sède were the ones discovered by Saunière. One other possibility is that Saunière concocted the parchments himself, but this begins to make nonsense of the whole

JESVSEVRGOANTCESEXATPESPASCShAEVENJTTbETh9ANTAMVRAT
FVERAOTIAZA•VVSMORTYVVS9VEMMSYSCTYTAVITIYESVSFEACERVNT
LAVIEM•TTCAENAPMTbTETOMARThAhMINISTRRAbATCbASARVSO
VEROVNXVSERATTE•dTSCOVMLENTATLVSCVJMMARTALERGOACbCEP
TTLKTbRAMYNNGENTTJNARATPFTJTTICT9PRETTOVJTETVNEXTTPE
dPESTERVAETEXTEJRSTTCAYPTIRTSNSVISPEPAESERTPTETAOMbEJTM
PLFTIAEJTEEXVNGETNTTOdAEREdTXATTERGOVRNVMEXAGTSCTPVhl
TSETVTXTVddXJCARJORTTS9VTYERATCVhMTRadTTIYRYS9TVAREhOCCVN
bENVTVMNONXVENVTTGRECENPdTSdENAaRÜJETddATVMESGTE
GENTES? dTXTNVFEMhOECNON9VJTAdEEGaENTSPERRTINEbEaT
adEVTMSEdqVhlnFVRELRTETLOVCVIOShCAbENJECA9VAEMVTTIEbA
NMTVRPOTRabETEdTXTTEJRGOTEShVJSTNEPTLLAMVNITXdIEMS
EPVLGTVRAEMSEAEJERVNETILL9VdPAVPJEKESENhTMJEMPGERhA
bEMTTSNOblTISCVMFMEaVTETMNONSESMPERhavbENSCJOGNO
VILIEROTZVRbaMV9LTaEXTMVdaCTSTqVTaTlOLTCESTXETVENE
aRVNTNONNPROTEPRTESVMETANT•MMSEdVTLVZaRVMPVTdER
Eh•T9VEMKSVSCTaOVTTaMORRTVTSCPOGTTaVKERVNTAhVTEMP
RVTNCTPEJSSACERCdOTVMVMTETLAZCARVMTNATCRFTCTTRENTY
LVTAMYLVTTPROP9TCRILhXVMAbThGNTCXVGTadETSNETCRCd
dEbANTTTNTESVM

NO ⊕ IS

JÉSV. MEdÈLÀ. VVLNÉRVM ✚ SPES. VNA. POENITENTIVM.
PER. MAGDALANÆ. LACRYMAS ✦ PECCATA. NOSTRA. dILVAS.

6.1 Parchment 1.

story about their holding the clue to the location of a treasure. We are being drawn to the conclusion that if Saunière found parchments while repairing the altar, they must have been as Descadeillas stated, a text relating to the construction of the church, and not the parchments illustrated by de Sède.

The Layout of Manuscript 2

Manuscript 2 (Fig. 6.2) – the one about the disciples picking and eating corn on the Sabbath – is very curiously laid out. The lines are of unequal length and some have gaps in them. Some words are split by the end of the line (for example *coeperunt* between lines 3 and 4, *manducabant* between lines 4 and 5). Three lines, the fourth, seventh and tenth, have crosses in the middle of the text. There are two strange little drawings, one at the top and one at the bottom of the text. The upper one is a triangle containing the letter I (just possibly a T) and above it is M. The lower one has P and S enclosed in a curled line.

6.2 Parchment 2.

De Sède gave no explanation or interpretation of the manuscripts in his book published in 1967, beyond saying that the texts of both contained coded messages. Yet the message hidden in Manuscript 2 is not hidden in a particularly obscure manner. As we have recounted, Henry Lincoln found it and gave it in his television programme, *The Lost Treasure of Jerusalem?* He noticed that the letter A at the end of the second line (actually part of the word *abire*) was slightly raised above the line. Closer scrutiny of the whole text revealed other letters which were raised. Line by line he found as follows: (on line 2) A D A, (3) G O, (4) B, (5) E R T, (6) I I, (7) R O I, (8) E T A, (9) S I O N, (10) E S T C E T R, (11) E S O R, (12) E T I L E S, (13) T, (14) L A M O R T.

Putting all these letters together, and spacing the words, we get the message

A DAGOBERT II ROI ET A SION EST CE TRESOR ET IL EST LA MORT.

There is an ambiguity in the meaning: it could be translated, TO KING DAGOBERT II AND TO SION BELONGS THE TREASURE AND HE IS THERE DEAD, or possibly and more likely, TO KING DAGOBERT II AND TO SION BELONGS THE TREASURE AND IT IS DEATH.[2]

It is hard to believe that if de Sède had known of the message at the time of publication of his book he would have deliberately omitted it. On the other hand, he did not include it in the revised edition of his book published in 1977,[3] although he did have an appendix describing the code which is hidden in Manuscript 1.

In the hidden message of Manuscript 2 is the connection between the Merovingian dynasty, treasure and Jerusalem (or Sion – Zion in English) which has led many treasure hunters to search in and around Rennes-le-Château for the lost treasure of Jerusalem. The creator of the manuscript does not want the link with Jerusalem to be missed. He draws attention to the word Sion by the arrangement of the last four lines of the text, which are split in such a way as to form a block whose right hand letters spell SION in a vertical line.

And that may not be all. Some analysts have found the word SION appearing in a diagonal line. If one joins the crosses in lines 4 and 10, and projects to the bottom, the line so drawn will pass through S of line 7, T of line 8, O of line 9, and finally it just touches the top of the O in line 14 and the bottom of N in the same line. The argument goes that the T and I look much alike, and if the O of line 14 is conveniently ignored, once more we get SION. We are inclined to the view that this is accidental. With a little change to the layout, for example adding three letters to line 6, thereby moving line 7 three letters to the left, the letter I could have been brought into the alignment instead of T. Just a small change in the position of the letters in line 14 would have helped. The word SION would then have emerged without any doubt.

Based on this discovery, Henry Lincoln proceeds to overlay Manuscript 2 with more and more lines. He extends the short lines of the device at the top left of the manuscript and finds that they pass through the little cross in line 3 and the N in line 14. This makes a triangle with the ends of the diagonal line explained above, and looks to be deliberate. He continues to add more lines, which to a sceptical eye seem to be somewhat arbitrary, and produces the irregular pentagon, which he showed in the film *The Priest, the Painter and the Devil*.

In comparison with the analysis of Andrews and Schellenberger,[4] Lincoln's seems modest in the extreme. They conclude that Manuscript 2 is in fact a map. They find a hexagram rather than a pentagram, and claim that one of the lines they deduce from the geometry represents the Paris Meridian, which actually passes about 6 km east of Rennes-le-Château.

It is hard to take this sort of analysis seriously. With sufficient time and ingenuity it is possible to find patterns and arrangements in almost anything – particularly in landscape. (This will be considered at length later.) It is no surprise to us that Pierre Plantard and Philippe de Chérisey were astonished when they saw in Lincoln's film, *The Priest, the Painter and the Devil*, a pentagon overlaid on Manuscript 2.

The Layout of Manuscript 1

Manuscript 1 is laid out in a neat block of twenty lines. Below that there is a little drawing and at the foot the two lines of the Latin prayer which we discussed in chapter 4. In the light of the style of Manuscript 2, we will obviously look for letters that are not written precisely on the lines. Clearly written below the lines are (on line 4) P, (5) A, (6) N, (7) I, (8) S, (10) A, (11) Ω, (12) S, (13) A, (15) L. These spell the Latin words *PANIS* and *SAL* (bread, salt) with the Greek letters alpha and omega in between them. We have here a clear allusion to Revelation 1:8 'I am the Alpha and the Omega, the beginning and the ending, saith the Lord.'

In very tiny letters we find (2) R, (3) E, (4) X, (16) M U, (17) N, (19) D, (20) I, spelling *REX MUNDI*, King of the World, a title used by the Cathars for Satan, whom they regarded as the creator of the physical world.

Interpolated in the Latin text are 140 extra letters (see Appendix A). The first 64 additional letters make no apparent sense, but on lines 9, 10 and 11, the 12 extra letters spell out *AD GENESARETH*. Finally there are 64 more letters as apparently random and meaningless as the first 64. *Ad Genesareth* means 'To Genesareth', or the Sea of Galilee, as it is known in the New Testament. Discarding *AD GENESARETH*, the 128 interpolated letters are those used in the code which will be explained later in this chapter.

The strange device at the bottom of the main text has attracted much attention. When inverted one can read the word SION, thus reinforcing the link between the two manuscripts (though there would seem to be no doubt that they are written by the same person).

The layout of Manuscript 1 is much less promising than Manuscript 2 for those seeking geometrical patterns. Nevertheless, Andrews and Schellenberger manage to find within it elevation and plan drawings of the Great Pyramid of Giza.[5]

The Cipher in Manuscript 1

The hidden message in Manuscript 2 was very simple: in Manuscript 1 it is fiendishly complicated. Basically the message was encrypted using a well-known method called the Table of Vigenère (Fig. B.1), which will be explained shortly. This method requires a keyword; in Manuscript 1 the message was encrypted twice, with two different keywords. A further complication was to reorder the letters by following a series of knight's moves on a chessboard. The detailed, step-by-step solution is given in Appendix B. In this chapter we shall concentrate on the method.

When de Sède published his book in 1967 he did not know the solution to the cipher. Lincoln received it from de Sède in 1971 during the making of *The Lost Treasure of Jerusalem?*[6] De Sède told Lincoln that it had been solved by French army experts, but he gave no names. He published the solution (with numerous mistakes) in 1977 in a revised and longer version of his book, now entitled *Signé:Rose+Croix*.[7] Lincoln gives the solution in detail in his book *The Holy Place*.[8]

The method of encryption was invented by a French cryptographer, Blaise de Vigenère, in the sixteenth century.[9] The alphabet is set out in rows; in each succeeding row the letters are advanced by one. This is shown in Figure B.1, in which it should be noted that we have used a 25-letter alphabet (omitting W, which was not used in French at that time, nor is it used in this cipher). The method is best illustrated by a short example.

To begin with one needs a keyword – we shall use BRAIN. Suppose the message to be encrypted is SAUNIERE IS CURE OF RENNES LE CHATEAU. We write out the message and above it the keyword, repeated as many times as is necessary to reach the end of the message. We then have the following:

```
BRAIN BRAIN BRAIN BRAIN BRAIN BRAIN B
SAUNI EREIS CUREO FRENN ESLEC HATEA U.
```

The letters are broken into groups of five letters simply to make them easier to read.

To encrypt the first letter S, we look down the left hand column to the row beginning with the key letter B, and across the top to the column headed by the plain text letter S, and find the intersection which is T. For the next letter we look for the intersection of the row beginning with A and the column headed by R, thus giving the letter R. Proceeding to the end we have the full encrypted message

TRUVV FJEQG DMRMC GJEVB FKLMP IRTMN V

Note that it would not have made any difference if we had interchanged the rows and columns in this process.

To find the clear message from the encrypted letters we follow the procedure in reverse. Writing the keyword above the encrypted message we have

BRAIN BRAIN BRAIN BRAIN BRAIN BRAIN B
TRUVV FJEQG DMRMC GJEVB FKLMP IRTMN V

We locate the row headed with the key letter B, look across as far as the cipher text letter T and then go up to the top to read the clear text letter S. As before, rows and columns are interchangeable.

For many years Vigenère's cipher was believed to be unbreakable, but it was found that providing the message was long enough and the keyword repeated itself, groups of letters would eventually repeat themselves and this could be the basis of a trial and error solution. Decryption relies also on the frequency distribution of letters (which is known for most languages) and the occurrence of likely words. Now the advantage of a short keyword is that it is easy to remember, but the key can be as long as the message, and if some pre-arrangement is made, even a series of randomly chosen letters can be used. The longer the key compared with the length of the message, the more difficult decryption becomes. If the key is the same length as the message, the cipher is almost certainly unbreakable.

In the section on the layout of Manuscript 1, we explained that there are 140 letters inserted in the Latin text, and of these the middle 12 appear to be of a different set because they make the readable phrase, AD GENESARETH. Discarding these 12 we are left with a sequence of 128 letters which constitute the encrypted message.

There are several steps in the decryption of the hidden message. Lincoln gives them as follows:

1. Using the Table of Vigenère and the first keyword, MORTEPEE, transform the 128 letters into sequence 2. (This keyword is a selection of eight letters from the inscription on the headstone of the grave of Marie de Nègre d'Ables. How these letters are selected for the keyword and the authenticity of the headstone will be discussed in chapter 7.)

2. Next shift all the letters down the alphabet by one, to make sequence 3.

3. Now make a second keyword of 128 letters by taking the entire text of Marie's headstone and adding the letters PS PRAECUM. The second keyword is these letters in reverse order.

4. With the second keyword and the Table of Vigenère, make a fourth sequence of letters.

5. Shift all the letters down the alphabet by one to make sequence 5.

6. Divide the 128 letters into two sets of 64, lay them out on two chessboards.

7. Starting on f6 on the first board and using a particular succession of knight's moves, such that each square is visited only once, read out the first 64 letters of the clear text. Repeat using mirror image moves on the second chessboard to get the second half of the clear text. The final clear message turns out to be an anagram of the second keyword, used in step 4 above.

Now the above procedure is not the only one that can be used to get the same answer. One can combine the two forward moves of one letter into a single step with a two-letter shift. In fact it would be quite all right to move forward, say ten letters at one step, and move back eight at another. Providing there is a net forward shift of two letters, the answer is the same. Alternatively one could shift the keywords by two letters, instead of shifting the text. But one can go a great deal further than this as the following explanation shows.

In the short example given above, we encrypted SAUNIERE IS CURE OF RENNES LE CHATEAU with the keyword BRAIN. If we now encrypt the encryption with the keyword BILGE we get:

```
BILGE BILGE BILGE BILGE BILGE BILGE B
TRUVV FJEQG DMRMC GJEVB FKLMP IRTMN V
```
giving
```
UAGCA GRPXK EUDSG HRPCF GSXST JAFSR X
```

Now this is exactly the same as we would have got if we had encrypted the original message with the keyword CALOR, as the reader can check. If we encrypt BRAIN with BILGE (or for that matter the other way round) we get CALOR, the combined keyword. No one can say that two keywords have been used, rather than one.

We can show that this is true arithmetically. In the illustration of the Table of Vigenère (Fig. B.1) the letters have been assigned numbers: $A = 0$, $B = 1$ and so on to $X = 22$, $Y = 23$ and $Z = 24$. By encrypting B (1) with T (19) we are adding the two numbers and 20 corresponds to the encrypted letter U. If the final number had been 25 or more, we would have subtracted 25: thus I (8) + R (17) gives A ($25 - 25 = 0$). Thus from our original little example, with first letter S, if we encrypt it successively with the codes words BRAIN and BILGE we get S (18) + B (1) + B (1) = U (20). The second letter A becomes A (0) + R (17) + I (8) = A (25 − 25 = 0), the third letter U (20) + A (0) + L (11) = G (31 − 25 = 6) and so on. It is obvious from this that the order of using the keywords is irrelevant and that the two keywords can be combined into one.

In a similar way it can be shown that rearranging the letters merely results in a new keyword – though of course it would have the appearance of a series of letters chosen at random.

This brings us back to de Sède's curious statement in *L'Or de Rennes*. Claiming no special expertise in ciphers, de Sède says he submitted the manuscripts for cryptographic analysis.

Thanks to the kindness of Commandant Lerville, President of l'Association des Réservistes de Chiffre, I made use of the services of several experts in this subject. . . . At the end of a very technical study their conclusions were as follows:
1. The texts have been encrypted by a double key substitution, followed by a transposition involving moves on a chessboard;
2. To the actual encryption, the author has added some puzzles;
3. Some mistakes have been intentionally introduced to frustrate attempts at decoding by setting investigators off on false trails.[10]

From the above discussion we can see that without breaking the cipher there is no way the experts could have known that either a double-key substitution was used, or that a chessboard was involved. And how can one tell that there are mistakes without finding the correct solution? One is led to wonder whether de Sède himself ever spoke to the experts. It seems more likely that whoever knew the encryption process had offered to show the manuscript to experts on his behalf, and then had concocted an answer which would be plausible to someone who admitted he had no knowledge of the subject.

Having worked through the decryption, the final message is this:

BERGERE, PAS DE TENTATION, QUE POUSSIN TENIERS GARDENT LA CLEF. PAX DCLXXXI. PAR LA CROIX ET CE CHEVAL DE DIEU, J'ACHEVE CE DAEMON DE GARDIEN A MIDI. POMMES BLEUES.

The punctuation is of course not available from the encrypted letters and has to be added afterwards to improve comprehension of the clear text. We could translate it as: 'Shepherd, no temptation, Poussin and Teniers hold the key. Peace 681. By the cross and this horse of God, I finish off (destroy) this guardian demon at midday. Blue apples.' Minor variations on this are possible.

In order to get this message, it is obvious that you have to start with the correct sequence of letters. Manuscript 1 has three errors: they are the 18th letter (O in the manuscript has to be changed to E), 19th letter (H to F) and 62nd letter (X to T). These are slips made by whoever was encrypting the text and were first pointed out by Lincoln. De Sède does not mention the errors in *Signé:Rose+Croix*. Although he arrives at the 'right' answer, it is impossible to get it from his initial sequence of letters, because he introduces more errors of his own making, and at one point has a whole block of cipher missing. It seems that he was badly served by his proofreaders.

One further point needs to be made. Lincoln states that when he first learnt of the solution, de Sède offered one based on a 26-letter alphabet (i.e. including W). He also states that it can be decoded using either alphabet, if one alters the letter shift to two at Step 5 above, making a total shift of three letters. This is not true: only with a 25-letter alphabet and a total shift of two letters does one reach the clear message given above.

Having arrived at the final result, one's immediate response is that it does not appear to make a lot of sense. But there is no doubt that this is the correct text, because the clear message is an exact anagram of the second keyword, and the chances of this having come about by accident are exceedingly remote.

On further reflection it is not surprising that it does not seem to have much meaning. Whoever devised this encryption set himself a tricky task by introducing the two constraints, first that there were to be 128 letters so that he could use the chessboard transposition, second that the final result would be an exact anagram of the second keyword. We have to admire the achievement; it must have been the outcome of a long series of trial and error. It was inevitable that the encryptor had to compromise with both message and keyword to reach his aim.

The first part, as far as LA CLEF, appears to be the main message: 'Shepherd, no temptation, Poussin and Teniers hold the key'. CLXXXI uses up the awkward letters of the date in the headstone, POMMES BLEUES is added at the end to consume surplus letters. Similarly, the inscription on the headstone had to be compromised; it was nine letters short for the knight's move routine and PS PRAECUM (which itself is pretty meaningless) had to be added to make up the deficiency.

In spite of the fact that much of the message never had any purpose other than to use up letters, many writers have expended a lot of effort, and great ingenuity, in trying to find significance in such phrases as 'blue apples' and 'guardian demon'. This brings us to comment on the purposes of encryption.

Encryption is a method of safeguarding a piece of information from the attentions of persons who should not receive it and at the same time make it available to those who should. The more important the information, the more trouble can be legitimately taken to protect it. Having decided that the information is significant and should be encrypted, the originator of the message would be expected to ensure that the recipient finally had something that was clear and unambiguous. During the war the famous Enigma machines were used, for example, to encrypt messages giving rendezvous points for German submarines. This vital information had to be guarded from the Allies, hence the use of the very complicated machine for encryption, but on the other hand ambiguity in the clear signal could also have led to disaster.

We might add that if the final message is not comprehensible when in the clear, why bother to protect it in the first place? And why complicate the process by introducing totally artificial devices like one of the keywords being an anagram of the message, which at the same time makes it more difficult to do and also increases the risk of blurring the sense?

For the moment we shall skip over the unanswered questions of who wrote and encrypted the message and when, and for whom it was intended and how they should find out how to read it, and concentrate on the internal evidence. The cipher and its 'message' give every impression of not being serious. The thing appears to be a puzzle, a mental exercise more for the enjoyment of its compositor than for any solemn purpose of conveying vital information that would lead, as some have supposed, to the discovery of treasure or some deep secret that if revealed would shake humanity. It is the work of someone who likes puzzles and mysteries, possibly a crossword addict, a prankster, a person who enjoys teasing others with hints and nudges. Couple this with the certainty that someone knew how to decipher it in 1967, when de Sède wrote his first book, and then fed him with a succession of little snippets which led eventually to exposing the 'clear' text, and we feel that we are looking, not at an important message from the past, but at a very clever game.

7

Stones and Inscriptions

The more one probes into the mystery of Rennes-le-Château, the more complicated it appears. In this chapter we will begin by looking at the keywords which were used in deciphering the message in Manuscript 1. The source of these keywords is not as straightforward as one might have hoped, and the further one progresses, the more elusive the trail becomes. We shall find that we are progressing a long way from Bérenger Saunière towards a shadowy world of ancient history and secret societies.

We have to start with the two keywords. The first is MORTEPEE, which we shall see is a word conjured from eight letters selected from the inscription on the tomb of Marie de Nègre d'Ables (Fig. 7.1). The second keyword is long, and requires the full inscription of 119 letters on the stone, together with an additional nine letters, PSPRAECUM, making 128 letters in all. The nine letters come, according to de Sède, from another stone (Fig. 7.3), which was also said to be on Marie's grave, though it does not bear her name. To distinguish the two stones, we shall call them Marie I and Marie II respectively. Some French authors have distinguished between the two stones by assuming that Marie I was an upright stone (*une stèle funéraire*) and that Marie II was flat on the grave (*une dalle tombale*).

In the whole story of Rennes-le-Château there are few facts that are quite incontrovertible. The existence of Marie de Nègre d'Ables is one of them. She was a historical figure who was born in 1713.[1] Different authors give various spellings of her name, such as Marie de Negri d'Ables – we have followed the version given by Bruno de Monts.[2] On 5 November 1732 she was married to François, Baron d'Hautpoul and Rennes, *marquis de* Blanchefort. They had three daughters, Marie, Elisabeth and Gabrielle. The baron's name is sometimes given as Haupoul without the T and de Monts is insistent that this is how the family wrote it themselves. It is also how it was carved on the tombstone. The baron died in 1753 and is interred at Limoux. Marie de Nègre d'Ables died on 17 January 1781 aged sixty-seven and was buried in the churchyard of Rennes-le-Château at the time when the *Abbé* Bigou was priest of the parish.

Stone Marie I

We noted in chapter 4 that Marie I was seen in the churchyard on 25 June 1905, the day of excursion to Rennes-le-Château by the *Société d'Etudes scientifiques de l'Aude*

(Aude Society for Scientific Studies) and that an account of the outing was published in their *Proceedings* in 1906. Fig. 7.1 is reproduced from their *Proceedings*.

This picture is clearly not a reproduction of an actual drawing of the stone. It does not have the right proportions: the original is stated to have a ratio of height to width of 2:1 – the ratio of the illustrated stone is only 1.65:1. The drawing does not show the break mentioned in the Proceedings nor indicate any signs of wear. It looks as though the printer has taken a rough sketch and copied it as far as he could by using available typefaces to reproduce it without the expense of a special plate.

It was a crudely carved stone. The first word of the inscription may have been intended to be CI, or (since there is a space) ICI, but it turned out as CT. One notices immediately that the mason has split two words, MARIE and SOIXANTE on to successive lines. He was obviously trying to use the full width of the stone available to him, with letters vertically aligned on both right and left sides of the stone. (This feature is not of course reproduced in the illustration because standard typefaces were used.) The mason's planning was a bit inaccurate, and on three of the first four lines he has not left quite enough space for large letters, hence three small Es were squeezed into the text. In addition to that he made a number of errors. He missed out the P of SEPT and had to put a little letter in below the line. On the third line he has carved DARLES instead of DABLES and the year 1781 has become MDCOLXXXI instead of MDCCLXXXI. The first word of the inscription may have been intended to be ICI but turned out as CT. There is space for the first I but since this is not on the illustration it probably means that by 1905 it was not visible owing to weathering or damage. One other error is worth mentioning: REQUIES CATIN should be REQUIESCAT IN; the space is in the wrong place. This might not have been too serious, except that the word CATIN is old-fashioned French for a trollop!

One might have thought that with as many faults as this, the stone would have been scrapped and another one carved, but this was not the custom of the period. Engraving was expensive and in any case it was possible to do some cosmetic work with a little mortar (which would have worn away faster than the stone) to correct at least some of the errors. Taking all the above points into account we have attempted to reconstruct what the stone might have looked like in its original, newly erected state (Fig. 7.2), a point to be borne in mind when looking at the works of authors who find 'clues' in the geometrical layout of the letters on this stone.

The gravestone may have been incompetently carved by a near illiterate workman, but the arrangement of the text can be accounted for quite simply. As Descadeillas wrote 'there is nothing mysterious in this clear and easily read text. Badly executed epitaphs like this are not rare'.[3] The four errors and the four small letters would not have been intentional or significant at the time the gravestone was set up. In the context of the cipher in Manuscript 1 they are highly significant and give, though obliquely, the first keyword, MORTEPEE, used in its decryption. One takes the

CT GIT NOBLe M

ARIE DE NEGRᴱ

DARLES DAME

DHAUPOUL Dᴱ

BLANCHEFORT

AGEE DE SOIX

ANTE SEₚT ANS

DECEDEE LE

XVII JANVIER

MDCOLXXXI

REQUIES CATIN

PACE

7.1 The tombstone of Marie de Nègre d'Ables – stone 1, reproduced from the journal of the *Société d'Etudes scientifiques de l'Aude*.

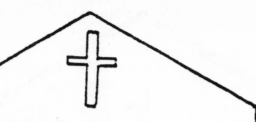

ICI GIT NOBLe M
ARIE DE NEGR E
DARLES DAME
DHAUPOUL D E
BLANCHEFORT
AGEE DE SOIX
ANTE SEpT ANS
DECEDEE LE
XVII JANVIER
M D C C L X X X I
REQUIES CATIN
PACE

7.2 The tombstone of
Marie de Nègre d'Ables
– stone 1, as it may have
appeared when first
erected.

erroneous T in CT, R in DARLES and O in MDCOLXXXI together with the isolated M on the first line to form the word MORT. EPEE comes from the four small letters which occur in the text in the order E, E, E and P, re-arranged to give the word EPEE. It has to be stressed, the keyword MORTEPEE is not based on the inscription on the stone, but on the picture of the inscription as it appeared in the *Proceedings* of 1906.

More would doubtless be learned if the stone was still available for examination. Unfortunately it has disappeared. De Sède had no doubts about its fate. He wrote in *L'Or de Rennes*:

> What Bérenger had more difficulty explaining was why he spent his nights shut in the cemetery. There against the church stood two tombstones marking the grave of Marie de Negri. . . . This lady had died a little before the Revolution and the *curé* Antoine Bigou, her chaplain and confessor, had lovingly composed her epitaph. . . . [Saunière] not only undertook to transport them from one end of the cemetery to the other, but also with quarryman's tools he patiently polished one to efface the inscriptions and a little after that got rid of the other.[4]

De Sède's theory is that Saunière had discovered treasure by deciphering the parchments and because he did not wish anyone else to be able to do this, he destroyed the stones on which were inscribed the keywords.

In retrospect that may not seem very convincing, because the deciphered messages are so obscure, but there is plenty of evidence that Saunière interfered with the tombs in the graveyard. The local villagers had objected to his activities and had petitioned the *Préfet* to stop him,[5] which he did. But this was in March 1895, ten years before the stone was seen by the members of the Society who found the stone lying in a corner of the graveyard.

The subsequent history of the stone is unknown for certain, but we have carried out an archaeological investigation of the graveyard and the surrounding area, which gives a few clues as to its possible fate. The results are reported in chapter 9.

Stone Marie II

We have already said that to make the second keyword we need to add PSPRAECUM to the text on Marie's tombstone, and that according to de Sède, these letters were carved on the second stone marking Marie's grave[6] (Fig. 7.3). His was the first book to mention the existence of this stone. He gives no dimensions or description, just a line drawing showing two vertical columns of Greek letters and four Latin words in the centre. Towards the bottom are the words PRAE-CUM, which are Latin for 'before' and 'with'. At the top we find 'P - S' in a curved line: this is almost identical to 'P S' in a similar line at the foot of Manuscript 2 (though on the manuscript the curved line is extended to beneath the P). Presumably this is the clue that we should link the stone and the parchments. At the bottom of the stone is a formalized drawing of an octopus.[7] Finally, in the bottom right-hand corner are the letters LIXLIXL, and in the bottom left corner what appears to be a signature.

De Sède published this drawing in 1967. After writing that Saunière had destroyed stone Marie II in addition to erasing the inscription on Marie I – this was four years before there was any hint that they might be important in deciphering the parchment – he continued: 'What Saunière didn't know was that he had taken a quite useless precaution. In fact, before he got rid of them, the significant inscriptions carved on the tomb of the Marquise de Blanchefort had been recorded during excursions by local archaeologists. One had been reproduced in the Proceedings of the Aude Society for Scientific Studies, the other figures in a work, today very rare, by Eugène Stüblein, *Engraved Stones of the Languedoc*.'[8]

Clearly a piece of information as important as this has to be checked very carefully, especially since the stone itself does not apparently exist and no person, except Stüblein, and presumably Saunière if he destroyed it, has ever been said to have seen it. The Society members made no mention of Marie II in their report of their visit to Rennes-le-Château on 25 June 1905, nor when they next visited the village on 16th August 1908.[9]

De Sède tells us nothing about Stüblein himself. The reference in his bibliography states that Stüblein's 'very rare' book, *Pierres gravées du Languedoc*, as it is entitled in French, was published in Limoux in 1884. He also says there was an offprint of Plates XVI to XXIII edited by a local *abbé*, Joseph Courtauly, and published at Villarzel-du-Razès in 1962.

Descadeillas describes how he first heard of Stüblein's book one afternoon in March 1966, when de Sède came to Carcassonne with some documents, including photocopies of the two parchments. De Sède told him the *Abbé* Courtauly, who was by then dead, had owned a copy of *Pierres gravées du Languedoc*. Descadeillas, who was the specialist in local history, was surprised he had never heard of the book and set out to investigate. He was unable to find a book of this title, either by Stüblein or anyone else in the *Bibliographie de l'Aude* (Aude Catalogue of Books).[10] Subsequent research has so far failed to produce any copies of Stüblein's book.

Descadeillas thoroughly researched the origin of *Pierres gravées du Languedoc* and also the life of Eugène Stüblein, with very interesting results, so we can do no better than to put forward his findings.

The Stüblein family originally came from Lorraine in the east of France. Eugène's father moved to the Mediterranean coast and ran a boarding school at Sigean, a little town just south of Narbonne. Eugène was born there in 1832 and he followed his father into teaching. From his youth he was interested in astronomy and meteorology

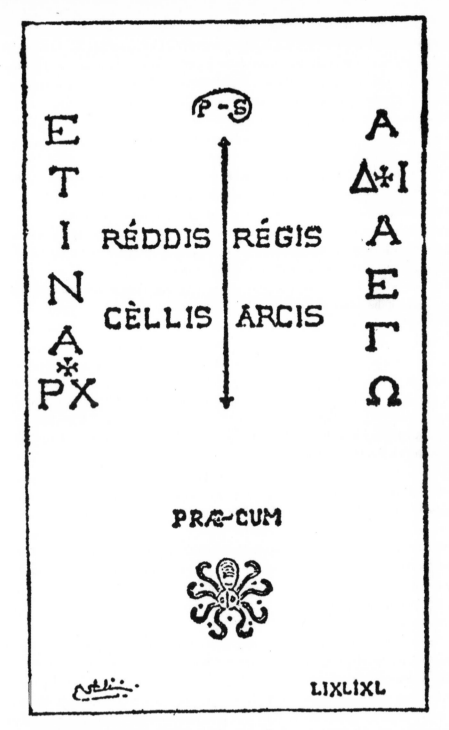

7.3 The tombstone of Marie de Nègre d'Ables – stone 2.

and wrote articles on these subjects in various local newspapers, including *La Dépêche du Midi*. He even wrote a book whose title in English would be 'Description of a journey to thermal establishments in the arrondissement of Limoux'.[11] This was published at Limoux in 1877 and was signed Stüblein of Corbières. Right up to his death in 1899 he continued to make meteorological observations, but never got involved with archaeology. In short, there is no evidence Stüblein wrote *Pierres gravées du Languedoc*. Apart from the offprints cited by de Sède, there is no evidence that the book has ever existed.

Well, if no one has found a copy of Stüblein's book, what about the offprints? They were located in a folder in the Bibliothèque nationale in Paris.

When de Sède visited Carcassonne he had with him copies of an unpublished work by Henri Lobineau – the one we mentioned in chapter 3 – *Genealogy of the Merovingian Kings and origin of various French and foreign families of the Merovingian line, following Abbé Pichon, Doctor Hervé and the parchments of the Abbé Saunière of Rennes-le-Château (Aude)*. There were 45 pages, including some illustrations in colour. The address of the author was given as 22 place du Mollard, Geneva.

This was another surprise to Descadeillas, as he had never heard of Lobineau either. He checked in the General Catalogue of French books (*Catalogue Général de la Librairie française*) for 1964 and found Lobineau's work listed on page 508 in the History section. He enquired at the Library of the University of Geneva, and was told that there was no Lobineau at Geneva, moreover there was no 22 place du Mollard. The street had only 11 numbers![12]

Descadeillas went to Paris to examine the Lobineau papers and there he found among them a pamphlet containing photocopied plates of tombstones, a map of Razès, an extract from an alleged will lodged with Captiers, the notaries in 1644, reputedly given to the author by *Abbé* Courtauly: all these supposedly from *Pierres gravées du Languedoc*, printed at Limoux in 1884. There was a lot of other material too, but we shall leave this until chapter 10.

On 20 June 1966 a small book was lodged with the Bibliothèque nationale in Paris. It contained drawings of gravestones and this was the Preface: 'The 1884 edition of Eugène Stüblein's book having become very rare, and I perhaps being one of the few people to have it in his library, in order to satisfy the numerous requests of researchers, I owe it to myself to have Plates 16 to 23 reproduced from this book, those concerning Rennes-les-Bains, Rennes-le-Château and Alet.' It was dated April 1962 and the name on it was *Abbé* Joseph Courtaly (*sic*). It was placed there by someone calling himself Antoine l'Ermite, whose given address was a hotel in the 17th arrondissement. This makes us suspicious immediately. His name means Anthony the Hermit, and we recall that Saunière was supposed to have bought a painting of St Anthony the Hermit on his alleged trip to Paris with the parchments.

The *Abbé* Joseph Courtauly, whose misspelt name was on this preface, was a local *curé*. He was born in Villarzel-du-Razès in 1890. He served in the army in the First World War and after demobilization went into the church. He worked in several parishes, none very far from Carcassonne, and in 1961 retired because of ill health to the village of his birth, where he died on 11 November 1964.

Descadeillas thought Courtauly was a very reputable person, who would not have become involved if the drawings were, as Descadeillas believed, fakes. He wondered how Courtauly got mixed up in the affair, and wrote:

We would be wondering still if we had not learned that in the last years of his life, when he was taking the waters at Rennes-les-Bains, he frequently met a strange person who, from the end of the 1950s, was often seen prowling about in those parts. This man lived in Paris. He had no connections and no known relatives in the area. He was a difficult fellow to place, drab, secretive, cunning, with the gift of the gab, but people who spoke to him said it was hard to follow what he said. He was not having a course of medical treatment. People asked about the reasons for his regular appearances, because he turned up unexpectedly even in winter. They also speculated about his interest in archaeological and natural sights, because he was not an intellectual. They were intrigued by the strangeness of his behaviour: he used to go around surveying the area and enquiring about the origin of properties. He would set his heart on scrubland or abandoned ground which did not interest anyone.[13]

Descadeillas went on to say that this man's comings and goings and his questions led to gossip. Some people thought he was mad, but he was building up a file of the locality containing all sorts of trivial information and opinions. He used to attribute to respectable people any old statements which he recorded on magnetic tape. He ascribed to the *Abbé* Courtauly remarks which did not tally with either the life or the character of the priest. And so it seems that Courtauly, old and ill at this time, came under the influence of a rather strange person who used him for his own ends. Descadeillas does not actually give this man's name, but he says he has reason to believe that he was the same person as the author of the Lobineau papers.

There is another thread to be followed, and this involves a man called Ernest Cros, who was born at Carcassonne in 1862. He lived in the area at the time of Bérenger Saunière and was interested in history and archaeology. He was not an archaeologist but a railway engineer and was involved in the building of the line south from Carcassonne to Axat. After quite a distinguished career, he retired in 1927, and from then, until his death in 1946, divided his time between Paris and a house at Ginoles, near Quillan. He knew and visited Saunière at Rennes-le-Château.[14]

Cros had an enquiring mind, and one of his methods for gathering information about the past was to question the older inhabitants. But without training in historical and archaeological techniques, he was inclined to accept uncritically what he was told. By talking to the older inhabitants of Rennes-le-Château, who remembered what the cemetery was like before Saunière moved the stones (and still resented his action), Cros came to the conclusion that there had been another tombstone, destroyed by Saunière. Through their recollections, he reconstructed the inscription as 'REDDIS REGIS CELLIS ARCIS'.

According to Descadeillas, Ernest Cros never saw the stone himself and he relied on the memories of local people who knew no Latin. If so, it is hardly surprising that the inscription makes little sense. Several investigators have tried to find a meaning in these words: one interpretation is 'At Rennes (*Reddis*), of the king (*regis*), in the caves (*cellis*), of the citadel (*arcis*)'. If one thinks there is a hidden treasure somewhere, this could be a spur to go hunting. But why have such an inscription on a tombstone? Cros's own records would be a help, but he died in Paris and no one knows what became of his papers. Descadeillas affirms that Cros never claimed there were any other words on this stone. Descadeillas wrote: 'the Greek characters inscribed on the stone here and there in the illustration given by M. de Sède are not part of the reconstruction offered by M. Cros: they have been added later. And – end of story – it's a stone that nobody has ever seen.'[15]

Yet, as seems to be almost always the case when dealing with Rennes-le-Château, we have information that never quite fits together. On the walls of the Museum at Rennes-le-Château in 1997 was displayed a paper entitled *Recherches de Mons. L'Ingénieur en Chef Cros* (Research by Chief Engineer Cros). The paper is ascribed to Noël Corbu, and the authorship is confirmed by Corbu's idiosyncratic spelling of the *curé*'s name – Béranger Saunières. Saul and Glaholm include it in their bibliography of Rennes-le-Château,[16] and date it to 1964. This seems plausible – it is likely it was written after Corbu's *Histoire de Rennes-le-Château* of 1962, and it must have been written before Corbu left the village in 1965.

Corbu does not say how he obtained the information which he presents in this note. It is unlikely he got it direct from Cros who died in Paris, aged eighty-four in 1946, the same year that Corbu moved into the *Villa Béthanie*, and years before Corbu started to publicize the *Hôtel de la Tour* with stories of Bérenger Saunière and treasure. Furthermore Corbu states that when he finally went to live permanently in Paris towards the end of his life, 'M. Cros had the objects that he had discovered and the notebooks of his work taken to Paris, either to his family, or more likely to the office of a society.'

Corbu agrees with Descadeillas, that Engineer Cros never saw the stone himself. He writes: 'It was by questioning the inhabitants of Rennes-le-Château that M. Cros, after the Great War, succeeded in partially reconstructing the inscription on the tombstone of Blanchefort; on the subject of supposed Greek characters engraved on the stone, M. Cros was persuaded that they were signs of some secret alphabet. Here is the partial reconstruction by M. Cros of the Latin letters P S REDDIS REGIS CELLIS ARCIS PRAE-CVM.'

Corbu does not show the Greek letters on his rough sketch or mention them again. Note also that he uses V instead of U, as indeed was usual in Latin inscriptions. (For the keyword we need U and not V.) Corbu's interpretation of the Latin is much the same as the one given above, with the additional interpretation of PS as the word PARS, and PRAECVM as an abbreviation of PRAECONVM (of the heralds), which he says refers to the Heralds of Christ, one of the descriptions of the Templars of the thirteenth and fourteenth centuries.

Then he adds a surprising verbatim conversation between Cros and Saunière, in which Cros asks, 'Why have you so carefully smoothed this stone so that nothing remains of the inscription?' to be told, 'this stone suits my project for an ossuary and there was no reason for keeping the inscription.' This paragraph itself leads us to doubt the reliability of the whole paper. If he had not met Cros, nor had access to his notebooks, could it be that Corbu, with or without the assistance of a third party, is making this up?

As to the Greek letters we have mentioned several times above, they are in two vertical columns, in capital letters (with two Maltese crosses which we can disregard), reading as follows: ETINAPX AΔIAEΓΩ. This inscription is probably unique among gravestones; certainly the authors have never come across anything like it before. It is not Greek, but a transcription into Greek letters of the Latin words ET IN ARCADIA EGO.

La Dalle de Coumesourde

There is yet a third stone we must describe, although its connection with Rennes-le-Château is more tenuous. This is the Dalle (or slab-stone) of Coumesourde. De Sède says in *L'Or de Rennes*[17] that the Marquis of Fleury, accompanied by the *Abbé* Bigou, went into exile in 1792, but before his departure he had a stone carved, which was lost. It was rediscovered in 1928 buried under a holm oak tree in a rocky hollow on the mountain of Coumesourde, about 2 km south of Rennes-les-Bains. He gives a drawing, which he attributes to Ernest Cros (Fig. 7.4). De Sède gives no reference by which we can check the circumstances of the discovery of this stone and does not say where it is at the present day.

On de Sède's drawing of the stone one face bears the words 'CEIL BEIL' and the date MCCXCII, i.e. 1292. (We presume that date should have been MDCCXCII, 1792, and

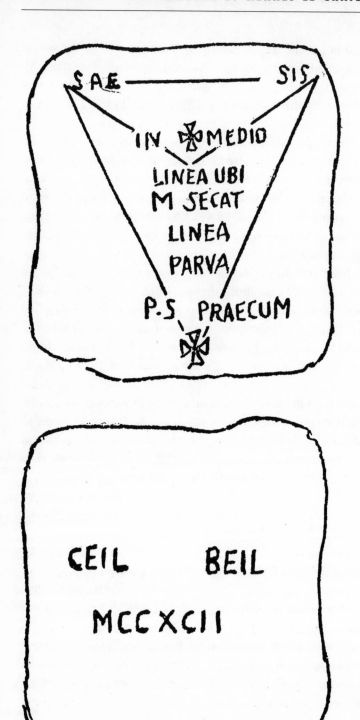

7.4 The Coumesourde stone.

that the error was made either by the person who made the drawing, or the mason, if indeed the stone existed.)

De Sède's drawing of the other face shows 'PS PRAECUM', a Latin inscription 'IN MEDIO LINEA UBI M SECAT LINEA PARVA', SAE and SIS at the top and two Maltese crosses. There is also a geometrical design of two triangles with a common side. No interpretation is given and de Sède draws no connections between the *Dalle de Coumesourde* and other aspects of the Rennes mystery. After mentioning the stone's discovery he does not refer to it again and we are left to draw our own conclusion that somehow it must be significant because of the words PS PRAECUM.

In the paper by Corbu on the work of Ernest Cros, the *Dalle de Coumesourde* is given more significance. He writes that in the opinion of M. Cros 'in order to find the sense of the tombstone of Blanchefort and to understand the relentless way that Béranger Saunières got rid of the inscription we have to study the Dalle de Coumesourde, discovered by M. Cros in 1928. . . . It was concealed in a rock fracture; its presence being indicated very discreetly, by an arrow and a Maltese cross, carved in a hollow in the rock.' In the text of the paper, Corbu gives two very schematic and different illustrations (neither of which is identical to de Sède's) and he shows only one side of the stone.

Corbu's interpretation (ascribed to Cros) is that it is a sort of map; the corners of the triangle indicate points on the landscape near Rennes-le-Château. The top left corner 'SAE' represents Sauzils; the top right 'SIS' the rocks of Blanchefort and Black Rock (Rouquo Negro); the cross at the bottom, the Castle of Bézu. The Latin inscription seems to be a guide to a location: 'in the middle of the line, where the large line cuts the small line is PS PRAECVM', and PS PRAECVM means 'share of the Heralds', i.e. 'treasure of the Templars'! So we are being led to believe that the *Dalle de Coumesourde* is a guide to finding treasure hidden by the Templars – if only we could discover how to interpret the clues.

Much of the Corbu paper concerns treasure. There is the hoard supposedly hidden by the *Abbé* Bigou: 'before leaving for exile, the *Abbé* Bigou used a hiding-place in the church, a hiding-place dating from the thirteenth century, prepared by the Voisins family, situated partly in the bell-tower, partly under the floor paving of the church: in 1891 the *Abbé* Saunières discovered this hiding-place and emptied it of its contents'. There are hoards hidden by various aristocratic families: 'since the 13th century the families of Voisins, Marque-Fave, D'Hautpoul, Fleury were in possession of the secret of the location of one or several hoards', and also the treasure of the Templars.

The emphasis on treasure tells us that it is Corbu writing and not Cros. In Cros's time there was no thought of treasure at Rennes-le-Château – the treasure only became part of the story in 1956 with the publication of the articles in *La Dépêche du Midi*. Having created the legend of 'the *curé* with billions'. Corbu convinced himself that it was true. He began a series of excavations himself. It was in the course of one of his digs that he found the bodies with remnants of hair and clothing dating from the last war. He was as enthusiastic as anyone in his search for hidden gold.

Corbu was also a writer. He had previously written a novel and had a feeling for adventure and mystery. He actively researched the history of Rennes-le-Château both for his talks to his clients at the hotel and because at one time he intended to write a book about the mystery. He would have heard about Cros's reconstruction of four words on the supposed second gravestone of Marie de Nègre. But that does not explain how he came to be aware that the stone was also reputed to have had Greek letters carved on it.

He could only have known this if he had seen the picture of the stone which allegedly came from Stüblein's book. Descadeillas saw illustrations in Paris in the Bibliothèque nationale, where they were deposited on 20 June 1966, after de Sède's visit to Rennes. How could Corbu have seen them before he wrote his paper of 1964? The answer is to be found in a letter written and signed by Corbu and dated 10 August 1962. This letter is filed in the Bibliothèque nationale in the *Dossiers secrets* of Henri Lobineau. Corbu's letter, only part of which is present, says 'The history of Rennes is very unsettling and it would be interesting to know what are the documents which *Abbé* Sauniéres (*sic*) showed to *Abbé* Hoffet. We will discuss it on your arrival.' So this letter tells us that Corbu was in contact with Lobineau in 1962, and Lobineau was involved with the murky matter of *Pierres gravées de Languedoc*. No problem then about Corbu getting an early look at the drawing of the stone Marie II.

Incidentally, the Corbu letter also implies that at the time he wrote it, he did not know of parchments containing encrypted messages. He could not therefore have been aware of the significance of the letters PS PRAECUM, which in his paper appear as PS PRAECVM. Perhaps he was told verbally of the extra letters, and the significance of the spelling was not made clear to him.

As we said earlier, the person who made the encryption had been constrained in two ways, firstly by using the double chessboard for a transposition, which demanded 128 letters, secondly by making the clear message an anagram of the second keyword. To achieve this would have required considerable trials, and only after the cipher was fully worked out could the extra nine letters PSPRAECUM be finally chosen. No author before de Sède in 1967 mentions ciphers, and the implication (which we shall see later is confirmed) is that the ciphers were devised not many years before this date. So even if stone Marie II existed, it would have been a truly extraordinary coincidence if the letters PS PRAECUM had been engraved upon it.

The paper by Corbu is largely overlooked by writers on Rennes-le-Château. De Sède uses it as one of his sources for his book *L'Or de Rennes*, though he does not include it among his references. It is from Corbu that he obtains his information about the *Dalle de Coumesourde* and from Corbu he also takes the idea of giving a verbatim account of the conversation between Cros and Saunière about defacing the gravestones – though not in the same words.

Summary of the Evidence

So in summary, what can we say about these three inscribed stones that figure in the story of Rennes-le-Château? None of them exists now, but there is sound evidence that Marie I really did exist. Its original appearance is uncertain however, because all we have to go on is the imprecise illustration from the Proceedings of 1905.

Stone Marie II is very doubtful. Since there is no evidence that anyone has ever seen it, we have to rely entirely on an illustration from a book. But no one has yet found either a copy of this book or a reference to it in a library catalogue. The collection of illustrations supposedly from the book was placed in the Bibliothèque nationale, not by the person who edited them, but a year and a half after his death by someone giving a false name. There is a folk memory of a stone with an inscription of four words, which may or may not have been associated with Marie's grave, recorded by Ernest Cros, whose written records of his researches have disappeared. The half-remembered words did not include PS PRAECUM, the vital extra for the completion of the second keyword. A paper by Noël Corbu, purporting to be an account of Cros's research includes PS PRAECVM, but if this is true the ciphers must have been already worked out by the time of Marie's death. We know this cannot be so, because the version of the Bible that was used was not published until about 100 years later. In any case, Corbu's paper is suspect, because it is likely that he was fed information by the very persons who seem to have been involved in manufacturing spurious illustrations of engraved stones.

The third stone, the *Dalle de Coumesourde* is just as elusive. It was said to have been discovered by Ernest Cros in 1928, but there is no contemporary written confirmation of this. The earliest known illustrations are two in the Corbu paper of 1964. They are not precise and differ from each other significantly. From these, with some artistic licence, de Sède prepared his drawing of the stone for publication in *L'Or de Rennes* (taking care to change PRAECVM to PRAECUM). Later authors have actually made use of the geometry in de Sède's illustration to substantiate their theories about the treasure of Rennes-le-Château or the mystical, even holy, significance of the landscape of the area.

It is on such gossamer evidence as this that the myths of Rennes-le-Château are founded. Who created the evidence, and when and how they did it, is the subject of later chapters.

8

Evidence from History

The story of Rennes-le-Château begins with an account of a parish priest who was supposed to have found a treasure. There's no doubt that he spent a lot of money and he refused to divulge its origins. Many people were convinced that he had found treasure but if so, where was it from? Many suggestions have been made – was it the treasure of Blanche de Castile as Noël Corbu supposed? Did it come from the Visigoths, who had taken from Rome treasure plundered from Jerusalem? Was it from the Merovingians, the Cathars, the Templars? All have been dragged into the story as possible sources of Saunière's wealth. But how much of this is likely to be true? Before we can consider these questions we have to look at events in the early history of what is now southern France. We have to see what were the links between these various people and Rennes-le-Château.

In modern times Rennes-le-Château is in the southernmost *région* of France called Languedoc-Roussillon, which includes the *départements* of Lozère, Gard, Hérault, Aude and Pyrénées-Orientales. It stretches from Avignon in the north of the *région* to Perpignan in the south. It is similar in extent, though not exactly the same, as the historic province of Languedoc.

This was a distinctive historical and cultural area of southern France, where the language was Occitan, the *Langue d'Oc*, which developed from the Latin of the late Roman world. It is still spoken by many country people, studied in universities in the south of France and learned in schools, particularly around Toulouse and Montpellier.

From 121 BC much the same area formed the Roman province of *Gallia Narbonensis*, the wealthiest part of Roman Gaul. Its capital was *Narbo Martius*, present-day Narbonne, which was within the old province of Languedoc but is outside the modern *région*. In AD 410 Rome fell to the Visigoths, and with the collapse of the Western Roman Empire in the fifth century they established a huge kingdom. It included most of the land south of the Loire, modern Provence, the Pyrenees and covered much of eastern Spain as far south as the Straits of Gibraltar. Though the rulers had changed, culturally there was very little change, and life in the towns and villas continued in much the same way for some time.

To the north and east of the Visigoths was the kingdom of Burgundy, and beyond them, in what is now Belgium and north-eastern France, were the Franks, the tribe from which France gets its name. They had originated to the east of the Rhine and had invaded Roman Gaul at the end of the fourth century. The kings of one of the Frankish tribes, the Salian Franks, were from a dynasty called the Merovingians, so named because the line was founded by a king called Merovich, about whom virtually nothing is known. The Merovingian kings believed, like Samson, that strength resided in the hair, and never had their hair cut nor their beards shaved, which earned them the nickname of 'the long-haired kings'.

In 481 Clovis I, grandson of Merovich, became king of the Franks and set about a policy of expansion.[1] He established the security of his kingdom by subduing the local tribes, married a Christian princess, Clotilde, and was himself converted to Christianity. Then he attacked and defeated the Burgundians. In 507 he drove southward and vanquished the Visigoths in a battle near Poitiers, and pressed south to burn Toulouse. He subjugated all the Visigoths north of the Pyrenees apart from those in Provence. Although he was not able to hold on to quite all of his conquered territory, he ruled over most of the area of modern France and some regard him as the founder of the French nation. Towards the end of his life he made Paris his capital city.

After the death of Clovis the laws of inheritance required that the kingdom be divided between his four sons. One of them, Chlotar, outlived the rest and for a while the country was reunited. But Chlotar also had four sons, who divided the country, each taking a share of land north of the Loire and a share south of the river. Not surprisingly there was family strife and intrigue and this prompted some re-organization of the kingdom. Towards the end of the sixth century the northern part was divided into two, Neustrie and Austrasie. Austrasie was the eastern kingdom, covering roughly the area of Belgium, Luxembourg, and the Rhineland, together with Picardie, Champagne and Lorraine. Neustrie was the western kingdom, occupying the rest of northern France except for Brittany.

For a while these two realms were again reunited under Dagobert I, but history repeated itself and on his death in 639, Neustrie went to Clovis II and Austrasie to Sigebert III. By then the Merovingian kings had lost much of their power to court officials, called mayors, who effectively ran the countries. The kings from this era became known as *les rois fainéants*, the enfeebled rulers.

Sigebert III died in 656. The events of the following six years are rather obscure.[2] The generally accepted view is that Sigebert's son succeeded to the throne as Dagobert II, but he was only a child and all power was in the hands of Grimoald, the mayor. Grimoald was not satisfied with his status; he wished to found a royal house of his own, and he had his own son crowned as Childebert III. To legitimize this act he put out the story that Sigebert III, believing his wife Himmechilde to be barren, had adopted Childebert as his own son before Dagobert was born. The young Dagobert had to be got out of the way. Humanely for the period, Grimoald did not have Dagobert killed, but sent him into exile in Ireland.

The usurpation was not popular with the rulers of the neighbouring country, Neustrie. War broke out, and both Grimoald and his son were imprisoned and disappeared. The Neustrians placed their own ruler, Childeric II (son of Clovis II), on the throne of Austrasie. Childeric was assassinated in 675, and a year later, after fourteen years in exile, Dagobert II reappeared to claim the throne of Austrasie. Dagobert was assassinated near Stenay (north of Verdun) in 679 aged about twenty-eight. He was interred at Stenay and later became the focus of a cult and was sanctified.

So over a period of seven centuries, the area around Rennes-le-Château had passed from Roman rule to Visigothic and then came under the influence of the Merovingian kings. Lincoln, in *The Shadow of the Templars*, claims an even closer connection. He states that Dagobert II had a son, Sigebert, who after his father's death, was taken to his mother's home at Rennes-le-Château. There it is said he became the Count of Razès and his descendants are supposed to be living in France to this day. Yet in the accepted historical records there is no mention of Dagobert having a son, or even being married. Where Lincoln got his information from and how reliable it is will be discussed in chapter 10.

Frankish territory was invaded by the Muslims in 711. In 732 they took Bordeaux and marched north to Poitiers. Here, in a famous battle, they were repulsed by Charles Martel, Mayor of Neustrie. The Merovingian kings were by now kings in name only. In 751 the last Merovingian king was deposed and Pepin, son of Charles Martel, was elected King of the Franks. It was the beginning of the Carolingian dynasty.

Under the Emperor Charlemagne the area was united for a short while, but later it disintegrated into princely dukedoms and counties. In 924 the county of Toulouse was created. In the tenth century the Counts saw their power diminish, as many new noble families emerged claiming authority over limited areas: by 1050 the Counts of Toulouse had control over a wide area, including Toulousain, Septimania, Quercy, Rouergue and Albi, making the county a powerful possession.

Michael Costen in his book *The Cathars and the Albigensian Crusade*[3] writes that the response to the loss of centralized rule was progressive militarization of the countryside, marked by the building of castles and the recruiting of knights. There was a rapid increase in the number of castles throughout the area, including the castle of Rennes-le-Château, which was in existence by 1002, and the nearby castle of Peyrepeteuse, first mentioned in 1020. Some castles were the property of families who lived in them, while others were granted to a castellan, or governor, on limited terms. Building castles was an expensive business, so it suggests that the area was rich enough and well enough organized to have surpluses which could be made use of. Contributions, in the form of taxes, were demanded from the local population.

Most of the estates in the south consisted of scattered holdings, whose land boundaries had descended from the late Roman Empire of the fifth century. The peasants were tied to the land and their lord's control. Development of the villages in the eleventh and twelfth centuries came with the rule of the Church and the protection afforded by the castles of the secular lords. Nucleated settlements gave the lords much more power over the activities of their peasants.

In Charlemagne's time the church had enabled the emperor to control his vast empire. In the Languedoc the bishoprics and abbeys are very ancient, some tracing their origins back to the third century. By the tenth century there was a growth of monasteries, reflecting a reform in spiritual life of the time, and by the twelfth century new spiritual orders had been established. The military religious orders of the Templars and the Hospitallers[4] were well thought of and benefited from gifts of land at this time. But both the geography of the Languedoc and the church's organization of different dioceses at Narbonne, Bourges and Auck meant that the church did not forge political unity with the secular princes.

In the mid-twelfth century there appeared in the Languedoc a sect called the Cathari, or Cathars, who won considerable support from both the nobility and the people of the Languedoc. Sometimes the Cathars were referred to as the Albigenses, as they were particularly strong around the town of Albi.

The Cathars were a dualist sect. They believed that there are two principles – one, the spiritual world of God, is good and the other, the material world of Satan, is evil.

The god of good and the god of evil exist alongside one another. The first is the god of light, goodness and spirit, associated with Jesus Christ and the New Testament. The second is the god of darkness, evil and all physical matter. It followed that anything material, including home, food and even the human body, was essentially evil. Thus Jesus Christ, who was an angel, could not have had a human body – his sufferings and death were an illusion.

Satan trapped the souls of fallen angels to animate the bodies of men and animals, as he could not himself, as a principle of death and negation, create life. Once trapped at the initial creation of matter by the Devil, souls could not leave unless they achieved perfection, and Christ came to show them how that might be possible.

The Cathars had no priests as such, but their leaders were the *perfecti*, or perfects. They followed a life of rigid asceticism. They renounced all possessions and lived through gifts from the other believers. They could not take oaths, have sex, or eat animal products. The *perfecti* were not priests and anyone who followed the necessary life of self-sacrifice, denial and ritual could become a *perfectus* through the confirmation of the Holy Spirit received at the laying on of hands, the *consolamentum*. Any Cathar could pray to God and the prayers of the *perfecti* did not have any special efficacy.

The Cathars believed that the Church with all its immense wealth and its corrupt priests was the work of the devil. The hostility of the Church is not surprising. The Catholic Church was infuriated by the unorthodox view of Christianity taken by the Cathars, and they were condemned as heretics. Pope Innocent III launched a crusade against them, and a French army from the north invaded the Languedoc in 1209. The series of wars which followed, often called the Albigensian Crusade, resulted in the near extinction of the Cathars, and the end of the independence of the Languedoc.

Some of the events of the Albigensian Crusade are well documented. The most dramatic event was the siege of the hill-top castle at Montségur (about 35 km west of Rennes-le-Château) in 1243. The castle was garrisoned by over 100 men under the command of Pierre-Roger de Mirepoix. It also provided refuge for a community of Cathar refugees.

In 1242 a band of men from Montségur killed members of the Inquisition at Avignonet. As a direct result of this, the Catholic Church and Blanche de Castile (mother of Louis IX, King of France, and regent during much of his reign) ordered the destruction of the castle. The seneschal of Carcassonne and the Archbishop of Narbonne were ordered to conduct the siege, which began in July 1243.

The attackers managed to haul a ballista, or stone throwing machine, up the cliff below the castle, and position it to breach the castle walls, and Pierre-Roger de Mirepoix was compelled to surrender, though his garrison was allowed to depart unharmed. This was not the case with the Cathars, who would consider neither flight nor the renunciation of their beliefs.

On the morning of 12 March 1244 the 207 Cathars marched down the mountain and were burnt to death in a huge funeral pyre. A monument stands on the spot today. It should be noted that the magnificent castle visible at the site today was built later in the thirteenth century. There is nothing left of the castle from which the Cathars walked to their death, and this is true of all the other 'Cathar' castles.

But in *The Priest, the Painter and the Devil* we are told that some Cathars had managed to get their treasure out of the besieged castle. The story goes that the night before the Cathars were burnt, a small band escaped down the cliffs carrying the treasure of the Cathars to an unknown destination. This story, for which there is no serious historical evidence whatever, has been skilfully incorporated into the myth of Rennes-le-Château.

What might the treasure of the Cathars have been? And how could it have ever have got to Rennes-le-Château to be found by Bérenger Saunière?

Some writers suppose the treasure to be that from Solomon's Temple. In AD 70 the Roman general Titus destroyed Jerusalem in a siege vividly recounted by the Jewish historian Josephus, who was present at the time. The temple was sacked, and its treasures carried off by the Roman legions. The treasure included the seven-branched candlestick, the menorah, which is described by Josephus in the triumphal procession in Rome.[5] A dramatic sculpture from the arch of Titus shows the menorah being paraded through the streets in Titus' triumph.

In AD 410 when the Visigoths under their leader Alaric captured Rome, they pillaged the city, no doubt taking away anything they considered of value.

That much is known fact: now we enter on the realm of pure speculation. If the treasure from Jerusalem had still existed at that time, and if it was still in Rome, it might have been part of the booty. Under Alaric's successor, Ataulf, the Visigoths settled in south-west France and Spain, and it may be that they took the treasure with them.

If the treasure ended up in the south of France, after passing through the hands of the Merovingian and Carolingian dynasties, it might just have come into the possession of the Cathars. After its rescue from Montségur, it might possibly have been hidden at Rennes-le-Château. Alternatively, according to other versions of the myths, the treasure might have been deposited with the Knights Templar for safe keeping. There was a Templar fortress only 40 km east of Montségur near the village of Bézu. Could it have gone there and then been taken later to Rennes-le-Château?

In fact these suppositions are fantastic in the extreme. To accept them is to believe in a long series of incredible events: that the treasure from the temple was preserved in Rome rather than melted down and used for Roman currency; that it still existed in AD 410, and survived the sack of Rome rather than suffering the same fate; that it was taken to the south of France and carefully preserved through seven or eight centuries to fall into the hands of the Cathars, all without any further historical reference to its existence; and that the Templars took possession of it, and somehow buried it in the Languedoc at the time of their own destruction. The chance of any one of these events being true is very small indeed. The chance of such a series of linked events being true is approaching zero.

The Knights Templar were certainly not supporters of the Cathars. There may have been the odd sympathizer among them, just as there were Catholic priests who secretly supported the Cathars. But it is unlikely that the Knights Templar would have looked after Cathar treasure. Their military strength made it possible to transport bullion to and from the Holy Land and their network of castles ensured that valuables could be safely stored. In effect they set up a banking system, used by both kings and pilgrims. There was much resentment at their wealth and this was fuelled by rumours of immoral behaviour. More significantly the king of France, Philippe le Bel, was desperately short of money.

The Templars did not long outlast the Cathars. They were attacked by Philippe in 1307. Many Templars were imprisoned and executed, some were burnt at the stake, including the last Grand Master, Jacques de Molay. When Pope Clement V dissolved the order in 1312 he ordered its wealth to be transferred to the Hospitallers or confiscated by the state. That any Templar treasure escaped the net is once again pure speculation.

But what about Blanche de Castile? According to Noël Corbu, the treasure was originally hers and she brought it to Rennes-le-Château for safekeeping at the time of the Barons' revolt.

Blanche was born in 1189, the daughter of Alfonso VIII of Castile and Eleanor, daughter of Henry II of England. Her early childhood was spent in Castile but at the age of eleven she left her childhood home to be married at Port Mort, near Les Andelys in Normandy, to Prince Louis of France. From then on Blanche lived mainly at the French court in Paris, although as was customary at the time, the court travelled around, staying at various royal castles, including Senlis, Compiègne, Pontoise and Etampes.

On the death of his father in 1223, Louis became Louis VIII. His reign was very short. He died in 1226 of dysentery on returning to Paris after a campaign against the Cathars. The heir was Louis, who was just twelve years old. Within weeks of his father's death he was crowned Louis IX at Reims and Blanche became regent during his minority.

She now faced a rebellion of the barons, supported by Henry III of England. Blanche was a strong and successful leader. She suppressed the revolt, established a truce with England, signed a treaty with Raymond, Count of Toulouse, and in fact brought peace to the whole country. During this revolt Blanche travelled from castle to castle in northern France, but not as far south as Rennes-le-Château, with or without treasure. At times she was short of money to provide for her army, especially during the long war against the Cathars.[6]

Louis came of age in 1236 and eight years later decided to go on a crusade against the Muslims. Once more Blanche took over running the country. The crusade did not go well. Louis lost a battle in Egypt and was imprisoned, leaving Blanche to find ransom money. Not having enough of her own resources, she was obliged to solicit contributions from her parents, her allies and the Pope.[7] Blanche died in 1252 at the age of sixty-four, while her son was still in the east.

Comparison of this account with that given by Noël Corbu in chapter 2 shows several discrepancies. The revolt of the barons was not during the crusade of Louis IX, but eighteen years before when he was still a youth. Blanche of Castile lived mainly in Paris. The detailed biography of Blanche by Régine Pernaud, who describes her campaigns and her travels, makes no mention of either Rennes-le-Château or treasure. We do not know where Corbu got his information and have to conclude that he made up his story for the benefit of the press.

1 The town sign of Rennes-le-Château.

2 'Excavations forbidden' – notice outside Rennes-le-Château.

3 Rennes-le-Château on its hilltop between the Rivers Sals and Aude.

4 Aerial view of Rennes-le-Château.

5 The dramatic Château at Arques, with Rennes-le-Château just visible on the hilltop above the left corner tower of the château.

6 Bérenger Saunière.

7 Marie Dénarnaud.

8 Remains of an arch which may have belonged to the former Church of St Pierre.

9 The Church of Ste Marie Madeleine at Rennes-le-Château.

10 The church porch.

11 The interior of the church.

12 The altar as it is today.

13 A plaster statue of a devil supports the holy water stoup at the door of the church at Rennes-le-Château.

14 A stone devil supporting the baptismal font at Montréal.

15 The bas-relief on the west wall of the church.

16 Statue of Ste Germaine and Stations of the Cross Nos V and IV in the church at Rennes-le-Château.

17 Station of the Cross No. VI in the church at Rennes-le-Château.

18 The statue of the Virgin Mary erected by Bérenger Saunière in 1891.

9

Evidence on the Ground

We noted at the beginning of chapter 2 that information about events that occurred in times past could be obtained not only from the written word but also from archaeological investigations, or evidence on the ground, which includes the site and its environment, artefacts and remains. These sources of information are many and various in Rennes-le-Château, although so far we have barely touched on them. In this chapter we consider them systematically, beginning with the geology and archaeology of the village and its surrounding area, then taking a look at the major buildings and artefacts in and around Rennes-le-Château which are relevant to this investigation. Finally we draw a few conclusions about the extent to which they confirm or refute claims relating to important points in the story.

Geology

Rennes-le-Château is in the Department of the Aude, which gets its name from its principal river.

The Aude has its source in the foothills of the Pyrenees close to the Spanish border (Fig. 1.1). From here it flows north in a deep gorge through Quillan and Limoux to Carcassonne, where it turns east to reach the Mediterranean between Narbonne and Béziers. At Couiza, 13 km south of Limoux, it is joined from the east by the river Sals, which drains the high and mostly forested ground of the west Corbières. On a prominent hilltop 2 km south-east of Couiza stands the village of Rennes-le-Château, overlooking the junction of the two rivers (Fig. 9.1).

Rennes-le-Château itself is in a dramatic location. It is a climb of almost 300 m from the town of Couiza by a very winding road. The village crowns a small hill topped with limestone conglomerate and areas of red marl, formed in the Quarternary period, i.e. last 2 million years. All of the rocks and soils are calcareous, that is to say limestone or derived from limestone. On several sides of the village are cliffs where the stone has been quarried. This is particularly true of the area north of the church where major quarries provided much of the stone from which the village houses are built.

The slopes below Rennes-le-Château, extending for some 4 km on the south as far as Granès, belong to the Cretaceous and Tertiary periods, are also predominantly

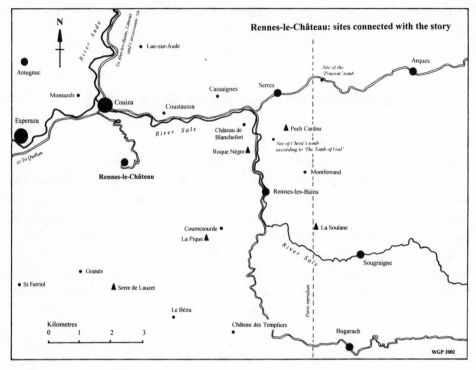

9.1 Map of the Rennes-le-Château area.

limestone conglomerate with some sandstone (the church at Rennes-le-Château is built from the latter). In the adjacent valleys there is tufa (of which the grotto at Rennes-le-Château church is made) and gypsum, extensively used in the building industry and for the manufacture of plaster of Paris.

During the Cretaceous period, about 144 to 65 million years ago, the dinosaurs flourished, and fossil bones and eggs are frequently found in this area. The limestone has often been quarried, and running water has carved out natural caves and underground tunnels. Such features have led to the discovery of traces of Old Stone Age cave dwellers, and also romantic stories about buried treasure.

Further afield can be found rocks of the Jurassic period dating from 213 to 144 million years ago. Some 11 km south-east of Rennes-le-Château rises the dramatic peak of Bugarach, and in this area gold was mined in the nineteenth and early twentieth centuries, and possibly earlier.

About 4 km east of Rennes-le-Château is the spa village of Rennes-les-Bains, famous for its hot springs, which have been in use since Roman times. A little to the north-east of Rennes-les-Bains are even older rocks of the Devonian period (about 408 to 360 million years ago), including the dramatic peak of Cardou. Mining has been carried out here for copper, iron, manganese, lead, silver, zinc, lignite and jet.

Rennes-le-Château

At the present time Rennes-le-Château is a small village of just over 100 inhabitants. It seems to have been at its largest in 1885; when Bérenger Saunière arrived there were 300 people. Some of today's inhabitants are farmers, some work in the neighbouring towns, and some depend on the tourist trade drawn by the extraordinary story of Bérenger Saunière. The inhabited area is entirely confined to the hilltop itself, and this may have always been the case.

Casual finds in the nineteenth and twentieth centuries, together with some recent excavation in advance of development, have confirmed that the hilltop was inhabited in prehistoric times. In 1930 a Neolithic (New Stone Age) tomb was found. There was substantial settlement by Iron Age people of the first and second centuries BC.

This is not surprising. One practice of the Iron Age tribes of north-western Europe (including Britain) was the fortification of strongholds, often but not always on hilltops, called *oppida* by the Romans. There is however no clear evidence of fortifications of this sort surrounding Rennes-le-Château. Although there are substantial dry stone walls visible on the south side of the village, these represent terracing of the hillside for agriculture, rather than ramparts. It may be that dry stone ramparts have been destroyed by reuse of the stone for building and farming activities, but it is equally possible that they never existed, and the settlement was simply an unfortified family farm, which owed its allegiance to a tribal centre elsewhere.

The local Iron Age tribe was probably the Tectosages, mentioned by the Roman authors Pliny[1] and Ptolemy as the tribe whose capital was at Carcassonne. There was certainly a major Iron Age settlement at Carcassonne, dating back to at least the sixth century BC, when Greek entrepreneurs traded up the Aude from the Mediterranean. The town's ancient name, Karkasone, is Greek.

Archaeological evidence from Rennes-le-Château, some of which was found and correctly interpreted by Bérenger Saunière, includes pottery, glass and mosaic pieces,[2] proving that the Iron Age settlement continued into the Roman period.

This is a little unusual. Iron Age hill forts or hilltop settlements were not normally transformed into upper class Romanized settlements. Romanized inhabitants preferred to live on warmer, more fertile sites on lower ground close to rivers and roads. Carcassonne was one such suitable location, and became a substantial Roman town on the trunk road to the west from Narbonne (*Narbo Martius*). *Narbo Martius* was a *colonia* (colony) of Roman citizens, founded in 118 BC. It later gave its name to the province of *Gallia Narbonensis* and became its capital.

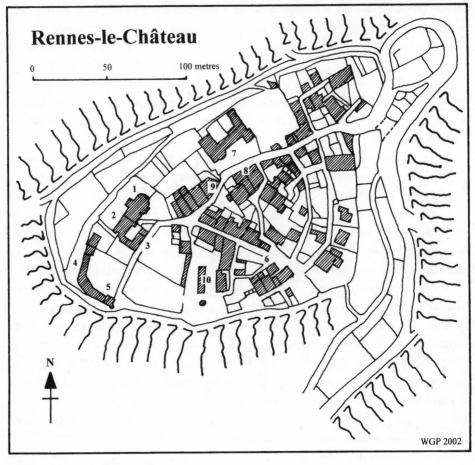

9.2 Map of Rennes-le-Château village.

1 Church of Ste Marie Madeleine
2 Old Presbytery (now the Museum)
3 *Villa Béthanie*
4 Belvedere
5 Tour Magdala

6 Site of the Church of St Pierre
7 Château
8 Atelier Empreinte (Bookshop)
9 Restaurant La Pomme Bleue
10 Mairie

There is no evidence at all of Roman roads to Rennes-le-Château, although a road did come up the Aude valley at least as far as the spa town of Alet-les-Bains. This may have continued south past Couiza and Quillan. It is possible that a hill fort at Rennes-le-Château became a small Roman town, but there is no confirmation whatever in Roman place-names or Roman topography, which is well established for the province of *Gallia Narbonensis*. It must be emphasized that we have no idea of the name of the settlement at Rennes-le-Château during the Roman period. The available evidence suggests that rather than a town there may have been a small Romanized villa with mosaic floors, or perhaps even a religious establishment devoted to the worship of a god whose origins were in the Iron Age period. There was almost certainly such a temple at Fa, 5 km west of Couiza. It is interesting to note that where the countryside was well settled, churches in this region seem to have existed since the fifth and sixth centuries. The churches were usually at villa sites.[3]

After Rome was sacked by the Visigoths, the Roman Empire in the west was effectively brought to an end. Although they were originally barbarians from beyond the Danube, the Visigoths admired and gradually adopted the Roman way of life.

Most of the Roman cities, towns and country houses continued their development without violent interruption. There are changes of artistic style, pottery, coins and mosaic designs, but it is difficult in an excavation to tell the difference between a late Roman villa and a Visigothic one. The Visigoths remained Christian. They continued to rule in France and southern Spain until the seventh century; and their empire only collapsed during the Muslim invasion of the early eighth century.

Any settlement surviving at Rennes-le-Château would have become part of the Visigothic empire. This is where the reported history of Rennes-le-Château becomes difficult to understand. It has been suggested that by this time the name of the hill-top settlement was Rhedae,[4] and that it was a major centre of the government of the Visigoths, and later of the Carolingian empire.

Claims have been made that it was a major city of upwards of 30,000 inhabitants,[5] spreading far and wide over the lower slopes of the hill. There used to be an aerial photograph on display at the Museum in the old presbytery at Rennes-le-Château which, it was suggested, showed extensive settlement on the slopes, including a great basilica and large mausoleum.

This is plainly nonsense. Close inspection of the photograph shows that there is little if any evidence of human activity on the slopes. The so-called mausoleum is caused by the temporary presence of manure heaps, and the 'basilica' by the presence near the surface of deposits of natural limestone conglomerate within a roughly rectangular area. This has been confirmed on the ground by the authors.

In fact extensive field walking on the lower slopes after ploughing in 1997 produced only a single shard of pottery of any sort. This was Roman samian pottery, dated to the second century AD. There was no other sign of human habitation. The only area with some occupation material lies close to the present village edge, and probably represents rubbish taken down from the village itself.

This of course does not dismiss the possibility that Rennes-le-Château was at one time a small Visigothic town, but with a population closer to 300 than 30,000. There has been extensive debate on this point since the publication in 1876 of a monograph entitled *'Rhedae', La Cité des Chariots* by Louis Fédié. This has recently been republished with an introduction by Jean Alain Sipra, by the *Association Terre de Rhedae*, which is based at the Bérenger Saunière Centre at Rennes-le-Château.

Louis Fédié was at one time Consul General of the Department of Aude and a prominent member of the *Société des Arts et des Sciences de Carcassonne*. His main study was of the counts of Razès, originally an administrative area under a military governor responsible to the Visigothic sovereign at Toledo. The term Razès appears to have been in use from the time of the Visigoths until the conquest of the Languedoc by Simon de Montfort in the thirteenth century. However, there is no great certainty about this until the appointment of Guillaume, the earliest Count of Razès, by the Emperor Charlemagne in 781.

There is substantial historical evidence that there was a city called Rhedae,[6] and that it played an important part in the history of Razès. The question is – was this Rennes-le-Château? There is no direct evidence to answer this one way or the other, and a conclusion must depend on a balance of probabilities.

It would be out of place to discuss this in detail here, but there cannot have been a large city on this site without leaving substantial traces, and no such traces are to be found. Furthermore, it is not easy to see how the name Rhedae could have been changed to Rennes. Rhedae was at the crossing point of four major roads; how could this possibly be the case at Rennes-le-Château on its isolated hilltop? There is no archaeological evidence of such roads either in the Roman period or at any time since. It is very difficult to believe that Rennes-le-Château was Rhedae.

Although Rennes had acquired its castle by the eleventh century, there is no record of the use of the name Rennes-le-Château until the nineteenth century. On a late eighteenth-century map of the Department of Aude held by the Bérenger Saunière Centre, Rennes-le-Château is simply called Rennes, and Rennes-les-Bains is called Les Bains de Rennes, suggesting that Rennes-le-Château was the more important settlement.

The Château

The Château, home of the Hautpoul Blanchefort family, is just to the east of the church (Pl. 25). There is no trace of the medieval château which once stood on this site. The present building, which is largely ruinous, dates from the seventeenth or eighteenth century. The castle consists of four main buildings around a central courtyard, with four corner towers, three square and one circular. Natural rifts in the rock on which it is built have led to tales of secret passages and troglodytes.

The Church of St Pierre

There were once two churches at Rennes-le-Château. In a fifteenth-century map of the Diocese of Alet in the Bérenger Saunière Centre there are two church symbols side by side. One street in the village is called rue St Pierre, and there is structural evidence in a workshop on the corner of the street of the existence of a substantial stone building, though only one side of a possibly Romanesque arch survives (Pl. 8).

It may be that Ste Marie Madeleine was the chapel for the medieval château, while St Pierre was the village church originating at a much earlier date. This is not certain however, and there has been no archaeological research at the possible site of St Pierre.

The Church of Ste Marie Madeleine

The interior of the present church is entirely the work of Saunière and his architect between 1891 and 1897 (Pls 11,12). There are no ancient features visible inside the church. However, some restoration of an earlier church took place in 1646, as indicated by the date stone preserved in the porch (Pl. 10) and in 1740 as shown on the date stone on the tower.

On the exterior of the apsidal east end of the church there are definite traces of its medieval origin. High on the north side of the apse are pillared arcades, though they have disappeared from the south side (Pl. 9). These are Romanesque features of the tenth and eleventh centuries – similar ones can be seen at the Monastery of Lagrasse and elsewhere in the Languedoc. The date is confirmed by the first mention of the church in an inventory of 1185.[7] The presence of the carved altar support and the Knights' Stone (described below) strongly suggests that a church, either this one or St Pierre, was already in existence in the eighth century AD.

Although it has been claimed that Bérenger Saunière's restoration was in some way extraordinary, this applies only to the amount of money he was able to spend on the work, which was far more than would be expected in a small village. It is clear that money was no object. The colourful decoration and the vigorous artistic work reflect late nineteenth-century fashions, and are paralleled in other churches, such as those at Couiza and at Montréal.

The entrance to the church is guarded by a plaster statue of the Devil (Pl. 13), supporting the holy water stoup. At first sight this might appear to be something very unusual indeed, but this is not the case. At Montréal, 32 km north-west of Rennes-le-Château, an equally startling devil supports the baptismal font (Pl. 14), this time in unpainted stone.[8] Above the water stoup at Rennes-le-Château are Saunière's initials, B.S. Above that is a sculptured group representing four angels before a cross, and the inscription *'Par ce signe tu le vaincras'* – 'By this sign you will conquer him.' The sign is of course the cross, and 'him' refers to the Devil.[9]

There has been much discussion of the inscriptions on the church porch.[10] The first inscription says *DOMUS MEA DOMUS ORATIONIS VOCABITUR*, 'My house shall be called a house of prayer'. This is simply quoted from Matthew 21:13 and was said by Jesus after he had upset the tables of the money changers in the temple. It is an appropriate quotation for a church porch.

The second inscription says *TERRIBILIS EST LOCUS ISTE*, 'Venerable is this place'. *Terribilis* in this context does not mean 'terrible' as used in English, but rather venerable, inspiring awe, which is highly appropriate for a church. This quotation is from Genesis 28:17, said by Jacob after his dream of the ladder to heaven. The same passage also provides the third, badly worn, inscription *HIC DOMUS DEI EST ET PORTA COELI*, 'This is the house of God, this is the gate of Heaven'. There is nothing remotely inappropriate or mysterious about these inscriptions, because this was the normal way of expressing Catholic beliefs.

Inside the church are the features ordered from Giscard of Toulouse in 1897.[11] These are the large bas-relief high on the west wall (Pl. 15) bearing the inscription *Venez à moi vous tous qui souffrez et qui êtes accablés et je vous soulagerai* ('Come unto me all ye that labour and are heavy laden, and I will give you rest' – Matthew 11:28); the fourteen Stations of the Cross; the piscina surmounted by a group representing the baptism of Jesus Christ by John the Baptist; other statues showing Mary with the infant Jesus, Joseph with the infant Jesus, St Mary Magdalene, St Anthony the Hermit, Ste Germaine with two lambs (Pl. 16), and St Roch; different pedestals to fit the statues; two pinnacles to go above Mary and Joseph; and three other small statues. All of these are in terracotta and painted in oil. They are in remarkably good condition today.

Much has been made of the possibility that these works contain references to hidden treasure or to Saunière's membership of various secret societies. When they are compared to works being installed in other churches in the Languedoc at this time by Giscard and comparable firms, it is clear that they are normal works of art for the period and contain no secrets.

The Knights' Stone

This stone, the *Dalle des Chevaliers*, is now displayed in the Bérenger Saunière Centre Museum (Pl. 24). It was discovered by Saunière, who showed his usual disregard for history by removing it and using it for paving one of the steps to the Calvary. It was seen by members of the *Société d'Ètudes scientifiques de l'Aude* on their second visit to Rennes-le-Château in 1908. They commented in their

Proceedings: 'At the foot of the Mission Cross we noticed a tombstone which had been discovered at the time of the church's reflooring, lying flat in front of the main altar. It is made of a very friable sandstone, and the carving which beautified it would have disappeared long ago if, at the time of its discovery, it had not been face down.'[12] The fact that the stone was found face downwards means that it had already been disturbed when placed in front of the altar as a paving slab, as the carving would almost certainly have been on view when originally set up. It is likely that it was not intended for a tomb at all, but had some other purpose. Maybe it had further damaging wear when it was in use as a paving slab in front of the Calvary. The top step, now of concrete, measures 131 cm x 83 cm. Allowing for a strip hidden under the kerb at each side, this matches the dimensions of the Knights' Stone.

It is often stated that the *Dalle des Chevaliers* was discovered on 21 September 1892 when Saunière recorded in his diary 'Discovery of a tomb, rain in the evening'. This cannot however refer to the Knights' Stone which was found, according to the Aude Society, in 1884–5,[13] though it is possible that it was found a little later than this during the reflooring of the church in 1886.

Depicted on the stone are two scenes within semicircular arches supported by pillars with spiral decoration. The arches themselves are covered with rows of beads or jewels, which are very reminiscent of the cross shown on the old altar support (see below). Above the arches, dogs are hunting in a wooded landscape. Within the left arch a lady sits side-saddle on a horse which is drinking from a trough. She appears to be blowing a horn. Under the right-hand arch a man rides a prancing horse with stirrups, apparently brandishing a spear and shield. The significance of the pictures is not understood, but the style conforms to that of the Carolingian Empire of the eighth century.

The *Dalles des Chevaliers* is the stone which figures in *The Lost Treasure of Jerusalem?* In Lincoln's interpretation the object that looks like a shield is a small child being carried by the horseman. He suggests the child is the baby Sigebert and the whole depicts his being taken to Rennes-le-Château for safety. Unfortunately the stone is so worn that it is impossible to know precisely what the carving represents.

The Old Altar

The altar support was taken from the church by Saunière during his restoration work. He used it, inverted, to support his statue of the Virgin Mary in the garden on the left of the church entrance (Pl. 18 and Fig. 9.3). He gave it a new base, and carved MISSION 1891 on what was now the bottom end, and PENITENCE PENITENCE on a new top. This was erected to commemorate the Mission conducted in the village that year.

The Aude Society also saw this in 1908 and reported: '. . . to the left of the church door, serving as the plinth for a Virgin of Lourdes, we found a pillar, which at one time supported the main altar. According to *Abbé* Saunières (*sic*) the main altar was in the form of a large slab, fixed on one side in the wall, and held up in front by two pillars, one of them rough, and the one already mentioned, which seemed to us to be of the same period as the tombstone.'[14]

One end (originally the top) has a mortise measuring 11 cm x 14 cm x 7 cm deep, into which another stone would have been fitted with a tenon prior to its use as an altar support. This recess has been incorporated into the story of the hidden parchments, but it is far too small to have contained documents.

The carving of the stone is sharp and fresh (Pl. 23). It seems that Saunière had the design recut to improve its appearance. His treatment of such antiquity in this manner emphasizes his disregard for the historical importance of ancient artefacts in his church.

The main feature of the decoration on the front of the stone is a cross attached to a spiral support. Three lines of jewels adorn the arms of the cross, together with spiral attachments to the ends of the arms. The lower two spaces between the arms are filled with branches, while the upper two hold the Greek letters Alpha and Omega suspended by bars from the panel above. An interlaced design fills the side panels.

There is no doubt that this is a Christian design. It could have been part of a tomb, or used elsewhere in the structure of a church. It has a strong connection with the Knights' Stone in its style of decoration, and probably also dates from the Carolingian period.

A search for a parallel to the altar support led us to the Archaeological Museum at Narbonne, where a very similar stone from the Eglise de Major is on display (Fig.9.4). At the top of this stone two doves or peacocks are pecking at a cantharus. Below there are two people, one of whom is sitting on a couch holding a jewelled cross, from which hang the Greek letters alpha and omega, as in the Rennes-le-Château example. Neither stone is fully understood, but the Narbonne stone may have been part of a chancel screen in a church with other panels amplifying the theme. Their presence suggests the existence in the Languedoc of a school of Christian stone carving with this distinctive and attractive style.

At the foot of the Virgin Mary's statue in the garden, which is now supported by a replica of the old altar support, lies a flat slab of marble (Pl. 21) with the inscription: *O MARIE CONCUE SANS PECHE PRIEZ POUR NOUS QUI AVONS RECOURS A VOUS* 'O Mary, conceived without sin, pray for us, who ask for your help'.

The inscription, enclosed within a decorative frame, clearly refers to the statue of the Virgin above it. The A of MARIE was at first carved as another M by mistake, and corrected. No doubt the error was camouflaged with cement at the time, but this has fallen out.

9.3 The old altar support from the church at Rennes-le-Château.

9.4 Decorated panel in the Archaeological Museum at Narbonne.

This large marble slab seems out of place among the sandstone blocks of the remainder of the paving and steps. On top of everything else, the front corners are curved while the back corners are rectangular. There is no apparent reason for the corners to be curved in an otherwise rectangular paving. It is quite likely that this slab, minus its inscription was in fact the altar table, which sat on the altar support and which Saunière removed from the church. Thus it would seem that two elements of the old altar have been used in the Mission memorial.

The Baluster

Once on display at the Bérenger Saunière Centre in Rennes-le-Château was a wooden baluster (Pl. 33) which features in the story of Saunière's discoveries in the church (see chapter 14). It may have been used to support the pulpit in an earlier church, in which case it would date from the church restoration suggested by the date stone of 1646. On the other hand, it may be the baluster referred to in the Parish Register of 1694.[15] What we do know is that when the Corbu family moved into the domain, the baluster was in the *Tour Magdala*.

The baluster consists of a short cylindrical column with an elaborate foliated capital, placed on an eight-sided base. It is 86 cm high and the top is 29 cm square. The top can be removed, but there is no cavity underneath. On one side a strip of wood at a slight angle to the vertical has been inserted in a notch from top to bottom of the capital, matching the mouldings. When this is removed there is no significant cavity behind the strip either.

The likely explanation for the strip is that the wood from which the baluster was made had a serious crack at this point, which was remedied by cutting a slot and inserting a patch. There is no cavity that could have contained either a phial or parchments.

The Churchyard

A survey of the churchyard (Pl. 9) carried out by the present authors in 1998 showed that there are no tombstones earlier in date than 1885. There are however some installed later than 1885 which mention earlier burials in the same grave. This confirms the accounts[16] of Saunière's work undertaken to clear the older tombs away, which led to objections by the people of the village.

In the western end of the churchyard used to lie the memorial to Saunière himself (Pl. 37). The inscription reads:

ICI REPOSE BERENGER SAUNIERE CURE A RENNES LE CHATEAU

1885 – 1917 DECEDE LE 22 JANVIER 1917 A L'AGE DE 64 ANS

('Here lies Bérenger Saunière, parish priest of Rennes-le-Château 1885-1917, died

22 January 1917 aged 64')

The stone was severely frost damaged and loose in its setting. It has been suggested that the stone was actually the re-used tombstone of Marie de Nègre d'Ables, but the dimensions are wrong and the underside of Bérenger Saunière's tombstone is blank. The slab actually measures 116cm × 35cm, while the true gravestone of Marie de Nègre was recorded by the Aude Society for Scientific Studies in June 1905 as 130cm × 65cm[17].

In September 2004 the body of Bérenger Saunière was exhumed and reburied in a specially built tomb within the grounds of the Villa Béthanie, in an attempt to reduce the risk of vandalism. The new tomb is designed to echo the semi-circular arch of the ossuary. Saunière's original inscribed stone has been removed to the museum.

On the churchyard wall close to the original burial site of Saunière was a simple tablet recording the burial of Marie Dénarnaud (Pl. 38):

ICI REPOSE Melle Marie Dénarnaud décédée le 29 janvier 1953

à l'âge de 85 ans P.P.E.

('Here lies Melle Marie Dénarnaud, died 29 January 1953 aged 85.

Pray for her')

At the time of writing this tablet has unfortunately been stolen. Close by is the tomb of Noël Corbu 1912–1968 and his wife Henriette (née Coll) 1902–1966.

According to Claire Corbu there is a vault beneath the memorials, which contained the bodies of Saunière, Marie Dénarnaud and the Corbu family. The steps leading down to this vault can be seen in a photograph reproduced in *Les Cahiers de Rennes-le-Château*[18], but this area has since been filled in.

The Temporary Altar

Close by the door to the cemetery is a small building called *Le Reposoir*, or the temporary altar (Pl. 18). Saunière established an altar here during the restoration of the church, and also used it as his office. Later it became his library until the construction of the *Tour Magdala*. Under the floor is a water tank, an important feature on this hill before piped water was available.

The Ossuary

Against the north wall of the churchyard and overhanging the quarry below stands Saunière's ossuary (Pl. 19). He built this to contain the bones from the graves that were disturbed during his reconstruction of the churchyard. It was restored in 2000, including the locked trapdoor to the cavity below.

In Henry Lincoln's film *The Lost Treasure of Jerusalem?* the ossuary is briefly shown as it was in 1971. On its floor lies a rectangular unbroken slab almost filling the area within the walls. Later in the film it is shown again with two corners fractured, though the corners are still lying there in place.

This slab, with further breaks and the corners missing is now displayed on the floor of the Museum. It was claimed by Lincoln and others to be the lost horizontal part of the tombstone of Marie de Nègre d'Ables, buried in the churchyard in 1781. Bérenger Saunière is said to have erased the supposed inscription. This is clearly untrue. The stone is a blank stone slab, roughly dressed by the quarry on the back, and smoothed for use on the front, perhaps as a gravestone. But it has never carried an inscription.

The Tombstone of Marie de Nègre d'Ables

The supposed horizontal part of Marie de Nègre d'Ables's tombstone (Marie II) is discussed in chapter 4 in connection with the parchments and in chapter 7 in connection with the inscriptions. However, there is no doubt at all about the existence of the upright slab (Marie I) belonging to her grave, which was removed by Bérenger Saunière. His lack of concern for this historic record is surprising, though the stone may well have been in very poor condition.

As we have noted previously, this stone was seen by members of the Aude Society for Scientific Studies on their visit to Rennes-le-Château in June 1905. The report in their Proceedings says: 'On visiting the cemetery we discovered in a corner a large slab, broken in the middle, on which it was possible to read an inscription which was carved very crudely. This slab measured 1.30 m × 0.65 m. But at that point someone comes to remind us that it is lunchtime. Served in one of the halls of the Château, the meal was of the highest quality. An excellent gateau closed the feast, and the first part of our programme.'[19]

It is ironic that the Society was swiftly distracted from something which interests us so much by the prospect of lunch! But the Society's Proceedings includes an illustration of the stone, so someone must have returned to take down the wording and dimensions. It is unthinkable that the supposed horizontal stone claimed by Lincoln existed at this time, as it would certainly have caused much interest and discussion among the Society members.

No one knows the present whereabouts of the stone that the Society saw: a terracotta replica based on the Society's illustration is displayed in the Museum of the Bérenger Saunière Centre. However, rubbish from the church and the churchyard has usually been disposed of even quite recently by throwing it over the wall into the quarry below. It is likely that Marie de Nègre d'Ables' tombstone lies with the rest of the rubble, well down in the heap.

The Calvary

In the churchyard at Rennes-le-Château stands the Calvary (Pl. 22), a monument commemorating Christ's crucifixion at the place of that name outside Jerusalem. It has recently been restored. Like other such features of the church it was built on the instructions of Bérenger Saunière. The Calvary was dedicated in 1897 by *Monseigneur* Billard, Bishop of Carcassonne, as a souvenir of his visit that year.

A mystery has been made of an abbreviated inscription on one side, which reads: *CHRISTUS A O M P S DEFENDIT*.

Lincoln suggests[20] that in full it might read: *CHRISTUS ANTIQUUM ORDINEM MYSTICUMQUE PRIORATUS SIONIS DEFENDIT*, which would mean 'Christ defends the ancient and mystical order of the Priory of Sion'. This is an ingenious attempt to provide evidence for a link between Bérenger Saunière and the supposed Priory of Sion, the mysterious organization to be discussed in chapter 12. There is no reason whatever to believe that this is the true meaning. On the obelisk of Pope Sixtus the Fifth in Rome, which was erected in the sixteenth century, the message appears in full:[21] *CHRISTUS AB OMNI MALO POPULUM SUUM DEFENDIT*, which means 'Christ defends his people from all evil'. There can be no doubt that this is the true significance of the inscription on the Calvary at Rennes-le-Château.

As we have already said, the Knights' Stone was initially placed at the top of the flight of steps leading to the Calvary.

The Grotto

The present grotto is a replica. The original was built for, or perhaps by, Saunière in person, with tufa quarried from the Valley of Bals, near the Ruisseau de Couleurs. It contained a statue of Ste Marie Madeleine, now also replaced by a replica.

Bérenger Saunière's Domain

To the west of the church Saunière built an extraordinary estate which survives to the present day. It includes a large and luxurious house (the *Villa Béthanie*), a curving belvedere overhanging the cliff with an iron glasshouse at one end and a new library (the *Tour Magdala*) at the other, crowned with a small circular tower and crenellations. There was a park with fountains, and a vegetable garden also with a fountain and paths that converged on a central circular area (see Pls 26–33). The buildings are now in the care of the Bérenger Saunière Centre.

The Tomb by the Road between Serres and Arques

As was recounted in chapter 5, this tomb figures in the affair of Rennes-le-Château because of the supposed resemblance between it and its surrounding landscape (Pl. 35) to the scene painted by Nicolas Poussin in one of his depictions of shepherds and a tomb, *Les Bergers d'Arcadie* (Pl. 34). The connections with the Saunière story are enhanced by the fact that in the painting two shepherds are pointing to the inscription on the side of the tomb, *Et in Arcadia ego*, the same words as were supposed to have been inscribed in Greek characters on the stone Marie II. Furthermore, Saunière is said to have purchased a copy of this picture (and two others) on his visit to Paris after the discovery of the parchments.

There is little one can say about the supposed purchase, except for the fact that Saunière's copies of the paintings have never come to light. If he had really brought three conspicuous pictures back to Rennes-le-Château, it is difficult to see how they could have all disappeared without trace and without any surviving record that they had been among his effects.

The tomb no longer exists, the site is bare. It was located on a little knoll on the south side of the road between Serres and Arques (Pl. 35), about 300 m east of the Paris Meridian. We have to rely on photographs[22] to see what the tomb looked like before it was destroyed in 1975. Roadside tombs are not uncommon in France, and are frequently of Protestant origin. The origin of this tomb is far from certain however. According to the local photographer interviewed by Lincoln, two American ladies had been buried in it in the 1920s. We have no reason to doubt this, but there is no independent confirmation of it either. The landowner, annoyed by the interest it aroused among treasure hunters, had it dismantled and its remains cleared away in 1988.

The similarity between the tomb as it was and the one painted by Poussin is not as strong as is often claimed. A photograph in *The Holy Blood and the Holy Grail*[23] clearly shows that its end is roughly square; the end of the tomb in the painting is taller than it is wide. Looking at the tomb from approximately the same angle as Poussin used gives a totally different background. Behind the tomb in the painting there is a distant crag; behind the roadside tomb there is the dominating mass of Pech Cardou. In the painting the undulating horizon said to depict Blanchefort and Rennes-le-Château is just to the right of the corner of the tomb; in reality if one had stood in front of the tomb in the correct place, one would have had to turn one's head about 30° to see Rennes-le-Château. Furthermore, close comparison of the painting and the real horizon shows only a slight resemblance. There is no real basis for the claim that Poussin had painted this view to perpetuate a secret in the landscape.

Shugborough Hall

Another site which has been associated with the Rennes-le-Château story is the Hall at Shugborough in England. This eighteenth-century house was rebuilt by Thomas Anson and owes much to his brother Admiral George Anson (1697–1762), a great sea captain and a reformer of the Royal Navy. In the garden of the house is the

'Shepherd's Monument'. A mock Greek temple front is used to frame a marble version of Poussin's *Les Bergers d'Arcadie*, though reversed left to right. It was carved by Peter Sheemakers in about 1750.

The purpose of the memorial is not clear. Beneath the marble picture is an enigmatic inscription: O U O S V A V V with the letters D and M below. Its meaning is not known, but it would surely have been understood at the time it was placed there.[24]

As the 'Poussin' painting has nothing in reality to do with Rennes-le-Château, the Shugborough monument is equally irrelevant.

Summary

The evidence on the ground supports some of the published statements about Rennes-le-Château but undermines others. To begin with it totally contradicts the assertions by Noël Corbu and other writers that Rennes-le-Château was a large centre of population, in the Visigothic period or any other. It shows that, although people have occupied its hilltop for many centuries, this was only ever a small settlement. There is no sign that Rennes was ever a great provincial capital.

There is evidence that there was a church at Rennes-le-Château from possibly the eighth century, but the existing building dates from the eleventh or twelfth century. The church was drastically reconstructed in the 1890s by Bérenger Saunière, in a form which is still intact in almost every detail. A large amount of money was spent, the origin of which is discussed in chapter 14. The interior fittings are lavish – some would say garish – but the architectural style and the decorative features are entirely in keeping with church style of the period. Most of the furnishings have parallels in other churches in the area, including the notorious devil. Strange as the pictures may seem to modern taste, there is no reason whatsoever to assume that they contain hidden messages.

Bérenger Saunière's domain was extraordinary for a village priest. Such mystery as there is lies in where he found the resources needed to build and furnish it.

One of the most important features of the Saunière affair is his discovery of four parchments (the two coded texts and genealogical tables) rolled in tubes secreted in a hole in the stone supporting the altar. The evidence does not support this story – the mortise hole is too small. This does not, however, preclude the existence of a void elsewhere in the altar construction. The alternative story, that the parchments were found in the baluster, is unlikely to be true since it has no internal cavity of any size.

There is no reason to associate features such as the tomb on the road to Arques with Rennes-le-Château at all. In chapter 11 we suggest how the 'Poussin' tomb, as it is sometimes called, came to be introduced into the story of Rennes-le-Château.

10
Secret Papers

We now come to a most peculiar collection of documents in the French National Library, the Bibliothèque nationale in Paris. They were an important source of information for Gérard de Sède when he was gathering material for his book, *L'Or de Rennes*. As we recounted in chapter 7, he showed photocopies of some of these files to René Descadeillas in March 1966 and Descadeillas was astonished that he, who had specialized in local history, had not come across them before. He investigated their origin, only to find that one of them at least was published by someone unknown, whose address did not exist. The documents are therefore suspect, yet important, because they mark significant steps in the development of the story of Rennes-le-Château.

In all there are about fifteen documents or collections of papers; six are in de Sède's bibliography, the others appeared in the Bibliothèque nationale after his book was published. Five are especially significant, and we have already mentioned three of them. In the order in which they were deposited in the Bibliothèque nationale, they are: *Généalogie des rois mérovingiens* (Genealogy of the Merovingian Kings), by Henri Lobineau, deposited in 1964; *Un Trésor mérovingien à Rennes-le-Château* (A Merovingian Treasure at Rennes-le-Château), by Antoine l'Ermite, deposited 13 May 1966; *Pierres gravées du Languedoc* (Engraved Stones of the Languedoc), edited by Joseph Courtauly, deposited 20 June 1966 by Antoine l'Ermite; *Le Serpent Rouge* (The Red Snake), by Pierre Fougère, Louis Saint-Maxent and Gaston de Koker, deposited 20 March 1967; and *Dossiers secrets d'Henri Lobineau* (Secret Files of Henri Lobineau), deposited 1967.

Genealogy of the Merovingian Kings

This is the file that was supposedly published in Geneva in 1956, from a non-existent address. Mostly it consists of genealogical tables; there is also a copy of a map of the old country of the Aude, supposedly drawn by the *Abbé* Pichon in 1814.

The first three genealogical tables give the lineage of the family of the counts and dukes of Bar from 850 to Marie Antoinette, wife of Louis XVI. The other tables set out the descent of the Merovingian kings, from Merovée (Merovich) of the fifth century, via Dagobert I and Dagobert II to a family called Plantard, continuing as far as the seventeenth century. All the charts have been most laboriously produced, each letter drawn separately with a stencil, in the style used by draughtsmen. A note on the summary page says that three copies were produced, in which case the charts must have taken very many hours of work. Most of the genealogical tables have amplifying notes and some are ornamented with illustrations of coats of arms.

Table 4, the Merovingian line from Merovée to Dagobert I, is in two sheets. The first states that it is based on the secret of the parchments of the *Abbé* Saunière, and it also has a note about Poussin, his painting *The Shepherds of Arcady*, and the motto *et in Arcadia ego*. The second sheet of Table 4 gives credit to *Abbé* Hoffet for furnishing Lobineau with the genealogical tables complied by Pichon and Hervé, with additional information from Saunière.

Table 8 (later descendants of Dagobert II) has the following slightly tortuous text with the heading 'The Enigma of Rhedae'. We gave the first sentence in chapter 4; here is the note in full.

One day in February 1892 the young *Abbé* Hoffet received an unusual visitor, the *Abbé* Saunière, *curé* of Rennes-le-Château from 1885, who came to ask this learned young linguist to translate some mysterious parchments which had been found in the pillars of the Visigothic high altar of his church. These documents, which bore the royal seal of Blanche de Castile, revealed the secret of Rhedae, the secret of the line of Dagobert II – which *Abbé* Pichon, between 1805 and 1814, had managed to establish following documents discovered at the time of the revolution. *Abbé* Hoffet, aware of the importance of the documents, kept a copy, but did not pass on the whole truth to *Abbé* Saunière. Saunière, being wise after the event, consulted other linguists, to whom he gave only fragments of the documents. During this period, thanks to this invaluable information, *Abbé* Hoffet constructed a very complete genealogy of the descendants of Dagobert II, the 'saint', assassinated by Pepin the fat; Dagobert II, the 'bear' king, whose ancestors were the kings of Arcady, the kings of Arcady who came from Bethany, near the Mount of Olives, from the tribe of Benjamin. Is this the reason why people have denied that Dagobert II existed? No, not entirely, because at the time of his assassination by the Pepin family (who had coveted the kingdom for several generations), Dagobert II had arranged for substantial treasure to be hidden at Rhedae, country of his second wife, mother of his son Sigebert IV, the future Count of Razès, and the existence of this treasure was a more important reason for the denial. However, neither Queen Blanche of Castile, nor Louis IX, the 'saint', even in the year 1251, dare touch this sacred hoard, about which the legend said anyone who took this treasure without having a right, be he pope or king, was in peril. In the great century – said one of the parchments – the heir will return to claim the inheritance of the great Bear.

So goes the legend in the parchments, where the gospel curses the wrong-doer who dares to steal a bit of the treasure, but one parchment also retells the history of an epoch of which we know almost nothing. The *Abbé* Béranger (*sic*) Saunière was summoned to the Court of Rome and refused to explain himself; he was suspended, died mysteriously on 22 January 1917, his servant and his heir, Marie Dénarnaud, who died in January 1953, ended her life in seclusion. Without the *Abbé* Hoffet, nothing would be known of the strange history of a family whose origin would be lost in the obscurity of time.

If the date (1956) on this file is genuine, it is the first account of Saunière taking parchments to Paris for examination, and the first time that Hoffet's name is brought into the story. But what were the parchments that Saunière is supposed to have taken to Paris? There's no mention here of ciphers – it is a matter of translation rather than decryption – and Saunière required a 'learned young linguist' to help him understand them. What language could this be? Being a priest, Saunière himself could have translated from Latin. When translated, these parchments are about genealogy. They enabled Hoffet to construct the family tree of the descendants of Dagobert II.

From this account of the meeting between Saunière and Hoffet, the parchments would appear to be quite different from the Latin manuscripts with the hidden ciphers, which were first shown to the world by Gérard de Sède. Hoffet is said to have kept a copy and given the originals back to Saunière. No one has ever seen these genealogical parchments, there is no independent evidence for their existence and it is extremely doubtful that they ever existed.

Nor is there any independent evidence for Saunière's trip to Paris or for his meeting with Hoffet, but Hoffet was a real person, sure enough. Descadeillas, ever thorough, researched his life.[1]

Emile Hoffet was born in 1873, at Schiltigheim near Strasbourg, the son of a Lutheran father and a Catholic mother. He was baptised in Paris at the age of eleven, where he began his studies at the choir school of Montmartre. He then went on to study at a seminary of a religious order, the Oblates of Mary, in the department of Meurthe-et-Moselle. His final studies were at Saint Gerlach in Holland and he took holy orders there in August 1892.

In the course of his career, Father Hoffet (as Descadeillas says he should properly be titled) went to Corsica as a missionary, spent some time in Rome and had several other appointments. From 1914 to his death in 1946 he lived in Paris. He wrote articles on church history and studied languages, Greek, Hebrew and Sanskrit. He had quite a reputation in this field, so it is fair to describe him as a talented linguist. But in February 1892, the date of his supposed meeting with Saunière, he was still a novice, aged only nineteen. Does it sound plausible that he would be capable of solving Saunière's problem of translation?

On studying the genealogical tables it is soon clear that the real purpose of the file has little bearing on the story of Saunière and his supposed treasure as it appears today. It is the genealogy itself that is important. Saunière's parchments are introduced as supporting evidence for lines of descent from King Dagobert II and to establish that some modern families, in particular one called Plantard, can claim him as an ancestor. The Lobineau papers claim Dagobert was married twice; his second wife, the supposed mother of Sigebert, being the daughter of Bera, Count of Razès. Yet, as we saw in chapter 7, Dagobert II's early life was spent in exile in Ireland, and he was assassinated while young. There is no record of his ever having had any children. His life is only sparsely recorded. He is an excellent choice if one wished to produce a spurious genealogy from a royal line.

As well as the genealogy of the line of Dagobert II there is another thread running through these tables; a myth about the distant origins of the Merovingians. In the note quoted above and the one on Table 4 we have six main elements: the line was descended from the tribe of Benjamin; they left Jerusalem and settled in an area near the River Rhine; there they established the land of Arcadia, which later became the kingdom of Austrasie; Dagobert II, with the aid of his second wife, hid royal treasure at Rhedae; the artist Poussin knew the secrets of the line of Dagobert and the location of the treasure; he tried to convey this in his painting of the shepherds gazing at the tomb and pointing out the inscription *et in Arcadia ego*.

So although these papers are primarily concerned with the descendants of the Merovingian line, and the parchments are only introduced to give credence to the genealogy, they contain the essentials from which the Saunière story was developed. Hence the message hidden in Manuscript 2: 'The treasure belongs to King Dagobert II and to Sion and it is death', and also the first few words of the message encrypted in Manuscript 1, 'Poussin holds the key'. The groundwork has been securely laid by Henri Lobineau.

But we have not yet asked the important question 'Who was this Henri Lobineau?' One answer comes from this file itself, in a quite curious way. Two years after the file was deposited in the Bibliothèque nationale, someone placed an extra sheet in it. It is a typed copy of a page of the periodical *Semaine Catholique Genevoise* (Geneva Catholic Weekly) for 22 October 1966. It is a letter, signed by one Lionel Burrus, protesting that Henri Lobineau has been vilified after his death by a Roman Catholic Bulletin.[2] The writer says that Henri Lobineau was a pseudonym, his real name being Léo Schidlof, and that Schidlof died in Vienna on 17 October 1966.

The gist of the protesting letter (which is written in a rather ranting style), is that the Lobineau/Schidlof genealogies are the work of a 'fellow-traveller, a notorious freemason, preparing a popular monarchy for France'. Apparently the Bulletin had said it was not true that the *Abbé* Hoffet in 1892 was given the task of translating the parchments brought to Paris by Saunière. The letter in reply says 'Hoffet in 1892 was following his studies in Paris; he met the *curé* Saunière at the house of Monsieur Ane, he was 19, it was his introduction to the Merovingian affair. Saunière had been sent by Monsieur Billard of Carcassonne, who was close to the *Abbé* Bueil, director of Saint-Sulpice, and Monsieur Ane was his nephew. Henri Lobineau never wrote that Saunière came to Paris to have the parchments translated by the *Abbé* Hoffet, who at that time was not yet ordained a priest.' This last sentence is hardly consistent with the note on the genealogical table, and we suspect that at the time the table was prepared, the author had not realized that Hoffet was such a young man.

So now we have to ask 'Who was Léo Schidlof?' He was an Austro-Hungarian,[3] and an art historian. In 1911 he had published in German an important work on miniatures; it was republished in English in 1965 in an enlarged edition under the title *The Miniature in Europe in the 16th, 17th, 18th and 19th Centuries.* For much of his life Schidlof lived in London. He was not connected with genealogy, and his daughter claimed that he had known nothing of Rennes-le-Château.[4] But why then did Lionel Burrus write the letter? In fact he did not. At the age of twenty, he was killed in a road accident in September 1966 – the month before the reported death of Léo Schidlof.

Léo Schidlof was not Henri Lobineau. His name, like that of Lionel Burrus, was used because neither man was in a position to object. We have stepped into murky waters indeed.

A Merovingian Treasure at Rennes-le-Château

This is a slight booklet of only ten pages. The author's name is Antoine l'Ermite and according to the title page it was published by Vié[5] at Anvers (Antwerp, but no address is given) in 1961, five years before it was lodged in the *Bibliothèque nationale.* It is print set, with justified vertical edges, and a typewritten sticker has been put on the title page reading *PUBLICATION de l'ALPINA.*[6]

The booklet reads rather like an interview given to a reporter from a local newspaper. Much of the text is set out as direct quotations of the words of Noël Corbu. So, as we would expect, the story of the treasure has many similarities with that written by him and placed in the archives at Carcassonne in 1962. But there are embellishments to the original tale. Memories seem to have improved with age.

The account of the discovery of the parchments is vivid:

The stonemason Babou from Couiza started work one morning at nine o'clock; he called to the *curé* to show him that in one of the pillars of the altar there were four or five hollow wooden tubes, sealed with wax.

'I don't know what this is!' he said.

The *curé* opened one of the tubes and took out a parchment, written, people think, in old French mixed with Latin, on which one could at first sight pick out passages from the Gospel.

'Bah', said he to the mason, 'these are old papers dating from the Revolution. They have no value.'

At noon Babou went to eat at the inn, but he was concerned and told the people who were with him. The mayor came for information; the *curé* showed him a parchment, which the good man didn't understand a bit, and the matter stopped there.

Not quite, however, for Béranger (*sic*) Saunière decided to stop the work on the church.

It continues in what are supposed to be the words of Noël Corbu: 'The *curé* tried to decipher the documents; he recognized verses from the Gospels and the signature of Blanche of Castile with her royal seal, but the rest remained a puzzle. Therefore he went to Paris in February 1892 to consult some linguists, to whom prudently he gave only parts of the documents.'

The discrepancies between this and previous accounts of the discovery of the parchments are clear: Babou makes the discovery (not the *curé*), there are four, maybe five parchments (not two or three), they are partly written in old French as well as Latin, they are extracts from the Gospels (not genealogies) and we have a hint that they may be in code.[7]

There are other colourful additions, for example the story of a shepherd boy whose lamb fell into a gully. When he climbed down to rescue the animal, he found himself in a cave with hidden treasure. He took some gold coins back to his village, but refused to say where he had got them – he was then accused of theft and was killed without divulging the secret of the hoard. (Sceptical readers will ask how anyone could know about the cave of gold if the boy said nothing about it before he was killed.) This legend is advanced as corroboration for the local belief that the treasure of Blanche of Castile was hidden in the area of Rennes-le-Château.

The booklet is revealing, for it shows how, from telling to telling, the story develops. Each little bit that has been added to make the story more entertaining becomes part of the accepted history, and from a few dimly remembered facts grows an account full of persuasive detail.

So where did this information really come from? It is in fact almost a word-for-word copy of a chapter that first appeared in a book by Robert Charroux *Trésors du Monde* (Treasures of the World), first published in 1962, five years before the book by Gérard de Sède. Charroux, a keen treasure hunter, visited Rennes-le-Château in the late 1950s, and we can presume did get his information directly from Noël Corbu. The fact that this text was taken without acknowledgement from another author indicates that whoever Antoine l'Ermite was, he was lacking scruples.

Engraved stones of the Languedoc

Five weeks after he had placed *A Merovingian Treasure at Rennes-le-Château* in the Bibliothèque nationale, Antoine l'Ermite was back there again, with a copy of the collection of Plates XVI to XXIII, supposedly from a book by Eugène Stüblein, and extracted 'in order to satisfy the numerous requests of researchers' by *Abbé* Joseph Courtauly. In chapter 7 we explained why there are good reasons for concluding that this work is a forgery. Let us see exactly what it contains.

The title page, dated 1884, and the preface (supposedly by Courtauly) are handwritten, as are all the captions to the plates. Plates XVI[8] and XVII[9] are Roman altar stones, and Plate XVIII[10] is a Roman tombstone. The drawings are signed 'E. Stüblein', but in fact appear to be copies of illustrations that were published in a book, *Ancient Inscriptions from the Pyrenees*, by Julian Sacaze, 1892.

Plates XIX and XX are of the same stone, viewed from front and rear. The drawing is captioned 'the Head of St. Dagobert' and is also signed 'E. Stüblein'. Beneath the drawing is a paragraph of text: 'The Dagobert Legend'.

Plate XXI is an exact copy of the drawing of the stone which we have called Marie I, as it appeared in the Proceedings of the Aude Society for Scientific Studies in 1906. We pointed out in chapter 7 that this was not an accurate representation of the stone's appearance. If Stüblein had seen the stone and drawn it himself, it would be amazing if he had made precisely the same errors in its proportions as were made in the Proceedings. We would have expected a genuine drawing by Stüblein to look more like our reconstruction in Fig. 7.2.

Plate XXII is the Marie II stone, signed, like the others, and captioned 'Sandstone slab, horizontal, in the cemetery of Rennes-le-Château, Aude. Tomb of the Dames Hautpoul of Blanchefort.'

The last plate, Plate XXIII, shows the *Dalle des Chevaliers*. The drawing is almost identical to the illustration of the stone that appeared in the Proceedings of the Aude Society in 1927.[11] Alongside the picture in the Proceedings there is a paragraph of descriptive text, 'A Carolingian tombstone (771), found in 1884–5 under the altar of the Romanesque church at Rennes-le-Château, one time capital, quite destroyed, of the Count of Razès.' This drawing was made by an artist, J. Ourtal, and he has put his name under the bottom right corner. When we compare Ourtal's drawing to Plate XXIII there is an important difference – the signature is not Ourtal's but Stüblein's.

According to the Proceedings, the stone was discovered in 1884–5. This would be just too late for inclusion in a book supposedly published in 1884. If we had any lingering thought that perhaps Stüblein's work might be genuine, it is immediately dispelled when we see, in the *Secret File of Henry Lobineau* (discussed on page 109), another illustration of the *Dalle des Chevaliers*. It is identical to Plate XXIII, except for two alterations: in place of Ourtal's signature there is the date 1884, and alongside it is the text that appeared in the Proceedings, with a significant change – the date of discovery is altered to 1882–3!

Two other pieces of evidence convince us that the work is a fake. The signature of Stüblein as it appears at the foot of the drawings is quite different from the one in his book about the journey to thermal baths[12] – and the name on the preface was misspelt Courtaly instead of Courtauly. Surely he would have got his own name right!

There is only one plausible explanation for all this deception. The stone Marie II had to be given credibility because some letters on it were essential to the encryption. After devising its inscription, a drawing was placed in a little collection of illustrations of real stones, in the presumed hopes that it would be accepted as genuine.

Le Serpent Rouge

This is a short and very peculiar work. It contains a Merovingian genealogy, two maps of France in the Merovingian period and a ground plan of the church of Saint-Sulpice in Paris. In addition there are twelve short prose poems, one for each sign of the Zodiac, plus a thirteenth for the constellation Ophiuchus, between Scorpio and Sagittarius. The poems are very obscure and full of symbolic allusions, but nevertheless are important: some authors believe that they contain clues to the secrets of Rennes-le-Château; we regard them as interesting sources for some of the material that has accumulated around the myths. We give our English translation in Appendix C, with notes, which regrettably do not make the text much clearer.

The author says that he is recounting a dream that he had on the night of 17 January, St Sulpice's Day (also the date inscribed on the tomb of Marie de Nègre d'Ables). Whoever wrote the text was familiar not only with the church of Saint-Sulpice, but also with the countryside around Rennes-le-Château and its church, for the poems contain several references to the latter's furnishings and inscriptions. In the poem 'Cancer', the black and white paved floor with Asmodeus looking over it is mentioned, as are the words that appear above the statue of the Devil – *Par ce signe tu le vaincras* (By this sign you will conquer him). The poem 'Leo' includes the words under the painting on the west wall, *Venez à moi vous tous qui souffrez et qui êtes accablés et je vous soulagerai* (Come unto me all ye that labour and are heavy laden and I will give you rest).

In 'Virgo' we find the words 'I was like the shepherds of the famous artist Poussin, puzzled by the riddle *"Et in Arcadia Ego . . ."*.' There are references also to P and S, to the meridian and to the Egyptian goddess Isis, which have inspired later authors to concoct ingenious interpretations.

But the very strangest aspect of this strange work is its authorship. The three named authors – none of whom knew each other – all committed suicide by hanging on 6 or 7 March 1967, before the document was placed in the Bibliothèque nationale. It would seem that the real author wished to remain anonymous and scanned the newspapers for reports of violent death. He then put an earlier date, 17 January, on the document and lodged it with the National Library on 20 March.[13] Such an act seems bizarre, and we would regard it as unlikely, if we were not aware that ascribing authorship to a dead person had not already been done with Stüblein (a book), Courtauly (a preface), Schidlof (genealogies) and Burrus (a letter). Despite the deception, there is no doubt as to the true identity of the author. The Merovingian genealogy and the maps of France in the sixth century (which also appear in the *Dossiers secrets*) point to the Plantard–de Chérisey stable, and this is confirmed by the fact that the same typewriter was used to create both documents.[14] The style, the obscurity, his known liking for puzzles and his familiarity with Rennes-le-Château all point to Philippe de Chérisey himself. Furthermore, the author is clearly addressing Pierre Plantard; in 'Aquarius' is written 'How strange are the manuscripts of this friend'.

The Secret File of Henri Lobineau

This file is a bizarre collection of scraps; letters (including one from Corbu, see chapter 7), maps, newspaper cuttings, genealogies, coats of arms and drawings. One page, with a genealogical table and two maps, is identical to a page in *Le Serpent Rouge*. The title page is hand drawn and dated 1967, which actually tallies with the date it was deposited in the National Library. This was after the reported death of Henri Lobineau (or Schidlof) and the Lobineau papers are collected by someone called Philippe Toscan du Plantier, whose address was given as 17 quai de Montebello, Paris. By now it will not surprise the readers to learn that this address is as fictitious as the Geneva one on the genealogies of the Merovingian kings.

The first page has a curious dedication, signed by Philippe Toscan du Plantier: 'To Monsignor the Count of Rhedae, Duke of Razès, the legitimate descendent of Clovis I, King of France, most serene child of the "King and Saint" Dagobert II, your humble servant presents this collection which make up the "Secret Files" of Henri Lobineau.'

Is this dedication to be taken seriously? If it is, du Plantier believes there is someone, unnamed and unrecognized as such, who is the rightful king of France through his descent from Dagobert II. Perhaps we are getting a little closer to the real background of the affair of Rennes-le-Château.

In a long, typed introduction, under the name of Edmond Albé, we are led through the events described earlier in this chapter, the death of Schidlof/Lobineau and the article by Lionel Burrus. Then we come to Saunière and the discovery, now dated to February 1892, of *four* parchments which are listed as follows:

1. A parchment in the form of litanies, which gave the genealogy of the descendants of Saint King Dagobert II from the year 681 to March 1244, the date of the marriage of Jean VII to Elisande de Gisors, dated 12 March 1244 and the seal of Blanche of Castile, Queen of France.

2. A parchment giving the text of the will of François-Pierre of Hautpoul, *Seigneur* of Rennes-le-Château, a text of the genealogies from 1200 to 1644, as well as six lines about St Vincent de Paul. This parchment bore the date 6 November 1644, recorded 23 November 1644 by Captier, notary at Esperaza.

3 and 4. Two parchments, extracts from the Gospels, whose date must be between 1781 and 1791; the text is encrypted by the former *abbé* of the place, Antoine Bigou.

This document, written eleven years after the first articles appeared in *La Dépêche du Midi*, is the first to be so precise. New information appears – that one parchment is in the form of litanies, that they include a will recorded by a notary, and that two of the parchments contain encryptions by Antoine Bigou. None of this is to be found in the first file we looked at, *Généalogie des rois mérovingiens*. What we see here is yet another elaboration of the story, whose purpose is to add credibility to the genealogical claims. The parchments have to be given a provenance. Now they are linked to a seventeenth–century will, signed and dated by a notary, no less, and by implication held at Rennes-le-Château until they were placed in the altar pillar by Antoine Bigou.

Superficially this might seem plausible, if one was unaware of the pseudonyms, false addresses and conflicting accounts in earlier documents. As well as that, there is the conclusive proof that the statement about the third and fourth parchments is false, because the version of the Bible used in Manuscript 1 was published a century after Antoine Bigou was supposed to have done this.

If the genealogical parchments had come to light we could take them seriously, but where are they now? The two manuscripts purporting to be the copies of the encrypted gospels were seen and published by Gérard de Sède. How was it that he did not also see the parchments containing the genealogical tables? In the *Secret File of Henri Lobineau* there is an answer to that.

These several texts were taken to Paris in 1892 on the advice of *Monsignor* Billard, Bishop of Carcassonne, and were entrusted to M. Bueil, Director of Saint-Sulpice, and got ultimately into the hands of Father Hoffet. Eventually the latter died, 3 March 1946, at 7 rue Blanche. The above documents 1 and 2, stolen from his library, passed unlawfully to the International League of Antiquarian Booksellers of England, and ended up in the secret files of the Order of Malta. (See the letter reproduced in this file.)

The file does indeed contain a letter, dated 2 July 1966 and written from Paris on the League's headed notepaper, in which two persons (the signatures are unreadable) who have recently visited Rennes-le-Château, inform M. Fatin, archaeologist there, that his castle is historically the most important in France. They add that this opinion is confirmed by 'two parchments bearing the seal of Blanche of Castile with the will of François Pierre d'Hautpoul, registered 23 November 1644, by Captier, notary of Esperaza, these items having been bought by our League together with part of the library of *Abbé* Hoffet, 7 Rue Blanche, Paris, who took possession of them from *Abbé* Saunière, one-time *curé* of Rennes-le-Château.'

We have contacted the Antiquarian Booksellers' Association in London, who confirmed that they did at the time have headed notepaper like that on which the letter was written. However they have no record in their files of any purchase of Hoffet's papers.

Turning now to the genealogical tables included in this file we find several compiled by *Abbé* Pierre Plantard, curate of the church of Saint Clothilde in Paris. On one table, headed 'House of Plantard (elder branch)' there is a note by the *abbé*, in which he claims his own descent from Dagobert II. At a corner of the sheet we see the coat of arms of Pierre Plantard V (1877–1922), 'Count of Rhedae'. On another tree the family of Plantard is linked with Blanchefort. Here we find small drawings of stones Marie I and Marie II. Other sheets in the file show large drawings of the two stones, Marie I (as we noted in chapter 4) having been drawn by hand to simulate the illustration and its accompanying text in the *Proceedings of the Aude Society for Scientific Studies,* at the expense of many hours of labour.

If there had been any doubt about the main interest of Henri Lobineau, whose papers these are said to be, it is dispelled with a full-page drawing of the arms of the Plantard family: on a red field, a circle and a fleur-de-lis (the badge of the kings of France) in gold. Above is an armoured knight; on a chain from his neck hangs a six-pointed star, signifying, no doubt, the claimed descent from the tribe of Benjamin. The wording on the Plantard arms is *et in Arcadia ego,* 'Even I, Death, am in Arcadia'. It may be an appropriate text for a gravestone but surely not for a family motto.

In the file we find more on the genealogy of the Merovingians. Two typewritten sheets give the line from Dagobert II, with a footnote saying 'Genealogy based on a parchment bearing the signature and royal seal of Blanche of Castile. It was found hidden in one of the four wooden rolls of the Visigothic pillar in the church of Rennes-le-Château. It was put there in 1788/1789 by *Abbé* Bigou, before that date it was attached to the will of François-Pierre, Baron d'Hautpoul of Rennes and recorded on 23 November 1644 by Captier, notary of Esperaza.'

These two pages have typed stickers, to the effect that they come from Joseph Courtauly. One sticker says that they are for Alpina (publisher of the booklet by Antoine l'Ermite), the other is dated 1961 (the year Courtauly retired to Villarzel-du-

Razès). There are also typed notes on the two large drawings of Marie I and Marie II, accrediting them to Eugène Stüblein. All of these stickers, as well as the one on l'Ermite's booklet, were typed on the same machine, presumably by whoever compiled the file.

Among the remaining papers in the file there is yet one other that merits attention. This is a table drawn up by Henri Lobineau about a curious organization, the Priory of Sion, also known as the Order of the Rose-Cross. According to this document, the Priory of Sion was founded in 1188 by Jean de Gisors, who called himself Jean II, and has had twenty-six grandmasters up to 1918, twenty-two male (each entitling himself Jean) and four female (all taking the name Jeanne). The list of grandmasters is astounding. They include Leonardo da Vinci (Jean IX), the scientist Robert Boyle (Jean XV), Isaac Newton (Jean XVI), Victor Hugo (Jean XXI), Claude Debussy (Jean XXII) and Jean Cocteau (Jean XXIII). The earliest grandmasters do not have household names, but we can find most of them on Tables 2 and 3 of the Genealogy of the Merovingian kings. The family of St Clair provided some of the early grandmasters, the dukes of Bar had several, the latest being Maximilien of Lorraine (Jean XIX), the brother of Marie Antoinette. We shall return to the Priory of Sion in chapter 12.

In spite of the false names, the non-existent addresses, the changes to drawings, the inconsistencies, the invention and the improbabilities to be found in the secret papers some authors still accept them. Picknett and Prince write: 'It is in our opinion, a great mistake to dismiss the *Dossiers secrets* simply because their overt message is demonstrably implausible. The sheer scale of the work behind them argues in favour of their having something to offer.'[15]

We disagree.

Summary

The documents from the Bibliothèque nationale show how, in the years leading to 1967, the story of Bérenger Saunière and Rennes-le-Château was steadily evolving. It begins with the genealogies: their compiler sets out to establish that there is a new, and as yet unrecognized, line of descent from the Merovingian kings. He picks on Dagobert II, whose history is not well recorded, as the source of the new line. Supporting evidence is needed, and it is claimed in the documents that this comes from parchments, found by Saunière when he restored his church, taken to Paris, and interpreted by Emile Hoffet. These are seen by Henri Lobineau, and the new genealogies are produced. A copy is placed in the French National Library, with a fake address on the title page.

There is no evidence that the parchments have ever existed, beyond the sensationalized reports of January 1956 in *La Dépêche du Midi*. Something has to be added to make the story more plausible. A 'popular' account is written, with new and vivid details of the discovery of the parchments, based very largely on the words of Noël Corbu. The author writes under an unlikely pseudonym, Antoine l'Ermite, whose address is an hotel; he gives no precise address for the publishers, and has cribbed the text from another author.

The Secret Files of Henri Lobineau gives us yet more information and a provenance for the parchments. They were said to have been seen, witnessed and dated by a notary of a town near Rennes-le-Château. Up to now we have not been given any means of checking the statements in the files, not one verifiable document has been cited. At last, it seems, a will can be consulted. But no, the will and the two genealogical parchments were stolen, and have passed beyond reach.

Behind this strange activity is Henri Lobineau, 'genealogist'. The files say that Henri Lobineau is a pseudonym, he is actually Léo Schidlof. But the real Schidlof had nothing to do with the matter – his name was borrowed without his knowing it. Schidlof died in 1966, so in 1967 the *Dossiers secrets* were deposited supposedly posthumously in the Bibliothèque nationale. The editor was someone called Philippe Toscan du Plantier. How he came by the files we are not told. The address he put on the cover sheet was false.

The genealogical tables in the files have all been laboriously drawn by hand and many months of work must have been required. The reason for the huge effort becomes clear from the dedication by du Plantier to the 'Count of Rhedae, Duke of Razès, legitimate descendent of Dagobert II, king of France'. The work of Henri Lobineau aims to prove that the heir to these titles is alive at the present day. He is obsessive in his efforts, determined to produce evidence to substantiate his thesis, and not too worried if the truth has to be bent a little here and there. No doubt most of the genealogy is correct, but a little tinkering can always help.

We ask whose claim is Lobineau advancing. Few people would work so hard if it were not for their own benefit. We know that Lobineau is a pseudonym and most likely the compiler thought he would have more credibility if he was not seen to be advancing his own personal interests. However, the name of the claimant is apparent in the documents. The lines of descent lead in one clear direction, to the family whose coat of arms is given prominence in the files, and that name is Plantard – the Pierre Plantard who was tracked down by the BBC and who appears briefly in the television film *The Shadow of the Templars*.

11

Plantard and de Chérisey

In spite of the fact that Gérard de Sède took much of his material from the files in the Bibliothèque nationale, you will not find the name Plantard in *L'Or de Rennes*. Nor does anyone called Plantard appear in Henry Lincoln's first two programmes *The Lost Treasure of Jerusalem?* (1972), or *The Priest, the Painter and the Devil* (1974). In the second programme he shows the drawing of the coat of arms claimed by the Plantards, but does not mention to whom it belongs.

Yet as we have recounted in chapter 5, it was Henry Lincoln himself who first came across the Plantard connection. In *The Holy Blood and the Holy Grail*[1] he writes that, while making the first television film on Rennes-le-Château, he requested some photographs from Gérard de Sède's publisher, and when they were supplied they had the name 'Plantard' stamped on the back. He also discovered that de Sède's book, *The Templars are among us*,[2] published in 1962, had an appendix which is in fact a lengthy interview with a Pierre Plantard. In this interview, Pierre Plantard is described as an archaeologist and an hermetist, or one who studies the obscure and the occult. Lincoln suspected that de Sède's book on Rennes-le-Château drew heavily on information supplied by an informant and '. . . eventually Pierre Plantard began to emerge as one of the dominant figures in our investigation.'[1]

It was not until March 1979, during the filming of the *Shadow of the Templars* that Lincoln managed to meet Pierre Plantard. He describes how this came about.[3] A BBC researcher made contact with a writer, Jean-Luc Chaumeil, who had interviewed Pierre Plantard for a magazine, and Chaumeil arranged the meeting. 'M. Plantard proved to be a dignified courteous man of discreetly aristocratic bearing, unostentatious in appearance with a gracious, volatile but soft-spoken manner. . . . After three meetings with M. Plantard and his associates we were not significantly wiser than we had been before.'

Lincoln interviewed Plantard in the *Shadow of the Templars*. Plantard looks dignified, but is enigmatic. The recorded dialogue goes like this:

Lincoln: Monsieur Plantard, is there still a secret at Rennes-le-Château?
Plantard: The secret is not only at Rennes-le-Château, it is around Rennes-le-Château.
L: Will the treasure of Rennes-le-Château ever be found?

P: Here you are speaking of a material treasure, we are not talking of a material treasure. Let us say, quite simply, that there is a secret in Rennes-le-Château and that it is possible there is something else around Rennes-le-Château.

L: And how does Poussin fit into this story?

P: To be seen in Poussin's paintings there are certain revelations. Poussin was an initiate and therefore created his paintings as an initiate. But he was not the only one in this story, there are other characters. In artistic expression the truth is concealed and one uses symbolism.

L: Tell us whether the Priory of Sion still exists today.

P: At this moment Sion still exists. One of its recent members – one of the last Grand Masters – was Jean Cocteau. Everyone knows this.

L: Monsieur Plantard, over the centuries you have – how shall I put it? – supported the Priory of Sion.

P: We have supported Sion and Sion has supported us.

L: We? Who are we?

P: We – I am speaking of the Merovingian line, for our line descended from Dagobert II. The Merovingians, it was they who made France. Without them there would be no France. The Capetians and the Carolingians followed on from the Merovingian line. The Merovingians represent France.

And that was as explicit as Pierre Plantard would be on film.

Of all the people involved in the saga of Rennes-le-Château, Pierre Plantard is one of the most important, probably the most important, yet at the time the *Shadow of the Templars* was made, very little was known about his life. Henry Lincoln had several meetings with him in the period 1979–1984 and also researched his background. Much of what he found was vague and contradictory. However in recent years his background has been studied thoroughly by two researchers, Jean-Luc Chaumeil and Paul Smith [4]. Both have collected original documents and letters, which throw much light on Plantard's activities and his personality.

Pierre Anathase Marie Plantard was born in Paris on 18 March 1920, the son of Pierre Plantard and Amélie Mari Raulo. A copy of his birth certificate, obtained by Lincoln from the *Marie* of the 7th *Arrondissement*, states that he was the son of a *valet de chambre*, a butler, but Plantard himself had given Lincoln a photocopy of a birth certificate on which the family name was given as Plantard de Saint-Clair and his father had the titles *Comte de Saint Clair* and *Comte de Rhédae*. On being challenged about the discrepancy, Plantard explained it by saying that during the war it was not unusual to insert falsified information to official records to deceive the Germans: the birth certificate Lincoln had obtained was the false one. The officials at the Marie said that this was a possibility,[5] their wartime records were not reliable. Taking into account what we know about Plantard's later activities it seems more likely that Lincoln had obtained a copy of the actual birth certificate, and that Plantard wished to mislead him about his origins.

Plantard was 19 when the Second World War began. He admired Field Marshal Pétain and in December 1940 he wrote a letter to him warning of a Jewish-Masonic conspiracy, an action which brought him to the attention of the French and German authorities. In 1942 he set up an organisation called the *Alpha Galates* (The First Gauls), for which he started a newsletter, *Vaincre* (To Conquer). Six editions, published monthly from September 1942 to February 1943 are in the *Bibliothèque nationale*[6]. The first edition has a photograph of the 22-year-old Plantard and an article by him, under the pen-name of Pierre de France. We give the text of this article in Appendix D. It sets out to rally a dejected French nation and recruit them to the Alpha Galates, an 'Order of Knighthood'. It is full of worthy phrases but rather short on specifics and as far as is known he had little success in recruiting members to the organisation.

In the context of the present study, the most interesting aspect is the light it sheds on the character of Pierre Plantard. Even at the age of twenty-two, in his own eyes he is someone apart from the crowd. He writes under an almost royal title, he aspires to be recognised as a leader. He looks to the past for inspiration; he wants to create 'A New Young Knighthood'. He is a fantasist, and already we have a glimpse of the character of a man who was later to see himself as a descendant of the royal Merovingian line.

Plantard's action in setting up the Alpha Galates was not with the approval of the Germans. He was arrested and served four months from the end of 1943 in Freynes Prison (near Orly Airport). Plantard told Henry Lincoln that he had been imprisoned for being in the resistance. When Lincoln tried to check this with the French authorities he was told that such information was personal and confidential[7]. Later researchers have had more success. It is known that there is a report on Plantard in the Paris Prefecture of Police (part of File Ga P7). French law prohibits precise details of convictions being made public, on the grounds that once one has served a sentence for an offence it becomes amnestied and should not be referred to henceforth.

Plantard married Anne-Léa Hisler on 6 December 1945. His movements after that are rather vague. According to a document written by his wife, he was living in Switzerland, having been invited by the Swiss Government in 1947[8]. In or about 1956 he moved to the town of Annemasse, near the border with Switzerland in the Haute Savoie and took employment as a draughtsman in a local company. His activities at Annemasse, which are rather crucial to unravelling the Rennes-le-Château story, are recounted in the next chapter.

In 1958, at the time of the crisis which led to Algerian independence, General de Gaulle came back into power as President of the Fifth Republic. Plantard set up a 'Committee of Public Safety', one of many that were being set up all over France at this time[9]. It was reported in three articles dated 6 June, 8–9 July and 29 July in *Le Monde*.

Mme Plantard wrote an article, a copy of which was deposited in the *Bibliothèque nationale* in 1965[10], in which she asserted that not only had Plantard been given this task, but after the General had successfully assumed power, he had personally written a letter of thanks to Plantard. Henry Lincoln drew a blank when he tried to check this with the *Institut Charles de Gaulle*, the official repository of the late President's papers.

While living at Annemasse, Pierre Plantard developed his interest in occult and esoteric knowledge and wrote a tract called *Gisors et son secret* (Gisors and its secret), which he deposited in the *Bibliothèque nationale* in 1961. About this time he got to know Gérard de Sède, and when the latter published his book *Les Templiers sont parmi nous* (The Templars are among us) in 1962, Plantard contributed a lengthy appendix. He is described as an archaeologist and hermetist, specialising in deciphering hermetic monuments. The Château of Gisors apparently has many mysteries, which Plantard attempts to elucidate with plays on words and numerology.

Two years later began the deposition in the *Bibliothèque nationale* of the series of strange documents written under a variety of assumed names. The first was the collection of genealogies supposedly by Henri Lobineau, deposited in January 1964, carefully and precisely laid out using stencils for the lettering, as was the practice at that date in drawing offices. The Plantard myth factory was now in operation, making the links between the Merovingian kings, the Plantard family and Rennes-le-Château.

Plantard himself wrote about his connections with Rennes-le-Château. He said that his grandfather Charles Plantard, 'the legitimate descendant of the Counts of Rhedae', visited Bérenger Saunière at Rennes-le-Château on 6 June 1892 and had lunch with him in the company of Henri Boudet. Also present was Elie Bot, described as consultant and building contractor.[11] Plantard adds a colourful touch: at the lunch 'a monkey called Méla, a present from a famous singer, played with a dog called Pomponet.'

At first sight this seems an account of a plausible event, but knowing the extent of Plantard's historical inventiveness, it is wise to be cautious in accepting this story as true. It was not written until 1978, is not supported by any other documents that we know of and may well be retrospective manufacture of evidence. The date 1892 is itself suspicious, because although Elie Bot was indeed one of Saunière's contractors, as far as is known he was not involved in the works at Rennes-le-Château until the construction of the *Villa Béthanie* and the gardens in 1901, nine years later. A surviving bill from Bot to Saunière covers work he undertook between June 1901 and June 1902.[12]

Pierre Plantard recorded his first visit to Rennes-le-Château as follows:

I went to Rennes-le-Château in August 1938 to recover some letters which the *Abbé* Saunière had received from my grandfather. It was during the holidays and I was not twenty years old. 'Marinette' as they called her in the district, received me very hospitably at the Villa Bethania; I stayed there for three days. We celebrated the seventieth birthday of the old lady. . . . It was impossible for me to keep the promise I had made to Mlle Marie Dénarnaud to come back and see her the following year. In 1939 was the war. The events which followed did not permit me to return to my land of Razès and to see Rennes-le-Château again until 1965. The marquis Philippe de Chérisey came with me. He was a friend whom I'd known for a long time and who was very interested in Rennes-le-Château. Mlle Dénarnaud, who had gradually got rid of the furniture which she possessed and who had sold the property to M. Noël Corbu, had been dead for a dozen years. The new proprietor, who had metamorphosed the Villa Bethania into an hotel, received us very well. He recounted to us the 'new history of the treasure of Rennes-le-Château' with far-fetched details that left us stupefied.[13]

This extract from the 1978 document is even more suspect than the first. It appears to be an attempt by Plantard to distance himself from the more sensational aspects of the story of Rennes-le-Château, even though he himself had primed Gérard de Sède with material for *L'Or de Rennes*. It conflicts with other information in several respects.

Plantard says he did not visit the area of Rennes-le-Château between 1938 and 1965. Yet according to Descadeillas, he made several visits to Rennes-les-Bains from the last years of the 1950s.[14] His visits attracted a lot of attention. As Descadeillas reported (see chapter 7), he behaved strangely and furtively, and though he talked a lot, it was difficult to follow his meaning. He was interested in archaeological and natural sights and seemed to be building up a file of the locality. He spoke to many of the local people, including the aged *Abbé* Courtauly, who died in 1964. Descadeillas did not name Plantard in his book – possibly after having written in such an uncomplimentary manner about him, he did not wish to risk a charge of defamation of character – but he said he had reason to believe the unwelcome stranger was the author of the Lobineau papers.

Confirmation of an earlier visit than 1965 comes from de Chérisey himself. Markale quotes him as saying that he (de Chérisey) was in Rennes-le-Château in 1961.[15]

Although Plantard does not say so specifically, the account of his meeting with Noël Corbu, only a few months before Corbu left the *Hôtel de la Tour*, reads as though it was their first contact. But we know they were in contact as early as 1962, because of the letter from Corbu found in the *Dossiers secrets*, which we mentioned in chapter 7. It ends 'we will discuss it on your arrival'. All this evidence points to Plantard visiting Rennes-le-Château in the early 1960s, and possibly in the late 1950s.

His motive for the initial visit, ostensibly to recover some of his grandfather's letters, may not be accurate either. We assume that from an early age he had come to the belief that he was the legitimate Count of Rhedae. This was his 'area'; in his view he was the local *seigneur* and it would only be natural to visit and to get to know it. In fact he went further than this and bought property in the area, including tracts of land around Rennes-le-Château and the mountain of Blanchefort.[16]

We shall try to reconstruct what might have occurred in the years leading up to the publication of the story of Saunière and Rennes-le-Château as it appeared in de Sède's book of 1967. Of course some deductions may not be correct, but with the framework of known facts and a modest amount of speculation, a plausible sequence of events might have gone as follows.

We recall that the first articles on the treasure of Rennes-le-Château had appeared in the press in 1956. In the last few years of the decade, there was wild enthusiasm for treasure hunting and excavation at Rennes-le-Château. Noël Corbu was giving exciting talks to his customers who dined at the *Hôtel de la Tour*. Saunière's treasure was the talk of the district. Pierre Plantard was staying only a few miles away. As would-be Count of Rhedae, and believing himself to be related to the Blanchefort family, it is inconceivable that he did not go to the village and hear the story of the *curé*, the parchments and the treasure.

In 1956 Plantard had already started his project of compiling genealogical tables under the pseudonym of Henri Lobineau, a name possibly inspired by *rue Lobineau*, near the church of Saint-Sulpice in Paris. He had completed the first three, the line of the Counts of Bar. His problem was to set out the descendants of Dagobert II without any embarrassing gaps. So when he heard the tale of the parchments and Saunière's sudden wealth, a course of action presented itself. Since the parchments were lost, unlikely ever to be rediscovered and their content not precisely recorded, why not make use of them to substantiate the genealogical trees? The parchments might have been genealogies, no one could say they were not, why not assume that they were? He annotated his later tables of genealogy with the name of *Abbé* Saunière as one of his sources of information.

But this required some explanation of how parchments found in the far south of France could have come into the hands of a genealogist in Paris. Saunière travelled a lot during his life. There is no record of his ever having gone to Paris, but on the other hand there is no record stating that he did not. Plantard annotated his Table 8 with the long note that we quoted in chapter 10 about Saunière's trip to Paris to meet *Abbé* Hoffet, thereby creating the link between the parchments and the genealogies.

On the fourth of the genealogical tables Plantard wrote a legend, rambling and somewhat incoherent, telling us that two thousand years ago some of the descendants of the tribe of Benjamin left the Promised Land and settled in Arcady. From them came the line of Dagobert. He says that Poussin knew this and was trying to explain it with his painting of the Shepherds of Arcady and the inscription *et in Arcadia ego*. What induced him to bring Poussin into the legend we are not sure, but in the course of his wanderings around the area of Rennes-les-Bains, Plantard could not have failed to see the prominent tomb, only a few kilometres away, at the side of the road to Arques. Its superficial resemblance to the tomb in the well-known painting may well have given him the idea.

That might have been as far as the matter went, except for the intervention of Plantard's friend, Philippe de Chérisey. They were two very different characters. Whereas Plantard was meticulous, obsessive, interested in arcane knowledge and the occult, de Chérisey was quick-witted, ingenious and outgoing. By birth a marquis, by profession a writer and humorist,[17] de Chérisey had been involved in the film industry, and wrote for the radio. Plantard told de Chérisey about Saunière and the parchments, and in turn de Chérisey told Francis Blanche, a radio producer. At that time Blanche was connected with a radio soap opera *Signé Furax*, a programme noted for innocent but plausible deception of its listeners. (One 'gag' was to invent a psychiatric hospital for mad plants.) It appears that Francis Blanche thought it would make good material, but he needed a new angle and suggested to de Chérisey that he should fabricate some parchments for use on the programme.[18]

The idea of how to set about a plausible fabrication seems to have occurred to de Chérisey on a visit to Rennes-le-Bains. Jean Markale recounts an interview he had with de Chérisey,[19] in which de Chérisey says: 'Being in Rennes-les-Bains in 1961, and having learned that after the death of the *abbé* the town hall at Rennes-le-Château had been burnt, along with the archives, I thought I would make use of this by inventing a story that the mayor had had a tracing made of the parchments discovered by the *abbé*. Then, following Francis Blanche's idea, I started to devise a coded copy based on passages from the Gospels, and then I decoded myself what I had coded. At last, by a roundabout route, I sent the fruit of my labours to Gérard de Sède. That worked beyond my wildest dreams.'

This admission is substantiated by Jean-Luc Chaumeil,[20, 21] when he quotes de Chérisey as saying 'The parchments were made by me. I took an old text, in uncials, from the work of Dom Cabrol.'

We think it likely that de Chérisey started with the shorter and simpler of the two manuscripts, Manuscript 2. He selected the New Testament story of the disciples picking corn on the Sabbath. Maybe he did not have a copy of the Latin Bible to hand, and translated into Latin from the French, making a few errors in the process. He wrote out the passage in uncials to give the appearance of antiquity and hid a message in the text by raising some of the letters – The treasure belongs to King Dagobert II and to Sion, and it is Death – in effect summarizing the ideas to be found in the genealogies. With his lines of irregular length he again picked out the word Sion, and for good measure he added PS in a monogram to hint that the origin of the manuscript was the Priory of Sion.

No doubt pleased with the results of his first effort, de Chérisey embarked on the more ambitious undertaking which led to Manuscript 1. Possibly Plantard wanted him to bring in the idea which he had put on Table 4 of the genealogies, that Poussin knew the 'secret' – 'Poussin holds the key'. During his visits to Rennes-le-Château de Chérisey would have learned about the inscription on the gravestone as recorded by the Society of the Aude (Marie I) and decided to make this the source of his two keywords. Then he added the (unnecessary) complications of the chessboard rearrangement and the solution's being the anagram of the second keyword. After trial and error he produced the message we have analysed in chapter 6. From there it was relatively easy to encrypt, and to insert it in a Latin text, but this time he made use of a Latin Bible published in 1890. Bearing in mind that Saunière's villa was called Bethania, and that the church was dedicated to St Mary Magdalene, the biblical passage almost chose itself. For good measure he wrote at the bottom of the manuscript the prayer he had seen in the church at Rennes-le-Château on a wooden panel below Saunière's altar, and he added a device which when looked at upside down gave the letters S I O N.

So far, so good, but de Chérisey had to find the extra nine letters to make up the 128 and that would have presented a problem. But if two keywords had come from a gravestone, why not the extra letters as well? Here, we think Corbu came unknowingly to the rescue. He had done quite a lot of research himself in order to provide material for his talks on Saunière, the village and the treasure, and would have heard about Engineer Cros and the verbal tradition that there was once another stone which bore the words *Reddis, Regis, Cellis, Arcis*. Suppose the stone had the extra nine letters as well? It is at this point that the manufacturing of evidence begins in earnest. We may deplore the deception, but we have to admire the effort.

The first task was to produce the picture of the stone we have called Marie II. Obviously it had to have the four Latin words, and the additional nine letters *P S PRAECUM*. Adding *et in Arcadia ego* was an embellishment, transcribing it into Greek letters was no more than an extra bit of fun. To give it credence it had to have been published in a book before Saunière rearranged the stones in the graveyard, hence the invention of Stüblein's work. It was obviously impractical to forge a whole book, but extracting a few figures was not too difficult, and would be more credible if it had been done by a local man of repute. Who better than the aged *Abbé* Courtauly? The newly forged material had to be deposited in an archive, but to avoid potential exposure, this was left until after the *abbé* died in 1964.

If the newly-devised parchments were to be accepted for the spoof radio programme, it would not come amiss to have some evidence for their discovery. With Corbu's aid, de Chérisey produced the little book *A Merovingian treasure at Rennes-le-Château*, under the pseudonym Antoine l'Ermite. (We attribute it to de Chérisey, because the style is not remotely like that of Plantard's in the genealogies.) For the first time it was stated that the parchments were extracts from the Gospels and that the inscription on Marie's tomb was an essential to understanding them. By this time Corbu was evidently getting confused. As we recorded in chapter 7, in July 1962 he wrote to Plantard, 'The history of Rennes is very unsettling and it would be interesting to know what are the documents which *Abbé* Sauniéres showed to *Abbé* Hoffet.'

Nevertheless, when Corbu was shown the picture of the stone Marie II, he accepted it as genuine, and described it in his paper on the research of Ernest Cros. We suppose that at about the same time he was given a sketch of the *Dalle de Coumesourde*. (This stone could not be included among those in the Stüblein set, because the accepted story was that Cros had discovered it in 1928.)

At some point the proposal to make a radio programme was abandoned. Plantard and de Chérisey were left with a lot of carefully prepared material. Surely this was worth collecting together and it would make a good story for a book. The author they selected was Gérard de Sède.

We do not know when de Sède undertook the project, but he was seen in the area of Rennes in 1965, and in March 1966, clearly on the trail of Stüblein's book, he called at the house of the deceased Joseph Courtauly, hoping to see his library and was turned away without access.[22]

Later the same year, when he saw the announcement of the death of Léo Schidlof, Plantard decided to 'kill off' the mythical Henri Lobineau, by the simple ruse of saying that Lobineau was Schidlof. We can only suggest that this was convenient in that it prevented de Sède demanding to meet Lobineau, which he would surely have done had he been a serious investigator. Inevitably this led to more deception, in the invention of a documented link between Lobineau and Schidlof, and the faked obituary from the young man, Lionel Burrus.

Plantard and de Chérisey supplied de Sède with most of the raw material for his book. They introduced him to the files they had deposited in the Bibliothèque nationale, which presumably de Sède took to be genuine. They let him see the manuscripts that de Chérisey had encrypted to reproduce them in his book, *L'Or de Rennes*, on condition that he was evasive as to how he came by them. They gave him a few hints on the method of encryption, but not enough information to enable him to arrive at the solutions, hence the hidden messages were not given in his book, and de Sède did not find the solutions until 1971.

Thus the story of Rennes-le-Château, Saunière's treasure, parchments with hidden messages, and all the other trappings, came to the notice of an even wider public. One of the readers of de Sède's book was Henry Lincoln, whose interest was captured, and his television films and writings introduced Rennes-le-Château to the English-speaking world.

But Henry Lincoln is not the only person to have made a film about Rennes-le-Château. On 17 September 1996, the BBC broadcast, in the *Timewatch* series, *The History of a Mystery*, made by an independent producer, William Cran, for Invision Productions. Cran looked at the evidence for claims made by Richard Andrews and Paul Schellenberger in their recently published book, *The Tomb of God*. We shall come back to this book in chapter 13; for the moment it is sufficient to say that these two authors, by making deductions from evidence which they believed they had found in the coded manuscripts, Marie's tombstones and the geometry of the surrounding countryside, had concluded that the body of Jesus Christ was buried near Rennes-le-Château on Mount Cardou. In the course of checking this the producer interviewed, among others, Pierre Jarnac,[23] Gérard de Sède and Jean-Luc Chaumeil.[24]

Jarnac comments on the supposed work by Stüblein on engraved stones. Holding a copy of de Sède's book, open at the page of references, he says to camera: 'I bought this book about thirty years ago because I am interested in treasure stories. Certain references in the index caught my eye, like Eugène Stüblein, *Engraved stones of the Languedoc*. I then consulted other works to see if Stüblein had published anything else. And I found a copy of *A Trip to Thermal Establishments*. What struck me when I compared the book with *Engraved Stones* were the signatures. In *Thermal Establishments* Stüblein's signature is completely different. This entire booklet on engraved stones is a complete forgery.'

In the film de Sède says of the characters of Plantard and de Chérisey: 'They were very different. De Chérisey's now dead. He was an actor whose stage name was L'Amadée. He was a very cultured man with a brilliant university degree. Unfortunately he led a life on the tiles, as we say in France. Plantard reminds me of a big nocturnal bird, very gloomy, very tall, very skinny. He's not that cultured, in fact he's quite ignorant.[25] But Plantard has a talent, a flair for symbolism. He finds symbols like other people find mushrooms.'

Chaumeil describes how he helped the BBC set up the interview between Lincoln and Plantard in 1979, in a small room over his mother's art gallery. 'This is the place where the BBC television has done the interview for Rennes-le-Château. Plantard was there, Harry Lincoln was there, and Roy Davies and all the team in this place . . . as for Plantard, he played his part to perfection.'

One of the most interesting passages in the film occurs when Jean-Luc Chaumeil reveals that he has the original parchments. He shows them to the camera. The one we have called Manuscript 1 is written on a sheet of yellowish paper, apparently of A4 size. Manuscript 2 is on a sheet of white paper, A5 size, with a note in red ink written diagonally across the top right hand corner. Chaumeil comments: 'Plantard trusted me because I was writing a book about him, and he gave me the original parchments. And here they are, Parchment 2 and Parchment 1. And this one – he's written a note in his own hand: "This is the original document, faked by Philippe de Chérisey, which Gérard de Sède reproduced in his book the *Gold of Rennes*". Here is the second parchment, which has earned thousands in royalties. It is written in Philippe de Chérisey's own hand. Here is an unpublished manuscript, called *Stone and Paper*. It is written by de Chérisey, and this 44-page document describes how the parchments were fabricated, and the ciphers set, and how they were decoded.'

Regrettably we have not been able to examine this book and have had to rely on the fleeting glimpses shown on the film and the voice-over, which continues: 'This is how de Chérisey solves the riddle he himself created. . . . He says 681 was the year in which King Dagobert was killed. . . .[26] Poussin is not the painter, but a play on words. In French poussin means a chicken, and Hautpoul, the local aristocrat, could be translated as big chicken. . . . Blue apples are not grapes or the blood of Christ, but another masonic in-joke, part of a rambling document full of puns and anagrams, by a man who calls himself the prankster.'

Without seeing the document it is difficult to know how seriously one should take it. Perhaps de Chérisey, with his own strange interpretation of the deciphered message, was having another private laugh.

The film corroborates our view on how it all happened – four people with different characters, different interests and different motives together produced one of the most famous historical puzzles of the century: Noël Corbu, anxious to make his hotel a commercial success, and cleverly exploiting the strange life of Bérenger Saunière to attract the visitors; Pierre Plantard, believing himself to be of the royal line of France, spotting an opportunity to manufacture evidence in support of his claim and hijacking the Rennes-le-Château legend for his own ends; Philippe de Chérisey, playboy and joker, making puzzles for his own amusement; and Gérard de Sède, writer on historical matters, who was none too rigorous in his acceptance of evidence, but was happy to write a best-seller. *L'Or de Rennes* was published, Henry Lincoln was captivated, and the mystery of Rennes-le-Château began to flourish even more.

12

The Priory of Sion

In the course of making his third film for the BBC Henry Lincoln teamed up with Richard Leigh and Michael Baigent. The culmination of their work was the publication in 1982 of *The Holy Blood and The Holy Grail*, a sensational work which became a best seller and ran into numerous editions. This book not only regenerated interest in Saunière and Rennes-le-Château but widened the horizons in a spectacular way, and it has led to speculation, hypotheses, theories and revelations that are so far from the original story that in later books by them and other authors the village and the *curé* are almost incidental.

We are told that the book was the result of ten years' research by the team of three authors, who also had the help of some research assistants. Certainly the amount of ground covered is immense. The bibliography includes over 250 works, many of them available only in French, and some very obscure indeed. The book begins with the authors' investigations into the Cathars and the Knights Templar, and quite early in the book they state their belief that behind these two organizations was a third, secret order, *Le Prieuré de Sion* or the Priory of Sion.[1]

Their prime source for the existence of the Priory of Sion was a single page in the *Secret File of Henri Lobineau*: a page which we have already mentioned briefly in chapter 10. According to this document a religious order called *L'Ordre de Sion* (the Order of Sion) was founded in 1090 by Godefroy de Bouillon. The monks installed themselves in the Abbey of Notre Dame on Mount Sion (or Zion) at Jerusalem, which is a small hill just to the south of the old walled city. About thirty years later in 1118, another order, the famous Order of the Templars was founded by Hugues de Payen, a French nobleman from Champagne who became their first Grand Master.

In 1187 Jerusalem fell to the army of Saladin and the monks of the Order of Sion returned to France. The following year, says the Lobineau paper, the Priory of Sion was set up, under its Grand Master Jean de Gisors. The full name of the new organization was The Priory of Sion, Order of the Rose-Cross. There is a note, supposedly from page 164 of the statute book of the Order[2] which tells us that between 1188 and 1306 the Order bore the name Ormus and that some of its members lived with monks of the Priory of Mount Sion: 'From 1306 there remained only one order, the Priory of Sion, which replaced the little Priory of Mount Sion and Ormus, the members of the 5th and 6th grades became the celebrated Rose-Cross because of their coats of arms.'

This paper is in fact claiming that the Priory of Sion was associated with the Rosicrucian movement from 1088. The Rosicrucians are a worldwide brotherhood who claim to have esoteric wisdom handed down from ancient times.[3] Among their fabled sages was an Egyptian called Ormus, whom some regard as a founder of Rosicrucianism. However most authorities take the origin of the Rosicrucians to be the appearance in 1614 of the *Fama Fraternitatis* or Account of the Brotherhood. It was written in German and published anonymously, though the author is known to have been one Johann Valentin Andreas (1586–1654). The book tells us about the journeys of Christian Rosenkreuz, who was reputedly born in 1378 and lived to the age of 106. He is said to have acquired secret wisdom on voyages to Egypt and other countries around the Mediterranean. It is doubtful that he ever existed, nevertheless the order flourished and possibly inspired those who founded the first Masonic Lodges in the seventeenth century.

Baigent, Lincoln and Leigh did a considerable amount of research to verify the account of the origins of the Priory of Sion. They found no reference to a medieval order with the name Ormus,[4] but they did come across some charters, confirming the existence of an Order of Sion in the twelfth century. But the Order of Sion is not necessarily the same thing as the Priory of Sion, and they have not been able to cite any medieval document which includes the words *Prieuré de Sion*.

Nevertheless they found in the Lobineau files several things which they could verify (names of early Grand Masters of the Templars, for example), and in spite of a few misgivings about the authenticity of the Lobineau papers, Baigent, Leigh and Lincoln ultimately came to the conclusion that the Priory had existed since its foundation in the twelfth century, and that it has continued to exist to the present day – an influential organization so secret that even its name was never revealed to the general public.

Having satisfied themselves that there really was an organization called the Priory of Sion, the three authors sought evidence of its involvement in various episodes of French history. They linked it to other secret societies, to the Knights Templar, to Rosicrucianism and to Freemasonry, and they equated it to the (possibly fictitious) *Compagnie du Saint-Sacrement* of the seventeenth century, which they say is the Priory of Sion operating under another name.[5]

Perhaps the most surprising feature of the Lobineau files is the list of supposed Grand Masters of the Priory, or *Nautonniers* (Helmsmen), as they were known. While the first seven were members of French noble houses (and appear on Lobineau's genealogies), some of the most eminent people of all time are among the later names.

Sandro Filipepi, better known as Botticelli, the painter, was said to have been Grand Master from 1483 to 1510. His successors include Leonardo da Vinci (from 1510 to 1519), painter, inventor and military engineer; Robert Fludd (from 1595 to 1637), physician; Robert Boyle (from 1654 to 1691), natural philosopher and chemist, Fellow of the Royal Society, discoverer of the law governing the expansion of gases; Sir Isaac Newton (from 1691 to 1727), President of the Royal Society, discoverer of the law of gravity; Maximilien de Lorraine (from 1780 to 1801), brother of Marie Antoinette; Charles Nodier (from 1801 to 1844), writer; Victor Hugo (from 1844 to 1885), author; Claude Debussy (from 1885 to 1918), composer; and Jean Cocteau (from 1918 to 1963), film director.

Several of these supposed Grand Masters studied both the Bible and the occult. Robert Boyle was enthusiastic for the dissemination of the scriptures; he wrote about alchemy and publicly endorsed a book on demonology by F. Perreaud by writing a preface to an English edition. Newton's theological writings began at an early period in his life. He was interested in the interpretation of prophecy and attempted to work out a biblical chronology from astronomical calculations. He too studied alchemy. Also among the names of the Grand Masters are two who had special connections with the Rosicrucian movement. One was Johann Andreas (from 1637 to 1654), who wrote the *Fama Fraternitas*, and the other was Robert Fludd. Fludd's attention was drawn to Andreas's book shortly after it was published and he wrote a manuscript vindicating the fraternity, which he addressed to James I. It is for his defence of Rosicrucianism that Fludd is most remembered today.[6] Charles Nodier and Victor Hugo were part of the same literary circle and were enthralled by the arcane and the esoteric. Claude Debussy as a young man met Victor Hugo and is reputed to have had contacts in Rosicrucian circles; Jean Cocteau painted a crucifixion scene in the church of Notre Dame de France in London, and added a rose to the cross. It begins to look as though these people might well have been associated with an organization such as the Priory of Sion.

But the lives of people as eminent as these have been examined in great detail by biographers. One would expect that if they really were members of an organization with links that spanned countries, and with a history of nearly a thousand years, something about it would have come to light. One can argue that the Priory of Sion was a secret society and therefore care would have been taken to avoid documents falling into the wrong hands. But for continuity of the Grand Mastership at least there would have had to have been contact between members, either in person or by correspondence; if the organization was anything other than a meaningless title, there would have been some activity which surely would have left its record. Yet nothing in these great men's papers relating to the Priory of Sion has been found.[7]

Nevertheless a Priory of Sion did actually exist in the twentieth century. It is a requirement of the French Government that all groups and societies must be recorded in a weekly publication, *Le Journal Officiel de la République Française*. The statutes of an organization called the Priory of Sion were registered in the sub-prefecture of St. Julien-en-Genevois, a town about 8 km south-west of Geneva, and notice of its formation on 25 June 1956 were recorded in *Le Journal Officiel*, no. 167, page 6731, published on 20 July. The location of the head office of the Priory of Sion was given as Annemasse and the four sponsors were André Bonhomme (president), Jean Delaval (vice-president), Armand Defago (treasurer) and Pierre Plantard.

The statutes of this modern version of the Priory of Sion comprise twenty-one articles.

In article II we read that the association takes the name of 'Priory of Sion', subtitled CIRCUIT (*Chevalerie d'Institutions et Règles Catholiques, d'Union Indépendante et Traditionaliste*), the meaning of which is explained in Article III. 'The aim of the association is to found a catholic order, with the intention of recreating in modern form, whilst preserving its traditional character, an ancient Knighthood, which by its actions promotes a highly moralising ideal and is a factor for steady improvement in the rules of life of the human personality.' The actual activities of this organisation are very vague, saying only that through active cooperation of its members, they will be able to give moral and material aid to those members who need it.

The organization and membership of the Priory are set out in some detail, listing nine grades in the hierarchy, each grade having three times the number of members of the grade above it. Thus there were supposedly 6561 novices, the lowest grade and one *Nautonnier*, the head of the organization. This is a very elaborate structure for what seems in fact to have been some sort of pressure group of residents opposed to the Annemasse local council who were in favour of low cost housing.

The association promised to set up in Haute Savoie, at a place they called mountain of Sion (Col du Mont Sion, 8 km due south of St Julien-en-Genevois), a priory which would serve as a centre for study, meditation, rest and prayer. It also undertook to issue a regular bulletin named Circuit, *Bulletin d'information et défense des droits et de la liberté des foyers H.L.M.* (Information bulletin and protection of rights and freedom of low cost homes.) The bulletin was edited jointly by Pierre Plantard and André Bonhomme. One issue was a special edition for the arrangement of school buses. The bulletin lasted for only twelve issues. The Priory of Sion was dissolved within the year. In the files kept by the French authorities it is noted that Plantard had broken sections of the penal code relating to crimes and offences against property and had served a six-month jail sentence in 1953.

Both the year of registration and the location are interesting. The date, 1956, is in the period when Plantard was compiling his genealogies, and it will be remembered that the file on the Genealogy of the Merovingian Kings was reputedly published at Geneva. There is a reference to the registration in the Lobineau files in the form of a note: 'Since 5 June 1956 in the *Official Journal* of 20 July 1956, No.167, the authority of the Priory of Sion, masonic order of the Rose-Cross, has again been recognised officially.'

Although the 1956 Priory of Sion lasted only a short time, that was not the end of it, because in 1961 Plantard formed a second version which lasted until 1984, when he resigned. Paul Smith's compilation of documents includes letters and articles in magazines, which show that by this time Plantard was in conflict with Jean-Luc Chaumeil who had researched Plantard's background and come to the conclusion that the whole episode of the Priory of Sion was a hoax.

Taking the evidence – and lack of it – into account, we are also driven to the conclusion that the Priory is nothing more than a Plantard invention. But one has to admit that the amount of work that has been put into the creation of the Lobineau files is staggering. Plantard must have done a considerable amount of research before he could have produced documents as superficially convincing as these. His knowledge of the Middle Ages must have been extensive and his choice of Grand Masters seems masterly, until one realises that similar lists of notable persons have been drawn up, for example by the Rosicrucian order, who claim Leonardo da Vinci, Isaac Newton and Claude Debussy to be among their past members.

We are not alone in our conclusions. David Barrett[8] quotes a masonic historian, John Hammell, as saying, 'As far as I am aware the *Prieuré de Sion* was never referred to before the appearance of *The Holy Blood and the Holy Grail*. With certainty I can say there is no reference to it in any Masonic literature.' Barrett goes on to add: 'we should beware of any complex theory which is largely based, as is the case of Baigent, Leigh and Lincoln, on lists of Grand Masters through the ages. The eighteenth century was awash with such. We should perhaps be even more suspicious when these lists include such luminaries as Leonardo da Vinci, Isaac Newton, Victor Hugo and Claude Debussy.'

Baigent, Leigh and Lincoln came to a different conclusion. Whereas we contend that because so much forgery and deception is to be found in the Lobineau files, one cannot admit any statement without independent corroboration, they give credence to the Lobineau files where we would not. They accept that the Priory of Sion really did exist while we contend that there is no evidence that stands up to scrutiny. From statements in the Lobineau files, they conclude that one of the aims of the Priory of Sion is the restoration of the Merovingian dynasty to the throne of France. Why it would be important to restore a seventh-century dynasty to the throne in a modern republic seems incomprehensible unless, as they remark, 'there was something else of immense consequence that differentiated the Merovingians from other dynasties. Unless, in short, there was something very special indeed about the Merovingian blood royal.'[9]

That brings the authors on to the legends of the Holy Grail. What exactly the Grail was is obscure; in some stories it is the chalice used by Christ and the disciples at the last supper. Lincoln suggests an alternative; in early manuscripts he finds the word *Sangraal*, or *Sangreal*. He interprets the word, not as *San Graal*, but as *Sang Réal*, royal blood. The controversial hypothesis advanced in *The Holy Blood and The Holy Grail* is that Christ was married to Mary Magdalene and had children, and that after the Crucifixion (which according to the book Christ may have survived by a plot), Mary Magdalene went to Marseilles with the Holy Grail, in other words with the royal blood, or the children of Jesus. From them, it is suggested, came the line of the Merovingian kings.[10]

According to Baigent, Leigh and Lincoln, this was a great secret, kept for nearly two thousand years by a small number of the initiated. *Abbé* Bigou, the eighteenth-century priest at Rennes-le-Château, was one of their number and it was he who concealed the parchments in the church before fleeing to Spain at the time of the

Revolution. Bérenger Saunière, 'a man who would do Sion's bidding', found them. The two genealogies revealed to him the secret of the Merovingian dynasty, but Saunière kept it to himself to his very death.

Baigent, Leigh and Lincoln published a second book on the same subject, *The Messianic Legacy*, four years after *The Holy Blood and the Holy Grail*. This book is in three parts, each so different that one gets the impression that they are three separate books bound together. Part 1, *The Messiah* is a very readable account of the political situation in Palestine at the time of Christ, the profusion of religious sects, the beginnings of Christianity and the diffusion of the gospel in the first centuries after Christ's death. There is no mention in this part of the Mary Magdalene hypothesis.

Part 2 of the book, *The Quest for Meaning*, is a long essay about the loss of faith in the modern era and its consequences, including a thoughtful section on fascist and communist ideologies as substitutes for religion.

The final part, *The Cabal*, plunges us into a detailed account of Lincoln's dealings with Pierre Plantard and (to a lesser extent) Philippe de Chérisey between about 1979 and 1984, a period which covers the publication of *The Holy Blood and the Holy Grail*. Lincoln also gives the results of his investigation on Plantard's activities during the war and at the time of General de Gaulle's return to power in 1958.

It is an astounding story. At every turn in his investigation, Henry Lincoln was fed with new information, some of it anonymously. An article written by one of his own team of researchers emerged with its text doctored by a supposed translator.[11] A totally different account appears about the two missing genealogical parchments that were supposed to have been acquired by the International League of Antiquarian Booksellers. The names of prominent Englishmen and Americans are cited. Lincoln follows trail after trail, yet firm corroborating evidence eludes him. He suspects that some documents shown to him by Plantard are actually forgeries. Many people at this stage would have concluded that they were victims of a deception; Lincoln thought that both he and Plantard were 'victims of disinformation'[12] and his suspicions turned to the secret services of Britain, France and the United States. Finally he suspects that the Knights of Malta are behind the machinations. His faith in the reality of the Priory of Sion remains unshaken.

It is not within the scope of this book to follow up every facet of Lincoln's investigation into the life of Jesus or the supposed origins of the Merovingian dynasty. Nor do we intend to comment on any of the subsequent theories which, based on the researches of Lincoln and partners, have produced even more astounding conclusions.

We have limited ourselves to matters relating either directly to the affair of Rennes-le-Château or to hypotheses that arise fairly directly from it. So far we have dealt with documentary and historical evidence, but that is not all there is to be examined. Studies by Lincoln and others of Rennes-le-Château in its immediate landscape have led to yet more bizarre theories. These are the subject of the next chapter.

13

Lines on the Landscape

Henry Lincoln's Studies of the Geometry

We have previously mentioned (in chapter 5) that in the 1970s Henry Lincoln started to study the geometry of the area around Rennes-le-Château following a suggestion from Professor Christopher Cornford. Lincoln published the results of his investigations in 1991, in *The Holy Place*. With the aid of the map of the local area published by the *Institut Géographique National* (IGN),[1] he looked first at the positions of three hilltops, namely Rennes-le-Château, Château de Blanchefort (Pl. 36) and Château des Templiers (the Templar Castle, which Lincoln refers to as Bézu), each of which was the site of a medieval castle, and found that they were located relative to each other so that they formed an isosceles triangle with angles 72°, 72° and 36° (Fig 13.1). This triangle is the right shape to fit into part of a regular pentagon. Lincoln remarks that 'the distance from Bézu to Rennes-le-Château is exactly the same as that from Bézu to Blanchefort. The coincidence of these natural features being so accurately placed is astonishing.'[2]

This discovery obliged him to return to the map to see what were at the other two points of the pentagon, and to his amazement he found two more peaks, La Soulane and Serre de Lauzet. He had discovered a gigantic pentagon, about 24 km around its perimeter. He says that if fires were lit on each of these peaks at night they would be visible from Rennes-le-Château. Even that is not all – there is another hilltop, La Pique, not far from the centre of the pentagon.

The regular pentagon was an important shape in mystical traditions. If we extend the sides until the lines intersect, we can draw a five-pointed star, the pentagram. When the star is surrounded by a circle which passes through the points, we have a pentacle, an ancient symbol used in magic, witchcraft and astrology. There is an astrological connection with the planet Venus, whose movements are said to describe a pentagram in the sky. For the geometry of the pentagon and its links to Venus and certain numbers, see Appendix E.

To mystics, Venus is linked with St Mary Magdalene. They looked on the planet as her symbol in the heavens. The church at Rennes-le-Château was dedicated to

Mary Magdalene; Venus is associated with the pentagon; near Rennes-le-Château is a pentagon of mountain tops – surely all these connections cannot be due solely to chance? Lincoln thought there was a deliberate connection, beginning with the discovery of the pentagon of mountains in ancient times. He writes: 'such a discovery would lie within the grasp of those more ancient astronomers, the builders of Carnac and Stonehenge. . . . For Christians, Venus had become the Magdalene, and so the church was dedicated to her. For an earlier culture, Rennes-le-Château was a gigantic god-given Temple to the Mother Goddess.'[3] This, he says, is the age-old secret of Rennes-le-Château.

We began by checking the geometry of the pentagon of peaks. This, and all the subsequent checks of geometry, was not done by an independent survey on the ground, nor by drawing lines on the map. On the outer edges of the map are printed co-ordinate numbers (in black) at 1 km intervals, equivalent to the Ordnance Survey's National Grid System. Tiny crosses on the map show where grid lines would intersect. We have a specially engraved and accurate graticule, with a grid of fine lines 4 mm apart, corresponding to 100 m on the ground. By placing the graticule on the map and positioning it accurately with the small crosses, it is just possible to read the co-ordinates of a place to about ¼ mm, which corresponds to 10 m on the ground. For extended objects such as churches, which are several tens of metres in dimensions, this is accurate enough. As an example, the grid co-ordinates of the centre of the little circle marking the position of the church at Rennes-le-Château are 593.97, 3069.82. Distances and angles are calculated, and the results given to the nearest 10 metres since there is no point in pretending to be more precise than this. This method is better than trying to make an accurate measurement directly from the map, because it reduces errors due to dimensional changes in the paper as humidity varies. Not only that, the calculations can be easily checked for accuracy. To enable the reader to check our arithmetic, we give a list of the grid co-ordinates of every site whose position we have used.

From the co-ordinates of the six points we calculated the lengths of the sides of the pentagon and also the distances from the hilltop marking the centre (La Pique) to each of the corners of the pentagon. The results are given in the table attached to Fig. 13.1. It is a surprisingly regular pentagon. The five sides are all about 4 km in length, with an average error of 70 metres, which is under two per cent. The angles at the corners of a regular pentagon would be 108°; the mean error of this pentagon is under 2°. La Pique is slightly off the true centre, but even so, the distances from there to the corners differ from the average by only 180 metres, that is about 5 per cent. This certainly looks an unusual natural configuration, but how unusual it is is difficult to say. It is worth bearing in mind that the area around Rennes-le-Château is extremely hilly with a lot of peaks and undulating ridges: we have not looked at other areas to see if similar geometrical figures can be picked out in the landscapes.

There is still an important question to be answered. Are these six peaks sufficiently prominent to have caught the eye of people in former times? We investigated this on a trip to Rennes-le-Château. We photographed the landscape and calibrated the camera so that we could relate the prints to accurate bearings.

From the village it is possible to see Blanchefort (on a bearing of 74.8°), but it is not above the horizon and does not stand out as a distinctive peak. It is just a slight undulation in the slope of the hill going down from the higher ground at Roque Nègre to the valley of the River Sals. Slightly to the right, and dominating Blanchefort is the peak called Pech Cardou (80.3°), which stands higher than any other hill in the vicinity. It is also possible to see la Pique (129.4°), but again it is not a distinctive rise, simply a point at the end of a long ridge. It too is dominated by a huge hill in the background, the massive Pech de Bugarach (127.0°). Château des Templiers (145.9°) appears as a tiny blip on an undulating horizon. Serre de Lauzet (182.5°) is difficult to identify, being, like La Pique, at the end of a long ridge. In fact it is not the highest point of the ridge and unless the lighting is favourable, it is almost invisible against the dark slopes of the much higher hills in the distance. As for La Soulane (109.4°), we completely failed to make it out with any certainty.

From the top of Serre de Lauzet however, Rennes-le-Château (2.4°) is very clearly seen, even though it does not break the horizon, because the buildings are usually brightly illuminated by the sun. Blanchefort (39.5°) is out of sight, since Roque Nègre is in the way. The view in this direction is dominated by Pech Cardou. None of the other peaks is seen from Serre de Lauzet, since nearer high ground intervenes.

So, far from being appreciated at an earlier epoch, it seems to us likely that Lincoln himself is the first person to have noticed that lines joining these five points would describe an (almost) regular pentagon, and he found the pentagon only because these points happen to have been chosen as spot heights on the map made by IGN.

David Wood's Studies of the Geometry

The pentagon of peaks is, of course, a natural formation, which may have been, or more probably was not, noticed in earlier times. The geometry takes on a totally different significance when one starts to bring in sites whose location is due to human activity, because this has implications on the state of human knowledge or technology a millennium ago (if we are looking at the sites of churches and castles), or maybe three millennia ago (if we think that the sites were originally selected in prehistoric periods). This was the next step in Lincoln's analysis. He took note of the work of David Wood (no relation to John Edwin Wood), whose background is in surveying and cartography. Wood was inspired by Henry Lincoln's discoveries to carry out his own investigations into the geometry of the area around Rennes-le-Château. His results were published in 1984 in a book entitled *Genisis* (sic), *The First Book of Revelations*.

This is a strange book and difficult to follow. You will not find in the index any reference to Gérard de Sède, Noël Corbu, or Philippe de Chérisey. Pierre Plantard is mentioned only in passing as a Grand Master of the Priory of Sion. Wood seems to accept without question de Sède's story of Saunière's discovery of the parchments, his trip to Paris, his association with such notables as Emma Calvé and the Duke of Hapsburg. He has no doubts about the existence of the Priory of Sion. What David Wood brings to the affair of Rennes-le-Château is a large amount of geometry, numerology, Egyptology and mythology, all of which combined leads him to a dramatic and unconventional theory about the origin of intelligent life on Earth. From his study of the alignments of natural and man-made features in the area around Rennes-le-Château, with additional material from Egyptian legends (but without the complications of conventional archaeology and geology), he deduces that the Earth was populated by beings who came from planets surrounding the star Sirius, and who lived on the lost continent of Atlantis until its inundation and destruction.

Though we may find it difficult to accept his conclusions, that does not preclude us from examining the evidence that he finds on the ground, some of which Lincoln makes use of in coming to very different conclusions about the significance of the area. David Wood began by studying *Le Serpent Rouge*. He seems to be quite unaware of the dubious provenance of the document. Nevertheless it provides him with 'clues', especially by linking Mary Magdalene with the Egyptian goddess Isis, a theme which he develops at great length.

His first observation came about, he says, when he heard of the local belief that on the Feast day of St Mary Magdalene, 22 July, if you stand at the church of Rennes-le-Château, the sun appears to rise over Château de Blanchefort. Actually, this is not quite correct: the sun rises over Blanchefort on about 21 August.[4] However, he records in his book that a continuation of his 'sunrise' line from the church at Rennes to Château de Blanchefort passes through the church at Arques. It also crosses the Paris Meridian and it has a bearing of 72° (a significant angle in a pentagon).

Then, working from the poem 'Pisces' in *Le Serpent Rouge* he looked at the southerly line from Blanchefort to the peak called Roque Nègre, which if extended would, he says, pass through the church at Rennes-les-Bains. These two lines are said to intersect at right angles. His other observations are to do with distances. He claims that from Rennes-les-Bains to Roque Nègre is exactly 1 English mile, that 'the distance between the sister churches of Rennes-le-Château and Rennes-les-Bains was exactly three miles',[5] and also that from Arques church to the Paris Meridian was one third of the distance from Arques to Rennes-le-Château (Fig. 13.2).

We have checked these assertions, using the method described above and the results are given in the table below Fig. 13.2. Firstly the line from Rennes-le-Château to Arques does not pass through Blanchefort, but about 100 m to its north. The distance from the Roque Nègre to the church at Rennes-les-Bains is as close as we can tell to 1 mile; the distance between the two Rennes churches is about 50 m short of 3 miles; where the Meridian cuts the 'sunrise' line is not quite at one third of the total distance but at about 30 m to the west. The bearing of Arques from Rennes-le-Château is 73.4°, and this line crosses the Blanchefort to Roque Nègre line at 89.1°. In short, these geometric claims are all correct to within about one per cent.

David Wood's next step was to project a line back from the site of the alleged Poussin tomb through the intersection between the 'sunrise' line and the Meridian on to the church at Rennes-les-Bains and then on for exactly one English mile. Using this point (Point X on Figs 13.2 and 13.3) as the centre of a circle with radius out to the church at Rennes-le-Château, he drew a circle on his map. 'I will never forget my surprise – even disbelief – as the compasses traced the circumference.'[5] On, or very close to the circumference of this circle he found the churches at the villages of Coustaussa, Cassaignes, Serres, Bugarach and St Just-et-le-Bézu. Also on the circle were the château at Serres and a rock formation which resembled a female head at Les Toustounes (Fig. 13.3).

As before, we have checked his claims (see the table beside Fig. 13.3). The tomb, the intersection with the meridian and the church at Rennes-les-Bains all fall on a straight line within the accuracy of measurement from the map. The co-ordinates of the centre of the circle can be found, as well as the distances to the churches. Here we did not get quite the results claimed by Wood, who lists the places on the perimeter of the circle as follows: 'Rennes-le-Château – the church of Coustaussa precisely [on the circumference] – Cassaignes a near miss – Château Serres – the church of Serres precisely – the strange rock feature on the side of la Berco Grando which resembled a female head – the church of Bugarach precisely – the church of Saint Just-et-le-Bézu precisely',[5] so we calculated the position of the centre of the circle which would pass through the churches of Rennes-le-Château, Serres and Bugarach and then worked out the distances to the other sites. This agrees reasonably well with his claims, except that it was necessary to put the centre of the circle about 80 m nearer to the church of Rennes-les-Bains than one English mile. However, it does remain as close as we can measure to the line through Rennes-les-Bains to the Meridian intersection.

Wood now observes that the circle passes through the intersection of the 'sunrise' line with the Meridian – which it does to within about 50 m. From now on his lines proliferate. He draws lines from St Just to Cassaignes, from Bugarach to Serres, and Bugarach to Rennes-le-Château. He produces a pentagram (Fig. 13.3) with four of its points lying on the circumference of the circle. The fifth, most northerly point, is about 6.8 km from the centre of the circle, on the side of a steep slope with no significant feature marked on the map.

Wood's subsequent analysis is more difficult to follow. He notes that in the painting on the base of the altar installed by Saunière in his church there is a tower to the left of the kneeling figure. This bears some resemblance to a conventional sign for a steep slope on the map at La Berco Grando, south-west of Arques. There is a conical hill in the painting – he believes it depicts the Berco Petito. He draws a line between these two points and finds that it is tangential to his circle. A line from the tangential point to the centre of his circle gives him the long axis of a rectangle. The axis of this rectangle is at an angle of 18° to the Meridian and has the same orientation as the Temple of Isis at Dendera in Egypt. Thus he is led to the view that there is a direct link between Rennes-le-Château and the civilization of ancient Egypt two millennia before Christ.

Continuing his analysis, David Wood finds more alignments, incorporating more points on the ground, both natural and man-made. He interprets these to represent the womb of the goddess Isis. Within the womb there is a 'seed' located about 700 m north of the centre of his circle (at 597.86, 3067.97), inside which he expects, should it ever be excavated, to find some important confirmation of his theories. His final conclusion is that the whole complex geometry was set out by survivors of Atlantis about 9000 BC and that its purpose was to indicate to posterity the site of the lost civilization. He locates Atlantis as being on the Mid-Atlantic Ridge at 26°06'W, 42°55'N.[6] Rennes-le-Château has the same latitude. As for longitude, Rennes-le-Château is halfway between his site of Atlantis and the temple of Isis at Sa-el-Hagar in Egypt (about 100 km WSW of Cairo). This, according to David Wood, is the real secret of Rennes-le-Château. It is interesting to note that in his analysis Wood totally ignores what to Lincoln was an amazing discovery, that five mountain peaks formed an almost regular pentagon.

The English Mile

We return now to Henry Lincoln's analysis of the site. While not happy with Wood's interpretation, he nevertheless accepts the geometrical relationships that Wood has found and incorporates them into a complex series of alignments which combine the pentagon of peaks and Wood's pentagram. Together they are shown in Fig. 13.4. In the course of his studies Lincoln has come to the conclusion that the sites were laid out using the English mile. In evidence he gives distances between various combinations of points: 'Point 1 to St Just is exactly 7 miles. . . . Point 1 to Point 2 is exactly 3 miles. Bugarach to Point 4 is exactly 1 mile'[7] and so on. His claims are compared with our calculations in the table associated with Fig. 13.4. We have used the same arithmetical method as before, this time calculating first the co-ordinates of points (such as Points 1 and 2 on the figure) that are defined by the intersection of lines. All his distances, although not exact, are correct to within about 30 m, except for Rennes-le-Château to the Château des Templiers, which we find to be nearly 200 m short of the 4 miles, and Point 1, the apex of Wood's pentagon, to Blanchefort, which is about 150 m further than 2½ miles.

Henry Lincoln noted that Wood's 'sunrise' line from Rennes-le-Château to Arques church did not pass exactly through Château de Blanchefort, but slightly to the north of it. He projected the line from Rennes-le-Château to Blanchefort beyond Arques and found that it '. . . arrived at a grotto. This grotto, clearly marked on the map, is beside the road and exactly 6½ miles from Rennes-le-Château Church! Moreover this grotto is placed with remarkable precision in exact relationship, not only with the church at Rennes-le-Château, but with the whole of the original pentagon.'[8]

His diagram shows the grotto as being on the intersection of the Rennes-le-Château to Blanchefort line and the Château Templiers to la Soulane line. Its calculated position is at 604.38, 3072.68; it is actually at 604.02, 3072.66, about 360 m west of the intersection of the lines. The distance of the grotto from the church at Rennes-le-Château is 6.49 miles. Lincoln notes that the grotto appears natural, but in view of its location relative to the five peaks of the pentagon, he suspects a human agency was involved in its construction. However it served to remove any doubts about the 'careful and sophisticated structuring of the artificial landscape'. [9]

As Lincoln proceeds with his analysis he becomes convinced that the English mile measure was the one in general use in this area in earlier periods. Not only that, the churches are sited so as to make an integral number of miles or half miles in the distances between them. If true this would completely change the accepted view of the historical development of English units of length and would imply, as

Lincoln argues, a grand design of great importance. He gives two sets of distances that we can test, from Bugarach church to ten churches, a cave and a calvary, all of which are claimed to be 'exact' miles or half miles (i.e. a whole number of half-miles), and from Rennes-les-Bains to six churches, two castles, the 'Poussin' tomb and the Magdala Tower at Rennes-le-Château. We give our analysis of these distances on page 160.

It will be seen that the word 'exact' requires some qualification. In the top half of the list the biggest differences between our calculated distance and a whole number of half miles is 0.08 miles, in the bottom half it is 0.09 miles. If we are willing to accept 0.09 miles difference and call it exact, then, say between 5 and 6 miles, we would allow all distances falling between 5.0 to 5.09 miles, 5.41 and 5.59 miles, and 5.91 and 6.0 miles. These account for 36 per cent of all possible distances! In other words, about one third of all possible distances would seem to fit his criterion of being 'exactly' a whole number of miles or half-miles.

In the area roughly defined by Bugarach, Missègre, the calvary at Alet, Antugnac and St Julia-de-Bec, there are thirty-nine churches, six castles, innumerable peaks and several calvaries. Taking just the churches, one would expect about twelve to be within 0.08 miles of a whole number of half miles from either Bugarach or Rennes-les-Bains. Lincoln's tables show nine and six churches respectively. On this evidence, there is no reason to believe that the English mile was used in laying out the churches to some grand design. It is much more likely that the locations of the churches were chosen because the site was convenient for some local reason or another.

The mile is not the only unit of length that Lincoln says he has found in the area and in *The Holy Place* he puts forward some unconventional ideas about the origin of English linear measure. We discuss these in Appendix G.

Alignments

Another aspect of Lincoln's investigation of the landscape around Rennes-le-Château was his discovery of alignments. These were mainly of churches but some link other man-made objects, castles, calvaries and various unidentified ruins, as well as natural sites, such as peaks, springs and sinkholes, which are not uncommon in limestone country. In total they constitute a grid pattern of some complexity. Lincoln finds two separate grids with lines at right angles; one grid is lined up on the eastern line of Wood's pentagon (Bugarach to Serres château) and the other on the western side (St Just-et-le-Bézu to Cassaignes). As before we have checked his claims and our analysis is given in the tables associated with the two grids.

The first grid (Fig. 13.5) has four parallel lines on a bearing of about 163°, i.e. parallel to the eastern side of Wood's pentagram, and seven lines on a bearing of about 73°, which is roughly the 'sunrise' line. The second grid (Fig. 13.6) has four lines on a bearing of about 19°, which is parallel to the western side of the pentagram, and two lines at about 109°. Lincoln shows a third line on the same bearing; we do not agree with this one, but it may be that we have not found the correct sinkhole on the map. Several of Lincoln's grid lines are defined by two points only, but where there are more than two, all points are usually very close to the line.

This looks very impressive. Surely such an array proves without doubt that care has been taken in times past (Lincoln suggests around 1500 BC) to set out a pattern on the landscape. Admittedly some of the churches and castles are medieval rather than prehistoric, but Lincoln does not find this a problem: the churches and other structures which mark out the design could certainly have been placed upon sites which were sacred to the early pagan inhabitants of the area. The alternative hypothesis, that these sites are located quite by chance and that the pattern is accidental, imposed in fact by the investigators themselves, may seem bizarre, yet that is just what we have to examine.

Claims that sites are aligned are not unusual. Most of our readers will have heard of ley lines: alignments of prehistoric sites, churches and so on in England. Ley line hunting has its own band of devotees, some of whom see in them remarkable properties. There are even those who contend that ley lines are indications of 'lines of force' by which extraterrestrials navigate over the earth's surface in their unidentified flying objects. While few people would agree with this, a considerable number accept ley lines as genuine survivors from the past.

The idea of ley lines, and indeed their name, came from a photographer and antiquarian, Alfred Watkins (1855–1935), who lived in the English county of Hereford. His father owned a brewery, and Alfred as representative of the firm travelled widely over the Herefordshire countryside, gaining an intimate knowledge of its topography. He was a prominent photographer, writing a book on the subject, and invented an exposure meter. In 1921, in the course of his travels, Alfred Watkins noticed that some prehistoric burial mounds, including long barrows of the neolithic period, and round barrows of the bronze age, appeared to lie in straight lines. Because many of these are on hilltops, he came to the conclusion that prehistoric man had deliberately made tracks using the barrows as sighting points. Later he found that barrows were not the only objects to be sited on lines; his maps include Iron Age encampments and Christian churches. In 1925 he published his observations in a famous book, *The Old Straight Track*. In it he gives instructions to the ley-hunter, to look out for 'ancient mounds, whether called barrows, tumuli, tumps or cairns; ancient unworked stones; moats and islands in ponds or lakelets; traditional or holy wells; beacon points; cross-roads with place-names, and ancient wayside crosses; churches of ancient foundation and hermitages; and ancient castles and old castle place names'.

To Watkins these alignments were simply markers to show the way to travellers. He concluded that they indicated tracks along which people walked or rode their horses. There was nothing magical in his interpretation.

Studying maps shows that alignments are usually genuine, and indeed, armed with a ruler and a large-scale map alignments can be readily found. The question is not 'Are the alignments there?' but 'Have sites been selected from a random distribution of them just because they happen to lie on a line?' Sometimes alignments are deliberate, Roman roads being perhaps the most obvious example, and it would not be surprising to find the sites of churches in villages strung out along a Roman road to be in a straight line. But some alignments must be accidental, and the problem is to know how many one would expect to find by chance. It is only if we get significantly more than this number that we can conclude that they are the results of deliberate activity.

Estimating the chance number of alignments is not particularly easy, and it is not possible to produce a simple formula that will give the answer. Fortunately, with the aid of a computer we can get an estimate, and how this is done is described in Appendix F. To begin with, we have to state what we mean by an alignment, because there is more than one way of defining it. The definition we have used is that an intermediate site is on the alignment if it is closer than a predetermined miss-distance to the line joining the two sites at the ends of the alignment. The miss-distance can be chosen to suit the circumstances. If we were measuring from a 1:25,000 map, where 1 mm on the map is equivalent to 25 m on the ground, a miss-distance of 25 m would not be inappropriate to use. But some of the sites, a church for example, could be more than 25 m across. Then perhaps 50 m would be more suitable.

The method of calculation, which is given more completely and more formally in Appendix F, is to let the computer pick randomly the co-ordinates of a set of points within the chosen area. Out of the set it picks a pair of points and then works out the probability that other points lie within the miss-distance of the line joining them. It then picks another pair of points, works out the probability again and continues until it has dealt with all the possible pairs of points. It adds all the probabilities together and produces the answer in the form of a table of numbers of two-point lines, three-point lines, four-point lines and so on to find the expected number of such lines. Though the amount of arithmetic needed to arrive at the answer is considerable, it is well within the capabilities of the average home computer.

142

Here are some typical results for points randomly scattered over a square 10 km by 10 km. The miss-distance is 50 m.

Number of points	2-point lines	3-point lines	4-point lines	5-point lines	6-point lines
20	173	16	1	0	0
30	378	53	4	0	0
40	644	121	16	1	0
50	958	229	34	4	0
60	1315	378	67	9	1

The program shows that the total number of lines increases rapidly with increasing number of points in an area. (With N points one gets a total of $\frac{1}{2}N(N-1)$ lines, which gives 190 lines for 20 points, 435 lines for 30 points.) Also the number of alignments with 3 and more points increases very quickly. If there is a large number of points there are bound to be numerous alignments.

This can be shown by looking at the area around Rennes-le-Château. If we take the area which is defined by the IGN Map 3615, but ignore the two folds on the left (west) side; that gives an area of 21 km by 20 km. Within this area are 43 churches and chapels, including ruined ones, 14 castles, 13 calvaries (at least 13, they are difficult to see on the map), 16 avens (sinkholes), 3 grottes (caves) and 119 sites marked 'ruins'. That makes 208 sites in all. In addition there is an unknown number of peaks and a scatter of menhirs, tombs and monuments. From the 208 sites alone there are 21,528 possible lines, which means there are about 120 within 1° of any compass direction. If we had a miss distance of 50 m, nearly 6000 of these lines would be three-point alignments, over 1500 would be four-point alignments and 350 five-point alignments. By admitting a whole range of categories of site, it becomes inevitable that alignments will be found, and the number found will be directly related to the effort spent in searching for them.

There is another possible test for the significance of alignments round Rennes-le-Château. As described in the second part of Appendix F, we have fed into the computer the grid co-ordinates of all the 40 churches in the area (just the churches, and missing out the ruined chapels), and programmed it to look for alignments with a miss-distance not exceeding 50 m. The number of three-point alignments is 77, compared with an expected 88, and the number of four-point alignments is 7, which happens to be the very number one would have expected by chance. It can be said with confidence that the churches have not been sited deliberately to make alignments, in spite of the apparently remarkable results obtained by Henry Lincoln.

The Work of Andrews and Schellenberger

Henry Lincoln and David Wood are not the only authors to have found geometrical patterns in the area around Rennes-le-Château. Two more authors, Richard Andrews and Paul Schellenberger, who have a strong background in surveying techniques, make use of alignments in their researches, and arrive at totally different conclusions from either Henry Lincoln or David Wood. Their results are published in *The Tomb of God*, and they have also been brought to public notice in a searching television production for the BBC's *Timewatch* series.[10]

Their starting point is the geometry of the two parchments as illustrated by de Sède and the design on the *Dalle de Coumesourde*. While admitting that there is some doubt about the provenance of all three, they have not been deterred by their dubious authenticity, nor by the fact that they have never seen the originals. Like Lincoln, they find a geometric pattern in the shorter of the two parchments. Though similar to Lincoln's geometry theirs is not identical, and pentagons are not part of it. They find an equilateral triangle, and add an identical but inverted triangle, thereby creating a regular hexagon. Whether or not the geometrical pattern in the parchment is deliberate or accidental they make a great leap of inference and conclude that the parchment is actually a map, and that the lines they have drawn on it relate specifically to features on the ground in the area around Rennes-le-Château.

Their analysis of Parchment 1 is somewhat different, because they concentrate on the decrypted message, looking for clues to identify locations on the ground. The number 681 led them to a map spot height of 681 m near the Col de l'Espinas (601.30, 3076.60). The cross in the message they take to be a cross beside the railway line north of Alet (592.88, 3078.77), and that gives them two primary points and the length of one side of their geometrical figure. They note that near the cross the railway line (which in their interpretation is the 'Horse of God') is straight and at right angles to the line joining the cross and the spot height. Projecting this direction southwards until it reaches Esperaza, and making it the same distance as the cross to the spot height, one arrives at the church. They now have two sides of a square. The south-east corner of the square is found to be quite near a col, the *Col Doux* (599.10, 3068.15) which they translate as Peaceful Col, thereby linking this corner with the word Pax of the message.

The next steps in their reasoning are complicated and involve a detailed examination of the paintings which Saunière reputedly purchased copies of on his supposed trip to Paris: Poussin's *Shepherds of Arcady*, Tenier's *St Anthony and St Paul* and *The Coronation of Pope Celestine V* by an unknown artist. They relate the geometry of the paintings to points on the ground which they believe correspond to the three apexes of the equilateral triangle of the smaller parchment. They locate its three corners: north-west (594.90, 3076.73), north-east (603.00, 3074.63) and south (597.15, 3068.66) and precisely in the centre of this triangle is the church at Peyrolles. Furthermore, the triangle and the square are related to each other – their northern sides are parallel.

Further geometrical analysis, too involved to summarize here, leads to the square being shifted, so that its north-west corner now coincides with the north-west corner of the triangle. The centre of the new square lies on Pech Cardou, about 800 m south-east of the remains of Château de Blanchefort. This site, according to the authors, is 'the most secret of hiding places and the location of the "treasure" of Rennes.'[11] And the hidden 'treasure'? According to Andrews and Schellenberger, it is the bodily remains of Jesus Christ.

One of the pieces of evidence that led them to this conclusion was the motto *Et in Arcadia ego*. They first added the word *sum*, I am, because they thought it made more sense, then rearranged the letters to give the anagram *Arcam dei tango. Iesu*, which they translate as 'I touch the tomb of God. Jesus.'[12] This is indeed an unusual method of historical research!

Andrews and Schellenberger claim confirmation of this remarkable deduction from the layout of the churches and châteaux in the area (Fig. 13.7). The triangle formed by the church at Peyrolles, the remains of Château de Blanchefort, the centre of the château at Arques they claim has a right angle at Peyrolles, and other angles of 30° and 60°. The western extremity of the château at Serres also has a simple geometrical relationship with this triangle, since it forms a near isosceles triangle with Peyrolles and Blanchefort, with angles of 120°, 30° and 30°.

To Andrews and Schellenberger these buildings have been located with regular geometry by those who know the secret of Christ's tomb in order to provide an alternative way of communicating the secret of its location. They take arbitrary clues from the two gravestones of Marie de Nègre. They note that on the drawing of Marie I as published in the Aude *Bulletin*, the top slopes at an angle of 60°, and also that on the alleged Stüblein drawing of Marie II a line joining the two crosses is at 60°. Taking these two illustrations at face value, they draw the same angles on the map. Two lines, on a bearing of 120° east from Blanchefort and a bearing 120° west from Arques, intersect on the slope of Pech Cardou at 598.75, 3070.43, the point *Y* on Fig. 13.7, very nearly at the same place as was found from the geometry derived from the parchments.

The Paris Meridian

In *Genisis* David Wood introduced another, seemingly unlikely addition to the geometry of Rennes-le-Château, the Paris Meridian. We have already mentioned this several times, in connection with various alignments and distances, and its appearance in the geometry would seem to require some explanation.

A meridian is simply the line showing the direction of the sun at midday; every place on the earth (except the two poles) has its local meridian, and every person who has accurately set up a sundial, has, without necessarily being aware of it, established their own meridian. This is fine for measuring the local time, but in order to know one's place on the Earth's surface relative to somewhere else, the latitude and longitude must be measured. The latitude presents little difficulty, since the elevation of the sun at midday gives it directly, but how to measure the longitude was a serious problem from the sixteenth century onwards when the great sea voyages were being undertaken. Basically, one had to measure the difference between the local time and the time at some place of origin, and astronomical methods were the only ones available for doing this. In order to measure longitude, in 1666 Louis XIV authorized the building of an observatory in Paris. The centre line of the building was established as the line of zero longitude – the Paris Meridian – and it has been in exactly the same place ever since. In 1884 at the International Meridian Conference in Washington DC, the Greenwich Meridian was set as the prime meridian of the world. The French Government was not happy with this decision, and French cartographers continue to the present day to indicate the Paris Meridian on maps of the IGN, including the one of the area around Rennes-le-Château. The Meridian passes about 350 m west of the 'Poussin' tomb.

There is a very famous local meridian in Paris in the church of Saint-Sulpice. It was set up in 1727 at the request of the *curé*, Languet de Gercy, who wished to determine precisely the date of the March equinox, and hence the date of Easter Sunday. The meridian of Saint-Sulpice, which is about 100 m west of the Paris Meridian, is marked in the floor of the church with a brass line. The proximity of the Paris Meridian to Rennes-le-Château and the occurrence of the church of Saint-Sulpice in the affair have caused some confusion. In *Le Serpent Rouge*, under 'Gemini', the reader is told to 'look for the line of the meridian', and 'place yourself in front of the fourteen stones marked with a cross', clearly referring to the interior of the church, but interpreted by David Wood as referring to the Paris Meridian on the ground near Rennes-le-Château.[13]

From his analysis of alignments, Henry Lincoln asserts that 'the Paris Meridian, which the Cassinis measured and which is still used by the French Geographical Institute, runs exactly along the line of intersections formed by the alignments of structures in *The Holy Place*. The Paris Meridian is demonstrably the line of intersections. It follows that the line was laid out and fixed by whoever conceived the overall geometric design.'[14] If true, this would be amazing. Lincoln's alignments include churches dating from the eleventh and twelfth centuries, at least 500 years before the Meridian was established. Lincoln says, 'It is difficult not to be drawn to the obvious conclusion that the Cassini Meridian line was based upon the "cromlech intersect division line".'[15]

The essence of his case is illustrated in two diagrams which appear in chapter 16 of *The Holy Place*. The first shows five alignments all intersecting at a point on the Meridian. We give a diagram of these alignments in Fig. 13.8 and the data in tabular form beneath it. Four of the five lines cut the Meridian within a distance of 220 m, which is hardly an accurate intersection. The third (through Castel Nègre and the centre of the circle of churches) is another 240 m away, but it is only fair to state that the location which we found to be the best fit for the centre of the circle is not necessarily where Lincoln would have placed it.

The above intersections define Point A on the Paris Meridian. Lincoln finds that the line from Antugnac church to Point A is just one of a fan of 10 lines radiating out from the church towards the Meridian (Fig. 13.9). He says that these lines cut the Meridian into equal segments, and that this confirms that the Meridian was sited in relation to existing structures. However, as Andrews and Schellenberger point out, this is not so: if there are equal segments on one line, one can draw any line parallel to that line and still get equal segments. In fact we do not find the segments to be equal, although we have tried to be as accurate as possible in taking the grid co-ordinates of the various places on the alignments. The table by Fig. 13.9 shows that the intervals vary from 1,310 m to 1,730 m, a difference between smallest and largest of 420 m or about 30 per cent. There is a similar scatter of intersections with other alignments intersecting the Meridian. For example, Ste Julia to Le Bézu, which Lincoln reckons meets the Meridian at Point D, is at least 100 m away.

One is thus driven to the conclusion that these results do not support the idea of a deliberate relationship between the Paris Meridian and alignments near Rennes-le-Château. As was said earlier, there are many churches, castles and so on in the area and it is not difficult, if one searches long enough, to find a pattern that can look very impressive.

Summary

In this chapter we have looked at three detailed studies of the area around Rennes-le-Château, all of which have been based, to a greater or lesser extent, on the geometrical arrangement of natural or man-made objects. All three have come to different conclusions. In each case the work has led to pinpointing a special site – a prehistoric temple; a 'seed' of unspecified nature connected with Atlantis and the goddess Isis; or the resting place of the remains of Jesus. It is quite inconceivable that all three studies have come to a correct conclusion, if they had, Rennes-le-Château would be a remarkable place indeed!

In each investigation a vast amount of work has been done by the authors, and arguments put forward in great detail. From looking at the same evidence – the Saunière story, the parchments, the *Dossiers secrets*, the natural landscape and the locations of buildings – they have arrived at very different endings. We have to ask why.

The answer, we believe, lies in the methods of investigation that have been adopted. Their conclusions may be different but their methodology has much in common, both in the way they select evidence and how they assess what they have selected.

Firstly they accept as sound evidence much that is doubtful. All the above authors take the story as told by Gérard de Sède to be essentially true. Yet it does not require a very critical reading to realize that de Sède wrote a sensational story with little hard evidence to back it up. The Rennes-le-Château literature is full of assumptions and possibilities, which when repeated often enough (and occasionally embroidered upon) become effectively the definitive account. In this book we have shown that many of the ramifications of the myths surrounding Saunière and the Rennes-le-Château story are not only dubious but fraudulent. They have gained authenticity simply by being repeated over and over again. The books we have looked at make astounding claims. It is a brave act to write a book which 'could constitute the single most shattering secret of the last two thousand years', or 'shed light on the origin of our species' or 'end with the discovery of the greatest secret of all' on such fragile foundations .[15]

Secondly, all of the authors have a narrow approach to the subject. Admittedly research has to have its constraints, or it can never be completed. But new results should be considered in the context of existing knowledge. If they are not in conflict, all well and good, they could before long be absorbed into mainstream learning. If they do not fit into the conventional framework, a situation which seemingly applies to any investigation starting off from the Rennes affair, it is only fair to point out discrepancies to the reader. Unfortunately there is little of that in the studies we have quoted. For the most part what the majority of the academic world accepts as valid archaeology, history and geology is ignored as though it is really of no great consequence. David Wood, for example, is happy to set aside all conventional anthropology and theories of human evolution on the basis of numerology and necromancy.

Thirdly, even with their highly focussed approaches, all of the authors are extremely selective in what they choose to admit and what to reject as evidence. If it fits into the hypothesis it is accepted, if not it is ignored. Nowhere is this clearer

148

than in their treatment of alignments. For the most part the claimed alignments are correct. However, we have already shown that if one is willing to consider a wide range of objects (churches, castles, crosses and so on), without even a thought as to whether they fit into a plausible chronology, a much larger number of alignments is created than one would expect intuitively: one will be able to find enough to suit any pattern. None of the authors seem to be aware of this nor give any thought to the possibility 'could what they have found be the result of chance?'. When one asks the question, the answer turns out to be an emphatic yes.

In short, surprising as it may seem at first, the explanation for all of these various studies coming to such different conclusions is basically a combination of selection of evidence and faulty methodology. The methods used are neither scientific nor rigorous. If one wanted, for example, to check whether churches in a particular area were sited in some pattern, a better approach would be to examine systematically the siting of each church relative to the others (a task best given to a computer) and then test statistically whether the outcome differed from a chance result by a significant amount. If it were done this way, and a statistically significant number of alignments was found, even the sceptical would be convinced. As it is, our quick look at the distribution of churches shows nothing unusual. The pattern of lines on the landscape, like almost everything else connected with Rennes-le-Château, fades and disappears before the searching eye.

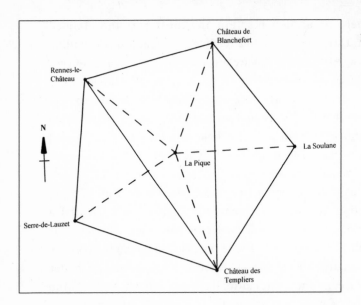

13.1 The Pentagon of Peaks.

Distances across the pentagon	km	miles
Rennes-le-Château to Templar Château	6.27	3.89
Templar Château to Blanchefort	6.29	3.91

Lengths of the sides		
Templar Château to La Soulane	4.01	2.49
La Soulane to Blanchefort	3.88	2.41
Blanchefort to Rennes-le-Château	4.11	2.56
Rennes-le-Château to La Serre de Lauzet	3.94	2.45
La Serre de Lauzet to Templar Château	3.89	2.42
Averages	3.97	2.46
Average difference from mean	0.07	0.05

Distances from the centre to the corners		
La Pique to Templar Château	2.98	1.85
La Pique to La Soulane	3.32	2.06
La Pique to Blanchefort	3.58	2.22
La Pique to Rennes-le-Château	3.62	2.25
La Pique to Serre de Lauzet	3.39	2.11
Averages	3.38	2.10
Average distance from mean	0.18	0.11

Data for locations listed

Place	Height (m)	Grid Co-ordinates	Angle
Rennes-le-Château	510	593.97, 3069.82	107.7°
Templar Château	832	597.48, 3064.63	111.9°
Château de Blanchefort	476	597.94, 3070.90	108.4°
La Soulane	587	600.09, 3067.67	105.7°
Serre de Lauzet	559	593.80, 3065.88	106.3°
La Pique	582	596.77, 3067.52	

150

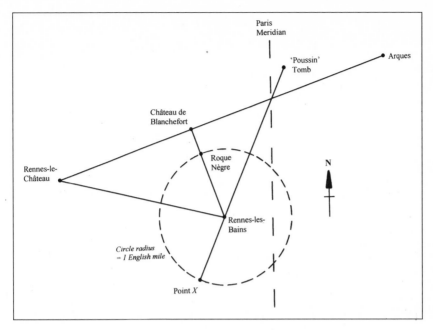

13.2 The 'Sunrise line' from Rennes-le-Château to Blanchefort.

Distances	km	miles
Rennes-les-Bains to Roque Nègre	1.61	1.00
Rennes-le-Château to Rennes-les-Bains	4.77	2.97
Rennes-le-Château to Arques	9.49	5.89
Arques to Meridian	3.19	1.98

The line from Rennes-le-Château to Arques Church passes about 100 metres north of Château de Blanchefort.

Bearings

Rennes-le-Château to Arques Church (1)	73.4°
Rennes-le-Château to Blanchefort (2)	74.8°
Rennes-les-Bains to Blanchefort (3)	162.5°
Angle between lines 1 and 3	89.1°
Angle between lines 2 and 3	87.7°

Grid Co-ordinates of locations listed

Rennes-le-Château, church	593.97, 3069.82
Château de Blanchefort, peak	597.94, 3070.90
Arques, church	603.06, 3072.53
Rennes-les-Bains, church	598.62, 3068.74
Roque Nègre, peak	598.10, 3070.26
Point where line Rennes-le-Château to Arques	
church crosses the Meridian	600.00, 3071.62
'Poussin' tomb	600.32, 3072.28

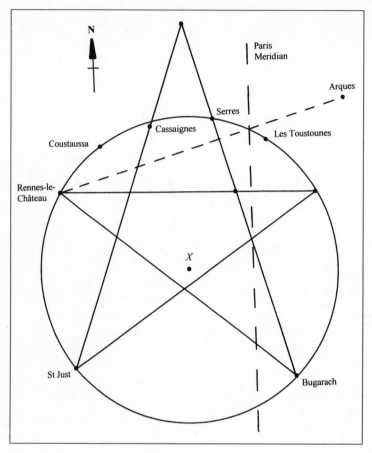

13.3 David Wood's Circle and Pentacle.

Distances from Point X

Place	Grid Co-ordinates	km	miles
Rennes-le-Château, church	593.97, 3069.82	4.68	2.91
Coustaussa, church	595.19, 3071.17	4.70	2.92
Cassaignes, church	596.84, 3071.78	4.56	2.83
Serres, château	598.88, 3072.00	4.73	2.94
Serres, church	598.97, 3071.92	4.67	2.90
Bugarach, church	601.23, 3064.02	4.68	2.91
St Just-et-le-Bézu, church	594.29, 3064.38	4.72	2.93
Les Toustounes, rock	601.03, 3071.02	4.78	2.97
Intersection: 'sunrise' line with Paris Meridian	600.00, 3071.62	4.73	2.94
Averages		4.69	2.93
Average difference from mean		0.04	0.03
X, centre of circle	597.95, 3067.36	0	0
Rennes-les-Bains, church	598.62, 3068.74	1.53	0.95

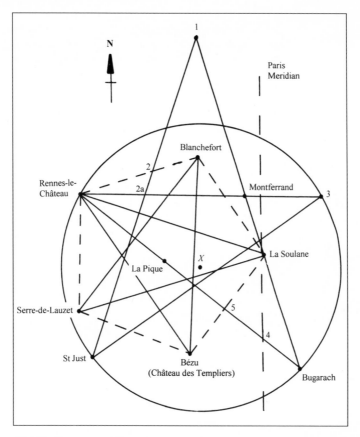

13.4 The Pentagon and Pentacle superposed.

Distances between points on Fig. 13.4

Lincoln's statement

	Our Calculations		
	km	**miles**	**difference**
Point 1 to St Just exactly 7 miles	11.30	7.02	+0.02
Point 1 to Point 2 exactly 3 miles	4.82	2.99	-0.01
Bugarach to Point 4 exactly 1 mile	1.58	0.98	-0.02
Bugarach to Point 5 exactly 2 miles	3.25	2.02	+0.02
Bugarach to La Pique exactly 3½ miles	5.67	3.52	+0.02
Rennes-le-Château to Montferrand exactly 3½ miles	5.56	3.46	-0.05
Rennes-le-Château to Templar Château exactly 4 miles	6.27	3.89	-0.11
Rennes-le-Château to La Soulane exactly 4 miles	6.48	4.03	+0.03
Point 1 to Blanchefort exactly 2½ miles	4.16	2.59	+0.09
St Just to Templar Château exactly 2 miles	3.20	1.99	-0.01
Point 1 to Point 2a, 3½ miles	5.61	3.48	-0.02
Point 2a to St Just, 3½ miles	5.69	3.54	+0.04
Mean difference from nearest ½ mile			0.045

153

Grid Co-ordinates of locations (on Fig. 13.4)

Point 1	597.99, 3075.06	Point 3	602.08, 3069.59
Point 2	596.41, 3070.51	Point 4	600.00, 3065.01
Point 2a	596.16, 3069.76	Point 5	598.69, 3066.05
Montferrand, château	599.53, 3069.68		

For other places see previous tables.

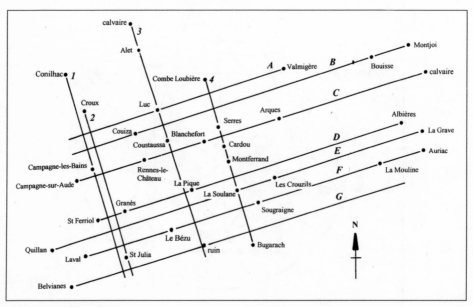

13.5 Lincoln's first grid.

Lines on Lincoln's first grid

Line	Place	Grid Co-ordinates	Off line (m)	Bearing
1	Conilhac, church	588.38, 3075.48		
	Campagnes-les-Bains, church	590.26, 3069.00		163.9°
2	Croux, church	589.56, 3073.03		
	St Julia-de-Bec, church	592.52, 3063.22		163.2°
3	Calvaire north of Alet	592.88, 3078.77		
	Alet, church	593.39, 3077.30	75	
	Luc-sur-Aude, church	594.52, 3073.20	13	
	Coustaussa, church	595.10, 3071.15		163.8°
4	Combe Loubière, Point 1	597.94, 3075.06		
	Serres, château	598.86, 3072.00	11	
	Pech Cardou, peak	599.24, 3070.72	10	
	Monferrand, château	599.52, 3069.69	16	
	La Soulane, peak	600.09, 3067.68	44	
	Bugarach, church	601.23, 3064.02		163.4°
A	Luc-sur-Aude, church	594.52, 3073.20		
	Valmigère, church	603.22, 3075.86		73.0°
C	Campagne-sur-Aude, church	589.41, 3068.45		
	Rennes-le-Château, church	593.97, 3069.82	12	
	Blanchefort, peak	597.94, 3070.90	90	
	Arques, church	603.06, 3072.53		73.3°
D	St Ferriol, church	590.80, 3065.79		
	Granès, church	592.73, 3066.31	50	
	La Pique, peak	596.77, 3067.52		73.8°
E	Quillan, church	587.56, 3063.84		
	La Soulane, peak	600.09, 3067.68	150	
	Les Crouzils, unknown ruin	603.08, 3068.40		73.6°
F	Laval, church	589.81, 3063.33		
	Le Bézu, church	595.60, 3065.08	<10	
	Sougraine, church	601.45, 3066.85		73.2°
G	Belvianes, church	588.80, 3061.40		
	Unidentified ruins	597.75, 3064.11		73.1°

The mean bearing of NW to SE lines is 163.5°; the mean bearing of SW to NE lines is 73.3°; and the difference between the two is 90.2°.

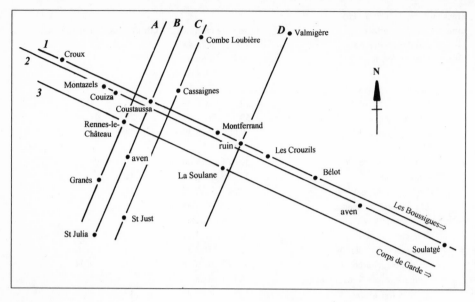

13.6 Lincoln's second grid.

Line	Place	Grid Co-ordinates	Off line (m)	Bearing
1	Croux, church	589.56, 3073.03		
	Coustaussa, church	595.19, 3071.17		
	Montferrand, château	599.52, 3069.68	74	
	Unidentified ruins	600.87, 3069.17	31	
	Les Crouzils, ruins	603.08, 3068.40	23	
	Le Belot, ruins	605.90, 3067.40		109.0°
2	Montazels, church	592.60, 3071.68		
	Couiza, church	593.21, 3071.44	32	
	Aven, sinkhole*	606.56, 3065.40		114.2°
3	Rennes-le-Château, church	593.97, 3069.82		
	La Soulane, peak	600.09, 3067.67		109.4°
A	Rennes-le-Château, church	593.97, 3069.82		
	Granès, church	592.73, 3066.31		19.4°
B	Coustaussa, church	595.19, 3071.17		
	Aven, sinkhole	594.05, 3067.73	16	
	St Julia-de-Bec, church	592.52, 3063.22		18.5°
C	Combe Loubière, Point 1	597.94, 3075.06		
	Cassaignes, church	596.84, 3071.78	12	
	St Just-et-le-Bézu, church	594.29, 3064.38		19.1°
D	Valmigère, church	603.22, 3075.86		
	Unidentified ruin	600.87, 3069.17		19.3°

* This may not be the correct sinkhole. Ignoring this line, the mean bearing of NW to SE lines is 109.2°; the mean bearing of SE to NW lines is 19.1°; and the difference between the two is 90.1°.

156

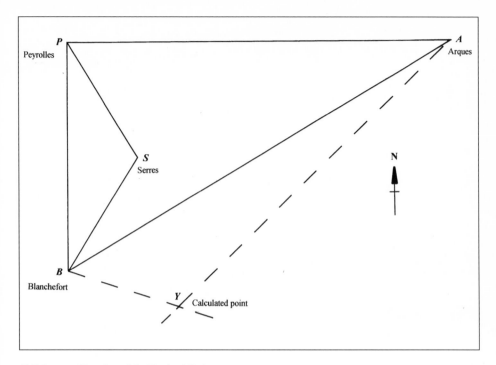

13.7 Supposed location of the Tomb of God.

Line	Place	Grid Co-ordinates	
P	Peyrolles	598.36, 3073.32	church
B	Blanchefort	597.94, 3070.90	château
A	Arques	602.49, 3072.59	centre of château
S	Serres	598.85, 3072.00	west end of château
Y	Calculated point	598.75, 3070.43	supposed site of Christ's tomb

Angles $BPA = 90.2°$, $PAB = 30.3°$, $ABP = 59.5°$
Angles $BPS = 30.1°$, $PSB = 120.1°$, $SBP = 29.8°$

BY is a bearing of 120°E, AY is a bearing of 120°W

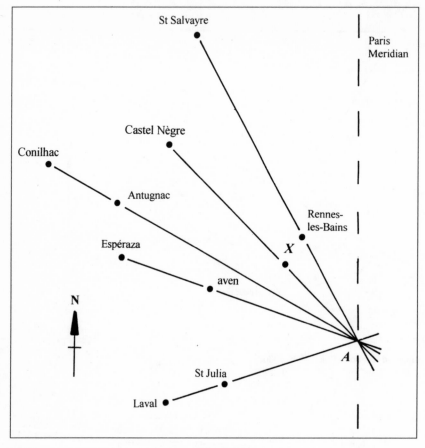

13.8 Intersections with the Paris Meridian: Fixing Point *A*.

From	Through	Intersection at
St Salvayre	Rennes-les-Bains	600.0, 3062.79
Castel Nègre	Point *X*	600.0, 3063.25
Conilhac	Antugnac	600.0, 3062.89
Esperaza	aven	600.0, 3063.01
Laval	St Julia	600.0, 3062.91

Mean point of intersection with the Paris Meridian is at 600.00, 3062.97

Grid co-ordinates for locations listed

St Salvayre, church	596.34, 3078.58	Rennes-les-Bains, church	598.62, 3068.74
Castel Nègre, church	594.16, 3074.97	*X*, centre of circle	597.95, 3067.36
Conilhac, church	588.38, 3075.48	Antugnac, church	590.89, 3072.76
Esperaza, church	590.60, 3070.44	aven, sinkhole	594.04, 3067.73
Laval, church	589.81, 3063.33	St Julia, church	592.52, 3063.22

13.9 The fan of lines
through Antugnac.

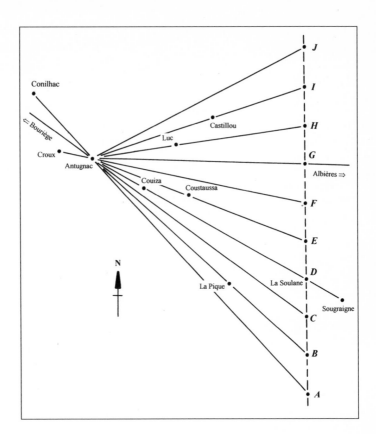

Line			Calculated position of intersection with Meridian	Intervals km	
Conilhac	Antugnac	A	600.0, 3062.89		
Antugnac	La Pique	B	600.0, 3064.62	AB	1.73
Bouriège	Antugnac	C	600.0, 3066.33	BC	1.71
Antugnac	Couiza	D	600.0, 3067.53		
Antugnac	La Soulane	D	600.0, 3067.72		
Antugnac	Sougraine	D	600.0, 3067.66	CD	1.31*
Antugnac	Coustaussa	E	600.0, 3069.39	DE	1.75
Antugnac	Luc	H	600.0, 3073.88	EF	1.48 x 2
Antugnac	Castillou	I	600.0, 3075.37	HI	1.49

* Taking the average of the three positions for D.

Grid Co-ordinates of locations listed

Antugnac	590.89	3072.76	Sougraigne, church	601.45	3066.85
Conilhac, church	588.38	3075.48	Coustaussa, church	595.19	3071.17
La Pique, peak	596.77	3067.52	Croux, church	589.56	3073.03
Bouriège, church	586.08	3076.15			
Couiza, church	593.21	3071.44	Luc, church	594.52	3073.20
La Soulane, peak	600.09	3067.67	Castillou, church	596.06	3074.25

Table of distances from two churches (see p. 138)

The column headed 'difference' shows the difference between the actual distance and the nearest half mile.

Place	Grid Co-ordinates	km	miles	difference
Distances from Bugarach church				
Bugarach church	601.23, 3064.02	0	0	
St Louis church	598.65, 3060.87	4.07	2.53	+0.03
Granès church	592.73, 3066.31	8.80	5.47	-0.03
St Julia church	592.52, 3063.22	8.75	5.43	-0.07
Valmigère church	603.22, 3075.86	12.01	7.46	-0.04
Campagne church	590.26, 3069.00	12.05	7.49	-0.01
Antugnac church	590.89, 3072.76	13.54	8.42	-0.08
Missègre church	602.98, 3078.27	14.36	8.92	-0.08
Les Sauzils church	586.57, 3068.05	15.20	9.45	-0.05
Calvaire near Alet	592.89, 3078.78	16.95	10.53	+0.03
La Pique, hilltop	596.77, 3067.52	5.67	3.52	+0.02
The aven, cave	594.05, 3067.73	8.08	5.02	+0.02
Distances from Rennes-les-Bains church				
Rennes-les-Bains	598.62, 3068.74	0	0	
Serres church	598.97, 3071.93	3.21	1.99	-0.01
'Poussin' tomb	600.32, 3072.28	3.93	2.44	-0.06
Le Bézu church	595.60, 3065.08	4.75	2.95	-0.05
La Tour Magdala	593.91, 3069.77	4.82	3.00	0
Granès church	592.73, 3066.31	6.37	3.96	-0.04
Missègre church	602.98, 3078.27	10.48	6.51	-0.09
Cavirac church	588.97, 3061.59	12.01	7.46	-0.04
Quillan church	587.56, 3063.84	12.10	7.52	+0.02
Roquetaillade château	588.94, 3077.17	12.84	7.98	-0.02

14

Bérenger Saunière

In earlier chapters we considered the evidence for the story that Bérenger Saunière found treasure. The trail led us to the conclusion that there was no treasure at all and that we were really dealing with a story of invention and deception. Yet if there was no treasure, there was certainly no lack of funds. The refurbishment of the church, the *Villa Béthanie*, the tower, the gardens and the new road, cost in all a large amount of money. So where did the money come from? Now is the time to look at the priest's life from the historical sources available to us, and to try to get closer to the truth of what really happened.

1852–85

Bérenger Saunière was born on 11 April 1852 at Montazels, a small village 1 km west of Couiza. His parents were Joseph Saunière and Marguerite Hughes. Joseph was Mayor of Montazels and manager of a grain mill. It was a prosperous period in the history of France and the family was fairly well off.

Altogether there were eleven children. Four died in infancy, leaving four boys, Bérenger, Alfred, Martial and Joseph, and three girls, Mathilde, Adeline and Marie-Louise. Alfred, who preceded Bérenger into the priesthood, was always very close to his elder brother. Joseph died at the age of twenty-five, while studying medicine in Toulouse.

Mathilde, the eldest of the three sisters, was not close to Bérenger and she had many disputes with her brother in later years over their inheritance and the problems of looking after their mother.

Bérenger was educated at the School of St Louis in Limoux, and took holy orders in the Grand Seminary in Narbonne in June 1879. In July of that year, aged twenty-seven, he was made curate at Alet-les-Bains, and in June 1882 the new Bishop of Carcassonne, *Monseigneur* Billard, made him priest-in-charge at Le Clat, where he remained for three years.

1885

Bérenger Saunière was appointed *curé* at Rennes-le-Château on 1 June 1885. It could hardly be said to have been a good preferment. The village was almost isolated from the outside world by its remote location and the people were very poor, the 300 inhabitants mostly working on the land.

The church of Ste Marie Madeleine was in bad condition. A report by the architect Girard Cals dated 25 October 1853[1] had concluded 'the building is in a dangerous state, but the danger is only superficial . . . the church is too small for a population of 500 souls. Its plan is irregular and bizarre. We do not recommend repairs or extensions, but to wait until the commune can afford a new church for about 4,500 francs.'

Urgent repairs had to be made by the commune in 1883, after a hurricane smashed two of the nave windows. These were boarded up, and the church was now more or less unusable.

The presbytery where the priest would live was also in a bad state of repair. Saunière had to take lodgings until its refurbishment was completed. He moved in with Guillaume and Alexandrine Dénarnaud, who lived in a house close to the church. They had two children, Barthélémy and Marie, who worked in a hat factory in Esperaza.[2] They also looked after an orphan, Julie.

Almost immediately after his appointment, Bérenger ran into trouble with the commune, who owned the church and employed him (his salary came from a government department). He had strong political views and during the election in October 1885, he read from the pulpit political articles from *La Semaine Religieuse de Carcassonne*,[3] urging his flock to vote anti-republican because the Republican Party was hostile to the church.

Unfortunately for him the republicans won the election. Saunière was reported to the Prefect of the Department and thence to the Minister of Culture who demanded that the Bishop of Carcassonne, *Monseigneur* Billard, remove Saunière and three others from their posts. The bishop was willing only to issue a reprimand, at which news the minister deprived the priests of their salaries. The bishop maintained a salary for Saunière by naming him a supervisor at the seminary at Narbonne. The commune demanded his return; after a year the suspension was lifted and Saunière finally took up his duties in his parish on 1 July 1886.

Meanwhile the problems of the church were pressing. The roof of the sanctuary might collapse at any moment. No funds arrived from the commune. At this point Bérenger's sympathy for the monarchist cause seems to have benefited him. He received a gift of money from the Countess of Chambord, who lived in Narbonne.[4] (The exact amount is not certain; it may have been 1000 or 3000 francs.[5]) She was the widow of the Count of Chambord, the Bourbon claimant to the throne and grandson of Charles X, king of France from 1824 to 1830. The count had died in 1883, while Saunière was at Le Clat.

The countess died in 1886, so Bérenger must have sought this gift during his temporary exile in Narbonne. Maybe this was in some way a reward for his anti-republican sermons. As soon as he returned to his parish, he lent the Parish Church Council 518 francs. Putting the sum in perspective, his initial salary was perhaps 900 francs per annum, so this loan must have been from the countess's gift. Since Saunière was now providing the funds, the commune could not control what he did.

Saunière was a determined man clearly ready to stand up for his beliefs. As a local, he gained the confidence of the population of the parish. He was handsome and broad-shouldered, and spoke the local language, Occitan, well. A number of Saunière's diaries, notebooks, and account books have survived, and they provide an insight into his character.[6] He wrote on the relationship of the priest with the parish and the people: 'The priest should show kindness with reserve and prudence, be popular without being familiar, visit his parishioners all the year, take an interest with discretion, and occupy the little children with prudence. He should dress simply, never go out without a hat, and maintain his dignity.'

Marie Dénarnaud, youngest daughter of the family he lodged with, eventually became his servant, and stayed with him throughout his life. It is interesting to read the principles on which he dealt with her:[7] 'Respect, but not familiarity. Not to permit her to talk about matters of his ministry. What you say to a servant should be able to be said to other women. She must avoid excesses of language, and he must not trust in her age or her piety too easily. She is not to enter the bedroom when he is in bed, except in case of illness.'

The young priest had strict principles, though it is clear that his relationship to Marie became much closer in later years.

1885–91

There are few records of what Bérenger Saunière did in the first two years. In 1887 the repairs were certainly under way and he is known to have ordered windows from Henri Feur of Bordeaux.[8] It is clear that in his earlier posts he had already established contacts with a wide variety of people. The village may have been isolated, but not the priest.

The new altar was ordered the same year from F.D. Monna of Toulouse, and installed on 27 July. This replaced the ancient stone slab which was partly supported by the sculpted pillar now on view in the museum (Pl. 23). The new altar, costing 700 francs, was paid for by a lady of Coursan, Marie Cavailhé, in accordance with a vow she made during a serious illness she suffered when she lived at Rennes.[9] In contrast, the bill for the windows (1,350 francs) was settled in four equal payments and not cleared until 1900.

So far we are on firm ground, but now comes the point where fallible memory and possibly fantasy begin to enter the story.

We have already shown that there are several versions of the discovery of the parchments. One, as recounted by Descadeillas, is that they were found in a cavity in the altar, another, as told by de Sède, is that one of the pillars was hollow. The latter is certainly not true, since there is only a small square hole in one of the pillars and it is clearly a part of a mortise and tenon used when the pillar was part of a larger structure. Another version is that a box containing documents was found during the replacement of the altar.[10]

Claire Captier, daughter of Noël Corbu, prefers an alternative account of the discovery of the documents.[11] It comes from the family of the bell-ringer at the time. The bell-ringer was called Antoine Captier, and his eldest grandson, Joseph, was Claire Captier's father-in-law, from whom she heard the story.

One evening when he came from the bell tower, Antoine saw a bright reflection coming from the capital of an old baluster which the workmen had left in a corner. He discovered a glass phial jammed in a slot in the wood, from which a piece of wood cut to shape to fill the crack had become dislodged. It contained a roll of paper, which he took to the *curé*. This may be a true story.

There is a reference to an obviously conspicuous baluster in the church in the parish register for 1694, when an unnamed lady was interred in the 'Tomb of the Knights which is beside the baluster'. It may have been the one which survives to this day and is displayed in the museum (Pl. 33). The present piece of wood filling the crack is not the original, and looks out of place. Perhaps during the manufacture of the baluster a fault was found in the capital, and a skilful patching job carried out. Someone may have taken the opportunity of leaving a message in a small phial, though it is difficult to see where there is space for its concealment.

Or perhaps someone left a note in the stonework when the old altar was built. Descadeillas thought that there could have been a text relating to the construction of the church. This is certainly possible, and might have led to the circulation of the more romantic versions of the discovery. As we now know, they inspired Plantard and de Chérisey to create the story of Saunière's trip to Paris with the parchments, leading to the supposed decoding and purchase of paintings from the Louvre. In fact at this period Saunière rarely left the Rennes-le-Château/Couiza area, and the furthest there is evidence for his travelling was to Carcassonne.

The fact that Saunière did not keep the document, if it existed, from either the baluster or the altar, confirms not that he was guarding a secret, but that he felt no interest in or responsibility for the history of the church. This was shown by his attitude to the grave of Marie de Nègre d'Ables. His aim was to create a modern and active church as the central feature of the village, and its past did not much concern him.

Another interesting event took place, probably in 1885 or 1886, during the complete reflooring of the church. A stone slab was lifted, and it was discovered that the side facing downwards was decorated with a carving. This is the *Dalle des Chevaliers*, or Knights' Stone, which we described in chapter 9.

According to the Captier family,[12] Saunière sent the workmen away, but not before they had caught a glimpse of shiny objects in the now exposed tomb. When one of the workmen asked what they were, Saunière said that they were 'medals of Lourdes', and were without value.

This is a critical point in the story of Saunière's wealth. Claire Captier and her husband Antoine accepted this story from the evidence of their own family, and the present authors are inclined to accept it too. Historians are tempted to decry tales of buried treasure, and they are usually untrue outside the realms of 'treasure hunting' with metal detectors. But the family evidence makes it at least possible that Saunière did find some valuable item in the tomb, and if he had in fact robbed a tomb, he would have been very reluctant to tell anyone, especially his bishop. The main objection to this theory is that no evidence survives in Saunière's records or elsewhere of the process of converting gold into cash. But what the *curé* found may have been only a small item. Descadeillas was told that Saunière had discovered a pot containing gold pieces, and he suggested that they had been left in the tomb by the priest's eighteenth-century predecessor, Antoine Bigou.

One of the high points of Saunière's ministry at Rennes-le-Château came on 21 June 1891. It was the occasion of the confirmation of twenty-four children. There was a procession around the village, with four men carrying a statue of the Virgin Mary on a richly decorated stretcher. The statue was a replica of 'Our Lady of Lourdes'. It was then set up in the garden on top of the old altar pillar, on which Saunière had had carved the words 'Penitence! Penitence!'

A detailed diary survives from 1890–1.[13] Two of its most-quoted entries occur in September 1891. Saunière recorded: 21 *lettre de Granès, découverte d'un tombeau, le soir pluie.* (Letter from Granès, discovery of a tomb, evening rain.) We do not know which tomb he discovered on this day. Eight days later he wrote: 29 *Vu Curé de Névian – Chez Gélis – Chez Carrière – vu Cros et Secret.* (Saw priest from Névian – Gélis's house – Carrière's house – saw Cros and Secret.) This has given rise to much speculation as to what secret Saunière could be sharing with his acquaintance Ernest Cros the engineer. However, at that time another Cros was the Vicar General and the entry actually records a visit by him to Rennes-le-Château accompanied by his secretary. There is no 'secret' – here as elsewhere in his diaries Saunière uses the word *'secret'* as an abbreviation for *secrétaire*.

At about this time Saunière had constructed – in defiance of the local regulations – a small building close to the cemetery door, which he called his library. It gave him somewhere to keep his books, housed a *reposoir*, or temporary altar, and made it possible for him to avoid constant contact with the Dénarnaud family with whom he was still living. A water tank was incorporated in the base to serve as a reservoir in this hilltop village. Later it also fed various running water features around the church.

Saunière turned the open area in front of the church into a garden, and continued work on the church to a total of 2,661 francs. But in September 1891 he suddenly stopped the work on the church. The money had run out, a sure indication that he was not in possession of unlimited wealth. In the autumn of 1891 he borrowed 500 francs from *Mme* Matte Barthelmy in the village, and there may have been others who lent him money.

Work resumed on 14 October with 'new masons'. Either he had quarrelled with the original team, or he did not have enough money to pay them. The pulpit arrived from the firm of Giscard of Toulouse on 11 November (price 750 francs),[14] and was dedicated eighteen days later. Work continued through the winter.

Saunière's detailed diary stops on 12 April 1892, after detailing expeditions to Les Bals and the Ruisseau de Couleurs (about a kilometre to the south-west of the village) to fetch tufa for his grotto.

1892–7

During 1892 Marie Dénarnaud gave up her job at the hat factory and became Saunière's servant, the job that her mother Alexandrine had previously been doing. Saunière and Marie seem to have become very close. He took her into his confidence and involved her in some obscure activities.

There is evidence that at this period Saunière was often absent for several days at a time.[15] There are multiple copies of pre-signed messages for Marie to send off, explaining, for example, that he had to visit a colleague, and it is likely that he did stay away and hid his absence from colleagues and correspondents. Much has been written about what he might have been doing. Ideas include a secret mistress, fund-raising excursions to wealthy ladies, treasure hunting in caves around the village, and smuggling people across the French/Spanish border. But there is no evidence of any of these things actually happening, and in any case there is no date for the use of the letters.

There are several accounts of Saunière and Marie digging together at night in both the church and in the cemetery. It is possible that these are only descriptions of the extensive work that was going on, inflated over the years by rumour. But it is also possible that the finding of something valuable persuaded the *curé* that a more general search might be profitable. If so, there is no evidence of either success or failure.

Certainly the churchyard was stripped of its earlier graves and tombstones, and the bones of the dead were collected and deposited in the ossuary which Saunière had built for the purpose. On at least two occasions the commune complained to the prefect. We quoted one letter of complaint in chapter 3, here is another written on 10 March 1895: 'We electors protest that the *curé* continues his work and we reinforce our earlier complaint and our desire to be free to maintain the tombs of our ancestors, and that the *curé* should not have the right to make embellishments, or place crosses or crowns, or shift everything or dump it in a corner.'[16]

The objections prevailed, and Saunière was ordered to stop.

The destruction of the churchyard was a very upsetting procedure for the older inhabitants. But Saunière's aim was probably to clear away the untidy remains of centuries of earlier use of the churchyard, and make it available for the well-ordered tombs that fill it today.

In 1894–5 work continued on a large scale. One bill for 917 francs was made out to a cabinetmaker, Mathieu Mestre of Limoux, for carpentry in the library. By this time the *curé*'s early good relations with the villagers had been destroyed by his work in the cemetery, and he was in constant receipt of complaints, most of which he ignored. On 14 July 1895 relations worsened further when there was a fire in a barn in the village which threatened the safety of the houses. The firemen wished to use water from the tank under Saunière's library, but the *curé*, who had the only keys, was away from the village. The firemen forced their way in and Saunière complained to the Gendarmerie. The Municipal Council was not sympathetic and ordered him to vacate the premises.[17]

In 1896–7 the restoration of the church accelerated. In September there is an estimate recorded for 2,400 francs to 'erect a vault . . . prick the old plaster, open up the old windows and get the walls and the vault ready for painting.'[18] This gives an idea of the scale of the work.

In November Saunière signed a contract with Giscard, sculptor and painter of Toulouse, for all the sculptural features of the church interior. Estimates for the work include such phrases as: 'Statues of the saints in terracotta, scenes in relief, people painted in natural colour, costumes of the period, background and countryside, all conforming to the model sent.' The total bill was for 2,500 francs. Saunière paid at the rate of 500 francs a month. In the same year he ordered the figure of the Devil supporting the basin for holy water from the same supplier at a cost of 300 francs.[19] All the work was done well, and the items are still in splendid condition today.

In *L'Or de Rennes*, de Sède wrote that there were hidden messages in the details of the paintings, sculptures and bas-reliefs, and this idea has been taken up by many later writers on Rennes-le-Château. They are of course encouraged in this view by the belief that Saunière himself might have outlined all the designs. However, it is clear from the estimates given that Saunière was sent a catalogue of the range of current fashionable possibilities for each item, and returned them with his preferred model marked. He did not design the church decorations himself.

In 1897 work on the church came to a climax. At this period, whatever his source of funds, Saunière was able to raise the money. There were five new windows, the chancel was enlarged and the church walls were doubled by a brick skin. The cemetery walls were rebuilt and the calvary erected. In addition the presbytery was totally renovated, and Saunière and the Dénarnauds moved in.

At Pentecost everything was ready for the visit of *Monseigneur* Billard, the Bishop of Carcassonne. Both the bishop and Saunière made speeches. Saunière listed his great achievements, but complained that he had been troubled by treacherous advice which had worked against everything he had achieved for the glory of God. Perhaps it is not surprising that such a complex piece of construction had caused problems.

He ended his speech (of which a draft still survives[20]) by explaining where he got the money. 'For all this, *Monseigneur*, I owe a little to my parishioners, much to my economies, and much to the dedication and the generosity of certain souls who are strangers to this parish.'

Up to this point he had spent something like 27,000 francs on the church and the presbytery, and it certainly needed explanation. The bishop seems to have accepted Saunière's account.

In spite of the triumph of his building programme, Saunière's relationship with the villagers was now at a low ebb. He was no longer welcome in their houses and became more and more solitary, relying heavily on Marie for support.

1898–1900

Between 1898 and 1900 there was a break in the building programme. Saunière was receiving bills for earlier work, and always requested time to pay. Although there was little spare money, shipments of rum and coffee continue to arrive, which he ordered directly from companies trading abroad.[21]

Nevertheless, from the end of 1898 the scheme for his domain began to take shape. He purchased almost all of the land needed west of the presbytery, and demolished the existing houses. The new plans obviously required expenditure on a scale that exceeded even that of the church. It is clear that he already knew how he could achieve his dream, and this must have required financial resources that are not recorded in his accounts.

1901–5

These years saw the construction of the *Villa Béthanie* and the *Tour Magdala*, together with the belvedere and the gardens (Pls 26–32). The architect was Tiburce Caminade of Limoux, who had also worked on the church. The Clerk of Works was Elie Bot from Luc-sur-Aude. All the land was owned by Marie, and much of the work was done in her name. This was clearly a legal device to prevent the church or the commune claiming ownership at any time in the future.

The work began in May 1901 and the parish was astounded. The amount and weight of materials coming from the station at Couiza was such that Saunière had to rebuild the winding road up to Rennes-le-Château.

The major structure of the Villa was complete by the middle of 1902. Few of the bills survive for this work as, along with many other documents, they were submitted to the Bishop of Carcassonne at Saunière's trial in 1910, and their whereabouts are not now known. However some bills do survive from 1905:[22] the railings in the park cost 2,500 francs and wallpaper from Paris for the villa cost 403 francs. There are continued financial strains – there was certainly not a large reserve of money available. The carpenter Mestre wrote in October 1905, 'The price I gave you is very competitive. If you can find someone who can do it cheaper, you are welcome.' A letter from the architect says, 'I imagine that present circumstances oblige you to restrain your expenses, but don't sacrifice a job which is going so well.'

1906–7

By this time the *Villa Béthanie* and the *Tour Magdala* were complete, but work continued on the belvedere and the gardens. Many tons of soil were delivered. A bill is recorded from the Clerk of Works for 10,305 francs. It was paid – in stages.

Over the preceding years, relations between Saunière and his own family had became strained. To them he appeared to have unlimited resources, yet he refused to take any responsibility at all for looking after his mother. After the death of his brother Alfred in September 1905, Saunière refused to have anything more to do with his family.

In September 1906 Saunière's sister Mathilde and her husband took the *curé* to court in Couiza to compel him to take responsibility for his mother for three months, or alternatively contribute three francs a day for that period. A draft of the reply in Marie's hand[23] says that Saunière could not afford such a sum. It is difficult to see how this can be reconciled with the huge amounts being expended on the domain, except in terms of the bitterness that had grown between Saunière and his family. He was however compelled to pay by the court.

Saunière made a will that year, leaving all his personal possessions, valued at 4,000 francs, to Marie. He owned none of the land or the buildings, which had been bought in Marie's name. The text of his will leaves no doubt about his feelings for his family: 'In view of the care given to me for many years by Marie, my cook, and in view of the lack of confidence I have in my relations whose conduct has been reprehensible on the death of my brother Alfred, I leave everything I have to Marie . . .'[24]

Marie's will stipulated that after they were both dead, the domain was to be left to the Bishop of Carcassonne. Presumably this was to ensure that Saunière's family did not get the opportunity to claim the estate in any circumstances.

1907–8

The multi-coloured glass in the villa, costing 950 francs, marked the end of construction work. Furnishings for the villa and the *tour* were bought from Maison Noubel at Carcassonne. The total cost on 20 December 1911 was 12,632 francs. The bill appears to have been settled in stages over several years. Yet though the *Villa Béthanie* was finished, Saunière and Marie continued to live in the presbytery (Pl. 39), for which they had to negotiate a new five-year lease with the commune.

The gardens were developed, and became a green oasis, watered from cisterns in the basement of the belvedere (Pl. 29). Saunière began to collect and trade in postcards and stamps on a large scale. He demanded help from all his many correspondents, and even sent them empty grocery boxes in which to send him their contributions. In 1908 he filled his new library in the *Tour Magdala* with books and journals. He hired a librarian, Henri Barret from Castelnaudry, for three months to sort things out. This cost at least 500 francs.

That year saw the culmination of Saunière's strange career. The villa was used for entertaining. Upper-class visitors were wined and dined on a lavish scale. Many receipts survive to give an indication of the luxurious food and drink provided.[25] There are many stories of famous people Saunière invited to Rennes-le-Château, but no confirmation that any of these people actually came.

By this time Saunière was in conflict with his bishop – a conflict which lasted to his death in 1917. *Monseigneur* Billard had retired in 1902, and the new bishop was *Monseigneur* Paul-Felix Beuvain de Beauséjour. Bishop Beauséjour was far less tolerant of the *curé*'s activities then his predecessor, and it has been suggested that the reason may be, in part at least, that Bishop Billard had similar monarchist leanings to Saunière, while Beauséjour was inclinded to republicanism.[26] The *curé*'s building works and his extravagant lifestyle were the subject of much gossip and comments among the clergy. Bishop Beauséjour asked Saunière for an explanation of his resources. Saunière replied vaguely. He told the Bishop that the *Villa Béthanie* was built as a House of Retreat for elderly priests, a purpose it certainly never served. Gifts of money, and there must have been many, had been solicited in the name of the Church. In the bishop's eyes the domain was church property, and he should control its use. This was of course totally in conflict with Saunière's ideas.

The bishop set about discovering exactly what was going on at Rennes with the aim of taking possession of the domain in the name of the Church. He knew that Saunière was saying Masses for various people outside the parish, and suspected that the *curé*'s income was in part derived from trafficking in Masses – charging for saying a Mass and then not actually doing it – a practice obviously totally contrary to Church rules.

1909

Early in 1909 the bishop named Saunière as priest-in-charge of Coustouge (about 40 km north-east of Rennes) to take up his appointment from 21 January. The *curé* of Esperaza was to come to Rennes. At Saunière's request the commune approached the bishop to object, but without success. It is interesting to note that the commune, although dissatisfied with Saunière's behaviour, nevertheless closed ranks with him when threatened by outside interference.

Saunière was determined not to leave Rennes-le-Château, and rather than be transferred to another parish, he resigned his post on 28 January. A draft of his letter of resignation survives.[27] In March he was interviewed by the bishop, who obtained no real clarification of what had been going on but made him promise not to solicit masses from outside the parish.

In May Saunière's mother died and his sister Mathilde demanded 30 francs towards the funeral expenses. In July *Abbé* Marty arrived to take over the parish. Saunière wished him well but Marty was not well received by the villagers, who preferred to attend mass in the little chapel which Saunière set up in the *Villa Béthanie*. The villagers now took Saunière's side against authority, perhaps to some extent revelling in his extraordinary reputation, and the fame it had brought to their village. The mayor refused the key of the church to Marty. Saunière even complained that *Abbé* Marty was neglecting his new parish!

During this time the bishop was in fact preparing a case against Saunière for the ecclesiastical court in Carcassonne. The main basis for this was the charge that Saunière was continuing to solicit payments by post for Masses which he could not possibly carry out.

1910

Constant correspondence from the bishop and the Vicar General was skilfully deflected by Saunière. He denied trafficking in Masses, and said his funds were essentially gifts, and that the givers wished to remain anonymous.

He was summoned to appear before the *Promoteur de l'Officialité* (ecclesiastical court) on 16 July. He pleaded ill health and the hearing was postponed to 23 July. Once again he did not appear, and in his absence he was found guilty of trafficking in the Mass and disobeying his bishop. He was sentenced to suspension for one month and ordered to pay back the fees for Masses he had not said. This was not done, as no one knew how much money was involved.

Saunière appealed against the judgement, and at the same time put up the domain for sale. He seems to have felt that his cause was lost. The new hearing was to be on 23 August, then adjourned to 15 October.

Saunière's advocate was *Abbé* Huguet, *curé* of Espiens, who entered into a long and complex correspondence with him. Saunière gave Huguet a detailed memoire[28], in which he refuted the accusation of making money from unsaid masses in the following words: "I answer that one would be mad to have such an idea. Where would I have been able to find from masses the 140 or 150 thousand francs to fund the cost of all these works, and this amount does not of course include the excavation and labouring work that I have done myself. Yes, one would be nuts to assert that." In the memoire he gives a list of his sources of money, beginning with his savings of 15,000 francs from his own income over 30 years. There were donations from various sources, the total coming to 71,600 francs. Saunière adds "It is pointless to ask me the names of other persons who have given me money as I don't have the authority to reveal their names."

But these were by no means the final figures submitted to the authorities, either for expenditure or income. His later list of sources of revenue totalled 193,150 francs. Among the many items, he has listed an anonymous gift from '*Monsieur de C*' of 20,000 francs and 30,000 francs obtained in gifts via his brother Alfred.

Early drafts of this document[29] show how he juggled the sums to inflate the total. The Countess of Chambord's gift appears originally as 1,000 francs, and later as 3,000 francs. The first draft has receipts for accommodation for two working hatters for twenty years, total 40,000 francs. Later this becomes providing lodging for a family (the Dénarnauds) at a rent of 300 francs a month, total 52,000 francs.

It is clear that much of the document is made up to show sufficient income to cover his expenditure. Is this because Saunière has lost all the accounts and is in a muddle, or is it because he has to conceal the real source of the money? The latter seems more likely in view of the care he is seen to have taken over so much of his record keeping.

Saunière, although in Carcassonne, did not attend the trial. He was formally accused of trafficking in Masses, exaggerated expenses, and disobedience to the bishop. He was found guilty of the first and third charges, and sentenced to go into retreat for ten days for spiritual exercises at the monastery of Prouilles. Saunière carried out the sentence in April 1911.

The sentence was a light one, and this was explained by the text, published on 5 November 1910: 'It is not sufficiently established that Saunière retained in his possession payment for Masses, and the judicial doubt must benefit the accused.' Proof was not possible because the documents were not available to the tribunal, who said: 'It is inadmissible that a *curé* who has solicited so many payments for Masses did not take care to keep the slightest record.'[30] Saunière did in fact keep records, and he took care to ensure that they were not available. Saunière explained in his defence that he burnt the notebooks when they were full.

Even as late as December 1910 there was an advertisement in Issue 13 of *Veillées des Chaumières* from Saunière offering to say Masses for 1 franc. Following this the bishop had a notice inserted in *La Semaine Religieuse* and other journals that Saunière was not authorized to accept further payment for Masses.

Letters confirm that he was still receiving payment for Masses as late as 1915 and 1916, though by that time there was some excuse in view of the many priests who were away in the First World War, and the large number of deaths in the fighting.

In his memoir addressed to his advocate, *Abbé* Huguet, Saunière claimed he had distributed the Masses he could not say to other priests, but when asked for proof, asserted that they were all dead.

The second charge alleging that Saunière had incurred unjustified expenses was cleverly referred by Huguet to the Sacred Congregation of the Council in Rome, where he hoped he had enough influence to secure an acquittal.

In spite of the problems of 1910 Saunière continued to live well, as receipts prove – for wine, liqueurs, rum, crockery, vases, upholstery, and the latest fashionable clothes from Paris for Marie. Saunière even ordered a bust of himself from Monna of Toulouse for 1,600 francs. But during this period there is some correspondence detailing problems with payment of the bills for entertainment.

1911

Investigations by an Inquiry chaired by the Vicar General in Carcassonne continued for the whole of 1911. Documents and proof were demanded. Saunière's replies made nothing clearer. Saunière did his ten days in retreat, and managed to avoid a meeting with the bishop. On 14 July Saunière presented his final summary of accounts for the whole of his stay at Rennes, listing his expenses at 193,000 francs, a sum considerably larger than the one in his memoire of some months earlier. (We gave the summary of his statement of expenditure in chapter 3.) His declared income, totalling 193,150 francs, balances this sum almost exactly – a surprising outcome.

Saunière was summoned to appear before the tribunal in Carcassonne again on 21 November 1911. The hearing was postponed to 5 December, and once more he did not turn up. For the second time he was condemned for defiance of his bishop and squandering and misapplication of funds, and he was sentenced to be suspended from office for three months. This suspension was to continue until he did what was requested, i.e. give a full account of his expenditure and income. This shocked Saunière, and from this time his health became a cause for concern, and financial difficulties began to escalate. The costs of the trial itself were enormous, although Huguet seems to have charged no fee, only expenses.

Saunière tried to raise loans from banks, but could not succeed as the property was not in his name. He was not destitute however, though the trial forced him to rein in his expenditure. Even in 1912 he was proposing to build a little kiosk at a cost of 2,500 francs.

Huguet obtained the return of the dossier, and insisted that the case be referred to Rome. He drew up a Certificate of Poverty for Saunière, which would have had the effect of a Legal Aid Certificate. But this required the approval of the bishop, which was not forthcoming.

The trial in Rome began late in 1912, and because of its endless complexity Saunière was to die before its completion.

The villagers were once more hostile – *Abbé* Marty had gone, Saunière was suspended and they had no priest to say Mass. Saunière took refuge in his stamp and postcard collection.

1913

According to Claire Captier the well-known photographic portraits of Saunière (Pl. 6) date from this year. They were done by A. Vaugon, a photographer from Montmartre in Paris. It seems unlikely that Saunière would have travelled to the capital for such a purpose, though he could have been photographed by the Paris photographer in a provincial centre. However, it is not entirely certain that the photographs are of Bérenger. It has been suggested that they are of his brother Alfred.[31] Alfred died in 1905, so if this is the case they cannot have been taken in 1913.

In spite of all his difficulties Saunière was still spending money. He ordered wine at a cost of several hundred francs. Clothes were ordered from Paris for Marie, and work in the domain suggests that he had abandoned the idea of selling.

1914–17

The final years saw Saunière increasingly ill, confined to bed for weeks at a time. His heart troubled him frequently. He made a pilgrimage to Lourdes in 1916. Visitors now became rare. Once more the bishop tried to arrange a meeting, but it did not happen. Being suspended, Saunière could not say Mass or accept fees for doing so. But the fees were still arriving in quantity, though some were intercepted by the dean of Couiza, who was now in charge of the parish. Saunière asked his correspondents to put his personal name on the letters[32] and made journeys by carriage to Couiza to collect the post himself.

Although his health seemed to improve towards the end of 1916, in January of 1917 Bérenger Saunière suffered a severe cardiac attack, and died the same month on the 22nd. The *Abbé* Rivière, *curé* of Esperaza, administered the last rites. Saunière was laid out in a room on the first floor of the *Villa Béthanie*.

In spite of all that had gone before, the villagers were shocked by the death of their famous priest, and flocked to the house to pay their respects and to sympathize with

Marie. On 24 January after a service in his church, Saunière was laid to rest in his tomb in the churchyard (Pl. 37).

Post-1917

After Saunière's death, Marie remained in possession of the whole of the domain. Her later years were distinguished only by poverty and hardship. The domain fell into partial ruin, and much of Saunière's library and other possessions were lost, stolen or fell into decay. There was no sign of Marie having access to hidden wealth of any sort. In 1946 she sold the whole estate to Noël Corbu, who allowed her to live there rent-free till her death in 1953 at the age of eighty-five. She was buried in the same tomb as Saunière and is commemorated in the churchyard by a small tablet (Pl. 38).

At her death Marie Dénarnaud was penniless. Although she must have known all of Saunière's secrets, she remained the faithful servant to the end and never revealed them to anyone. Three years after her death, Corbu gave the interview to the reporter from *La Dépêche du Midi* and thus began the affair of Rennes-le-Château.

Saunière's Sources of Money

So where did Saunière's wealth come from? Not, it seems, from the discovery of a large cache of treasure he could dip into over the years. While we cannot rule out the fraudulent retention of a small valuable find from the tomb under the church, or even his finding some more valuables in his mysterious nightly churchyard activities with Marie, there is no evidence of gold or antique objects being converted into cash and Marie was left in poverty at her death. Furthermore, it seems that his income was variable; there were some periods when money was readily available, others when it was in short supply. Most bills were paid in instalments, and there are letters from tradesmen demanding their money.

In his speech in the presence of Bishop Billard in 1897, Saunière said he had practised economies, and received gifts from both his parishioners and others who lived outside the parish. Saunière had certainly contributed some money from his own limited resources, and money had been contributed by his parishioners. It is very difficult to assess how much came in the way of donations from other people. He was always very careful to avoid mentioning names, as we have noted in chapter 3.

Claire and Antoine Captier have preserved an interesting letter from an unnamed close friend:

You have got some money, it's nobody's business to probe the secret you are keeping; you have spent it as you pleased, that concerns only you. As no one is asking for it back, no one accusing you of theft or fraud, and as your conduct in this matter has been blameless, no one has the right to incriminate you, especially a third party like the bishop.

If someone has given you money under a pledge of secrecy, you have to keep the secret and no one can release you from it except the one person who gave it to you and even then you have to see if the disclosure that you may have been authorized to make would not lead to your moral detriment, and in that case you should still remain silent.[33]

Although at first sight this letter might be taken to refer to a secret treasure, it is clear on careful reading that the writer is referring to money that has been given to Saunière to further his building projects under promise of secrecy. This is quite understandable. Although the Countess of Chambord allowed her name to be known, other gifts from wealthy individuals, charmed perhaps by the entertainment offered in the *Villa Béthanie*, had to be kept secret. Saunière's correspondent sympathizes with his problem and agrees that he cannot reveal details to the bishop in open court.

There remains the trafficking in Masses of which Saunière was accused at his trial. There is plenty of evidence for this. Claire and Antoine Captier contend that Saunière accepted money by post for far more masses than he could possibly carry out or was legally allowed to do by the church. They have in their possession at least two notebooks containing long lists of applications for Masses,[34] and he was soliciting Masses from all areas. He contacted colleagues, other congregations, hospices, boarding schools, hospitals, orphanages and lunatic asylums. Masses were sometimes ordered in bulk, as in a letter from the Sisters of Nevers at St Etienne 'I enclose the sum of 250 francs to cover 250 Masses at 1 franc each . . .'.[35] In 1892 he received 904 francs, and this represented about three Masses a day, the most a priest was allowed to perform. In 1897 he received 5,500 francs, about twelve times his salary.

The author Jean-Jacques Bedu[36] provides a penetrating analysis of the notebooks that survive for January 1896. This shows that Saunière was receiving money for between eight and fifty-five Masses a day, leading to an illegal income of 970 francs in January alone. On this scale it becomes clear that the major part of the *curé's* income was from the trafficking in Masses, and that the sums involved were indeed enough to account for much of his building programme.

A priest was allowed to say three Masses for the dead daily except on Sundays, when only one was allowed. To say fifty-five Masses in a day would be ridiculous. Of course Saunière was not saying them at all, but using the system in an entirely illegal way to fund his expenditure on building works. He made the trafficking in Masses a vast industry at which he became a master. Jean-Jacques Bedu estimates convincingly that in the period for which some record survives, Saunière collected about 90,000 francs, and during the whole of his ministry received as much as 146,000 francs.[37] This, with gifts, his salary and other income, is more than enough to cover the overall expenditure of 193,000 francs claimed at his trial.

Saunière advertised extensively that he was available to say Masses that other priests were unable to say because they had requests beyond their daily allowance. There is a list of the towns in which he was advertising.[38] Most were in France, but some were in Belgium, the Rhineland, Switzerland and north Italy. At one point Bishop Beauséjour had notices placed in several journals to the effect that Saunière was not authorized to solicit Masses directly in this way. Normally such arrangements for passing Masses from one priest to another (and of course the payment for them) was carried out by the Bishop's Secretariat.

Most of the requests for Masses were received from priests, religious organizations and particularly nunneries, where the nuns themselves were not allowed to say Mass. Although the sums involved in payments for a Mass were small (typically 1 or 2 francs), when the number of requests ran into thousands then the income was considerable. Inevitably, it was impossible for Saunière to declare this source of income to the bishop, as it was completely illegal. It is clear that the bishop knew only too well what Saunière was doing, but proving it in court was another matter. Saunière declared that, although he kept a record of Masses, he destroyed them at the end of every year, and so could not produce them. A few of those records whose existence he denied still survive today.[39]

Among the various theories about the source of Saunière's wealth, there is one more that has yet to be mentioned – that Saunière received large sums of money from *Abbé* Henri Boudet, *curé* of Rennes-les-Bains. The origin of this suggestion seems to be none other than Pierre Plantard, who wrote in 1978[40] that Boudet had financed Saunière, via his housekeeper Marie, to the extent of 3,679,431 francs in the period 1887–91 and 837,260 francs from 1894–1903. There is no evidence for Boudet's largesse, except the single statement of Pierre Plantard. For the reasons set out in Appendix H, we believe it to be yet another of his many deliberate attempts to confuse and mislead.

Summary

When he arrived in Rennes-le-Château, Bérenger Saunière was energetic, devoted to his faith, and not afraid to speak his mind in public, even on sensitive political matters. He was determined to rekindle the faith of his parishioners and bring them back into the church. He knew that the provision of a building which would inspire worship was essential to his aims. He set about raising the money needed, and he was outstandingly successful in creating a beautiful church, which still stands today.

Saunière raised money by borrowing and by encouraging gifts. Some of the donors were known, but others remained secret. He was able to use his charming personality to bring in gifts, particularly from wealthy women. In some ways he was ruthless in his aims. Historical features in the church and churchyard were destroyed in his drive towards a modern place of worship. He upset his parishioners by his clearance of the churchyard, but swept aside all opposition.

The exciting years of rebuilding the church undermined Saunière's character. He began to enjoy wealth for wealth's sake, and started his programme of building a luxurious domain which tended to the glory of Bérenger Saunière rather than God. There was a limit to the money he could obtain by gift, and he succumbed to the temptation of dishonest and illegal methods. In order to complete his works, he began systematic abuse of the system of saying Masses for the dead, and did so on an epic scale. He spent large sums on the pleasures of high living, entertaining lavishly in the *Villa Béthanie*, which was supposed to be a rest home for retired priests.

His relations with his superiors deteriorated rapidly and he was called to account before the ecclesiastical court. His bishop demanded an explanation of his large income but he was unable to provide one. Many of the gifts he received were donated in confidence. He may have found and kept something valuable in his clearance of the church and churchyard, which amounted to tomb robbing. He made many thousands of francs by illegally selling Masses which he did not carry out. His final years were spent in a desperate struggle to maintain his lifestyle and to avoid final condemnation by the church. He died in poverty before the courts had finished their work.

15

History and Pseudo-history

The Presentation of History

It is not surprising that the story of Rennes-le-Château has generated so much interest in the forty years or so since the first news of the *curé*'s treasure was made known. Nor is it surprising that books are still being published which either elaborate on the basic tale or at least refer to it, often as though it was established fact.[1] Everybody likes a mystery and the story has generally been presented in such a way that there is mystery in plenty. Hidden treasure also fascinates, especially if it is hinted that some remains to be discovered. Marie Dénarnaud was supposed to have held the secret, promising great wealth to Noël Corbu, but she died without revealing it.

If there was a treasure maybe it could still be found. Some people thought so. There were clues in abundance. In *L'Or de Rennes* Gérard de Sède described the interior of the church in such a way as to indicate that it was full of mysterious 'clues', which could lead to the hidden fortune if they could only be interpreted. He also showed pictures of the two parchments, and said that they contain hidden codes, by implication relating to the treasure. When, through the investigations of Henry Lincoln, the solutions to the codes were published, there were even more clues to be followed up. The story is almost irresistible. It would appeal to anyone with a liking for solving problems.

Thousands took up the challenge and the ground in the village was turned over to such an extent that the local authorities were obliged to put up the famous notice *LES FOUILLES SONT INTERDITES*. Rennes-le-Château was treated as though it was a genuine riddle waiting to be solved, like the one invented by Kit Williams in his famous book *Masquerade*.[2]

As well as a treasure hunt we have a historical mystery, with more than a suspicion of intrigue. There is a *curé* who seems to have had some shady dealings. As presented in various versions of the story, Saunière's source of money is a mystery. We are led to wonder if he really did discover a treasure which he concealed from his bishop, or if his source of wealth was from illegal activities such as selling Masses or worse. Moreover there is a touch of spice in the suggestion that he may have had close relations with a famous opera singer. There are hints of even darker mysteries; we are told that on his deathbed his confession was so shocking that the priest who heard it never smiled again. There is conspiracy in the background – suppression of information by the Church of Rome, and involvement of the secret services of some European powers.

Even this is not all there is to the story. Rennes-le-Château itself is a very unusual place. The nearby mountains are said to be in such locations as to represent the occultists' pentagon and since this would have been noticed in ancient times (so various authors tell us), the site would have had special historical significance. The geometry has led some researchers down amazing paths, to conclude either that Mary Magdalene came with Christ's children to found a royal line, descendants of which are living to the present day; or that Christ's body was buried near Rennes-le-Château, or that Rennes-le-Château was founded by people from the lost continent of Atlantis.

This is a dramatic story and as entertainment could hardly be bettered, but we have shown in this book that there are no grounds for taking it seriously. We have examined the affair of Rennes-le-Château and Bérenger Saunière in detail from the first accounts as they appeared in the press to books written three decades later, by which time the story had acquired its elaboration and ramifications of considerable complexity. We have compared the published accounts that have appeared in these books with the historical facts on which these accounts are based, checking wherever possible with the original documents in archives. We have cross-checked for consistency and contradiction between the different accounts, and also looked at the evidence remaining on the ground. The overall conclusion leaves no room for doubt. While some of the basic facts are incontrovertible, for example that Saunière found a source of money and spent it on elaborate building projects, we have also found that there is little firm evidence to support the more sensational aspects of the stories. It seems that almost everything that has appeared in print and on the screen has been the result of combining a few facts that can be substantiated, some apparent facts that have been deliberately falsified and a very large amount of speculation.

Yet there is no doubt that the story of Rennes-le-Château has been taken as serious history by many people – the large number of web sites devoted to it testifies to that. It is natural to ask why this should be so. The first (and most influential) books that were written on the subject, by de Sède in French and Lincoln and co-authors in English, have an air of authority. They are clearly not novels, and contain a large amount of material which is true. The village of Rennes-le-Château is real enough. Saunière was *curé* of the church, built the villa and the tower, which are there for all to see. Furthermore these books look like weighty works of history; they include photographs, diagrams, and a considerable amount of text on some little-known episodes in French history. In the honourable tradition of all academic investigations there are references to other publications, and some of those referenced are obscure indeed. They could only have been unearthed by devoted study. They have all the outward appearances of serious historical research, presented in a convincing yet semi-popular style.

But this is not history. At the end of the BBC's *Timewatch* programme on Rennes-le-Château, from which we have already taken extracts, Robert McCrum, Literary Editor of the *Observer*, expressed his concern at the presentation of historical subjects without the strict application of historical evidence and historical method:[3] '. . . if you look around the bookshelves there is a lot of it published, and people mistake this kind of history for the real thing. These kind of books do appeal to an enormous audience who believe them to be history, though actually they aren't history, they are a kind of parody of history. Alas, one has to say that this is the direction history is going today.'

What McCrum is complaining about can be called pseudo-history. In this chapter we shall look at the characteristics of pseudo-history and consider how it differs from history. Perhaps the most obvious of the differences is that it is often presented in a sensational manner. Admittedly much academic history (and archaeology) does not make very exciting reading and has little appeal to the general public. It is, of course, a worthy aim to make the results of historical research widely available and no one would deplore the presentation of history in an easily accessible form, whether in books or on the screen. Historical and scientific subjects – for our comments apply with equal force to the presentation of science – frequently appear on television. Some of the programmes (especially on wildlife) are undoubtedly excellent, but increasingly television programmes fall into the trap of seeking out the sensational at the expense of significant knowledge.

Two examples will illustrate the point. We may cite a programme about the Roman city of Pompeii, which was destroyed by the eruption of Vesuvius in AD 79. The producers concentrated on the pyroclastic flow and the horrible deaths of those trapped in their houses. Yet the main importance of Pompeii lies in the extraordinary preservation of the life of a great Roman city frozen at an instant in time. Alas, the reporting of the lives of ordinary people, their homes and their workplaces, their works of art, their clothes, their furniture, their recreations, the election that was in progress when the calamity struck – these will not attract the headlines and are rarely thought worthy of a programme.

For the second example we take the recent and much promoted series on the life of Christ, *Son of God*, presented by Jeremy Bowen. One could argue that the course of western European civilization has probably been determined more by Jesus Christ than any other individual and therefore his life merits serious historical study on television. But this programme was weird in the extreme. An attempt was made to reconstruct the seating plan at the Last Supper, and even the menu. There is no evidence for this that would be acceptable to a historian. The programme tried to explain the resurrection by claiming that Jesus was rendered unconscious by a herbal anaesthetic administered on a sponge by a Roman soldier. The final absurdity was to reconstruct the face of Jesus from a skull which had no proven connection with him at all.

Dramatic presentation of history is not solely a modern activity. Medieval writers did it. On a foundation of a few half-remembered facts, they wove elaborate stories, and some of the myths that have emerged, for example those about Robin Hood and King Arthur, are now so familiar that they are part of our collective culture.

Arthur (or Artorius) was probably the real name of a local leader who came to power somewhere in south-west Britain after the end of Roman rule. But all the stories of the Knights of the Round Table reflect the condition of society closer to the thirteenth century than the fifth. The kernel of historical truth is buried under a mountain of fantasy, which as time passes grows ever larger in the process of telling and retelling the story.

A story can be influential without being true. The Arthurian myth has considerable power and it provided substantial assistance in obtaining funding for the excavations at South Cadbury Castle in Somerset in the 1960s. The director, Professor Leslie Alcock, was not averse to encouraging the *Observer* newspaper to dwell on the possibility of uncovering dramatic evidence about the real King Arthur, in return for substantial funding. Ironically the dig actually revealed the remains of a large hall belonging to an important post-Roman local leader who was still importing wine from the Mediterranean. Whether or not his name was Arthur is another matter. The name Arthur attracts the tourists, and sites associated with the legend, such as Tintagel in Cornwall, benefit from the interest.

We could perhaps regard the Arthurian myth as simply the result of medieval storytelling that gained acceptance by constant repetition. Pseudo-history, which has given rise to some modern myths, is somewhat different, in that commonly it is presented in such a way as to try to convince the reader that the author's interpretation of events is supported by evidence. (Of course, unless the reader happens to be well informed about the particular period it is almost impossible to judge whether the author's conclusions are valid or not.)

Apart from Rennes-le-Château, many historical episodes have given rise to contemporary myths. From remote periods to modern times there are plenty of subjects: Atlantis; ancient Egypt; the Knights Templar; Jack the Ripper; the fates of Martin Bormann, Rudolf Hess, President Kennedy and Diana, Princess of Wales; all have been worked and reworked with ever more bizarre results. Wherever there is scope for uncertainty, there is an opening for a pseudo-historian.

Martin Kemp, Professor of Art History, Oxford University, summarized the situation as follows in the *Timewatch* programme :

There are certain historical problems, of which the Turin Shroud is one, in which there is a fantastic fascination with the topic, but a historical vacuum, a lack of solid evidence, and where there is a vacuum – nature abhors a vacuum and historical speculation abhors a vacuum – it all floods in. But what you end up with is almost nothing tangible or solid. You start from a hypothesis, and that is then deemed to be demonstrated more or less by stating the speculation. You then put another speculation on top of that, and you end up with this great tower of hypotheses and speculations and if you say 'where are the rocks underneath it?' they're not there. It's like a house on sand – it washes away as soon as you ask hard questions of it.

The Turin Shroud, which Kemp refers to, is an example of a recent historical myth. This is supposed to have been the cloth used to wrap the body of Christ after the crucifixion, and the image that appears on it has been claimed to be staining caused by contact with the corpse. The belief has long been widely held, yet a moment's consideration will show that the cloth could not have come by its discoloration in this manner, for if it had, the stains would not look like the picture of a face. This is because the cloth would have been wound around the head, and upon unwrapping, the pattern on the cloth would be distorted. The face looks like an image caused by painting or dyeing,[4] and is reminiscent of the medieval style, quite unlike first-century portraits. The shroud has the appearance of a processional banner, which would have been folded in the middle and hung from a horizontal bar at the top of a pole, so that from one side the front of the figure could be seen, and from the other the rear.

After a long period of persuasion the authorities permitted radio-carbon dating on a fragment of the Turin Shroud. It was shown to have been made in the thirteenth century, rather than the first century AD. While scientists and historians were no doubt relieved at the result, it was not long before the appearance of claims that a conspiracy among the researchers had led to these results. The myth had its own momentum and those who wanted to believe in it were not easily dissuaded by contrary facts.

The examples we have given above, together with Martin Kemp's comments, give us a guide to some of the characteristics that distinguish pseudo-history from history. They are: a sensational presentation; the revelation of a mystery; lack of solid evidence; assumptions coming to be taken as facts; and repetition giving an appearance of validity.

This list is not comprehensive. We could add for example: citing evidence without giving the source; presentation of evidence in a misleading way; coincidences taken as evidence; selective use of evidence; disregard of conflicting evidence; failure to explore the consequences of derived conclusions; conflict with accepted chronology; and conflict with accepted history (or archaeology). All of these factors can be found in the literature of Rennes-le-Château (though not all necessarily in any one book).

In much writing of this genre there is another aspect, the suggestion that the reason why the author's revelations have not been made public before is that the evidence has been deliberately suppressed by some powerful organization, such as the Church of Rome or the CIA. This too is evident in works about Rennes-le-Château.

Although in earlier chapters of this book we have attempted to show instances where events and actions are assumed to have taken place on evidence without sufficient regard for historical rigour, here we recall a few examples and relate them specifically to points in the above list.

Lack of Solid Evidence

As we have shown, very few facts in the story of Rennes-le-Château are supported by any firm evidence. One striking example is the supposed purchase of the three pictures by Saunière during his alleged visit to Paris (for which there is also no evidence) after the discovery of the parchments.

There is a well-known axiom in archaeology: 'absence of evidence is not evidence of absence' and one must be careful to keep this in mind. Thus, in spite of the facts that there is no record of Saunière's ever having purchased the paintings, there are no copies of these paintings today at Rennes-le-Château, there is no record, either written or verbal, of their ever having been at Rennes-le-Château, and no mention of them has ever been found in any of Saunière's, the village's or the church's papers, we still cannot be absolutely certain that Saunière did not in fact purchase copies.

But if we think of the balance of probability, it is barely conceivable that he would have been able to bring objects as large and noteworthy as copies of the old masters back to his village, display them, then somehow get rid of them without any record of these occurrences surviving.

The crucial point however is that the paintings play a significant part in the story, and those who claim their existence should prove it; the onus is not on the critics to disprove.

Citing Evidence without Giving the Source

The cautious reader of *L'Or de Rennes* is put on his guard in the very first chapter, when de Sède, writing more than sixty years after the event, quotes word for word a conversation between Saunière and the town mayor on what should be done with the recently discovered parchments.[5] This is clearly an important conversation, which, if it could be verified, would go a long way towards confirming that parchments were discovered at the time. However, de Sède gives no indication as to how he came to know what was said between the two men.

On the following page is another verbatim conversation, the private discussion between Saunière and the Bishop of Carcassonne, introduced with the words 'Here is the dialogue between the two men, as it was reported to us'.[6] This is an even more important passage, because the bishop is allegedly instructing Saunière to take the parchments to

184

Paris for examination, and even offering to pay his fare. If this conversation were substantiated, it would give considerable credibility to the whole affair. But who could have reported the conversation to de Sède? Only someone who was close to either Saunière or the bishop in the 1890s. In the absence of a written record of their meeting, the passage of time ensures that de Sède could have learned it only second or third hand. If ever a passage of text required a reference to establish its authenticity, this is it. Alas, no source is given, and we draw the conclusion that this passage is simply author's licence, put in to make the text more readable. By including this passage without substantiation, de Sède weakens the credibility of his whole account.

De Sède quotes another important conversation, between Saunière and Ernest Cros, when the latter challenges the *curé* about defacing the gravestones. The significant point here is that this is the only evidence for the fact that Saunière obliterated the inscriptions. In the letters we have quoted in chapters 3 and 14, the villagers complain that the *curé* uprooted the stones and dumped them in a corner, not that he defaced them. Once again we are not told how it was that de Sède knew what Saunière and Cros said to each other.

Presentation of Evidence in a Misleading Way

De Sède leads the reader to believe that the defacement of the stone on the tomb of Marie de Nègre took place in or before 1895, by saying that in this year the local inhabitants objected to what he was doing in the churchyard. He then tells us that the inscription on the stone had been recorded by members of the Aude Society of Scientific Studies, thus rendering Saunière's obliterations ineffective, implying that the visit took place before 1895. Although he references the Society's journal, he does not give the date of publication.[7] On checking the reference (which admittedly the casual reader would not be likely to do) we discover that the actual day on which the members saw the stone was 25 June 1905, when they found it lying in the graveyard.

Nothing that was written was actually incorrect, but the readers have been misled. De Sède wanted to create the impression that Saunière had to destroy vital evidence quickly, because the stone was somehow important to the decryption of the ciphers. The reality was that Saunière simply pushed the stone out of the way, having no real interest in it. Once one realizes this, an important piece of the Saunière myth disappears.

Coincidences Taken as Evidence

In *The Tomb of God* by Andrews and Schellenberger there are several examples of the use of coincidences (or near coincidences) taken to support their thesis. Mostly they involve the authors' geometrical interpretation and as such are lengthy to describe, so we shall give only one example.

As we have indicated in chapter 14, these authors concluded that the letters DCLXXXI in Manuscript 1 (which we have argued arises simply because of the need to use up the awkward Xs) indicates a spot height of 681 metres.[8] Even if the message were genuine, there is no reason to assume that this is what 681 means.

Andrews and Schellenberger find a place of this elevation on the modern IGN map, the Col de l'Espinas. A line from the cross by the railway line north of Alet to the Col has a bearing of 105°, i.e. it cuts the Paris Meridian at 75°. The cross is on a stone inscribed with the words 'RESURREXIT 1801–1876' (presumably indicating it was set up originally in 1801 and was re-erected in 1876 after the construction of the railway).

To Andrews and Schellenberger this is confirmation of their interpretation of 681, because 1876 - 1801 = 75, the angle of the line crossing the meridian. Thus several totally unrelated facts are adduced as proof of their deductions because two numbers (which had to be manipulated anyway) happen to be the same.

Failure to Explore the Consequences of Derived Conclusions

The above example is particularly interesting because it illustrates another of the characteristics of the genre. Let us suppose Andrews and Schellenberger had been right in their deductions and the numbers on the cross had been deliberately put there as a clue to lead future investigators to the location of the tomb of Christ. Then whoever had the cross erected and inscribed must have been party to the great secret which they claim to have uncovered. Here is an important lead which the authors did not follow up. They ought to have investigated who erected the cross and when, and then how that person came by the secret knowledge which was handed down from earlier times. Instead they passed on to other topics with the phrase 'forcing aside thoughts of likely candidates'.[9]

Disregard of Conflicting Evidence

One of the most striking examples of this concerns the identification of the tomb on the road to Arques with the tomb painted by Poussin. We noted in chapter 9 that the skylines behind the tomb were not at all alike. De Sède[10] and Lincoln appear not to be worried by this discrepancy. Andrews and Schellenberger, on the other hand, do recognize that the backgrounds are not alike, but they nevertheless accept the identification with caveats, and write 'This discrepancy should be enough evidence on which to reject the identification – unless, that is, Poussin had made the alterations on aesthetic grounds, or someone had later changed that part of the painting. . .'.[11]

Conflict with Accepted Chronology

In chapter 13 we looked at the lines claimed to have been found in the landscape by Lincoln, David Wood and others. Geometrical analysis by these writers incorporates the Paris Meridian in various ways – for example on Fig. 13.8, where we have lines joining pairs of sites intersecting at a point on the Meridian. Lincoln contends that this is a deliberate arrangement, and if this is the case, the only way all of these lines can intersect at one point is if the intersection point is fixed before the locations of all the sites are established. Apart from the sinkhole, which is a natural feature, all the sites are medieval churches; hence according to Lincoln's hypothesis the Meridian line must have been fixed at least a millennium ago. As we pointed out earlier, the events leading up to establishing the Paris Meridian are well known and documented. The Paris Meridian line was fixed in 1666, hundreds of years after the churches were built.

Conclusion

Although one or two books have appeared in French which cast doubt on some aspects of the Saunière story,[12] little has appeared in English to show how insubstantial is the evidence. A notable exception was the BBC's *Timewatch* programme broadcast on 27 September 1996, made by Bill Cran of Invision Productions. In it, he applied basic rules of historical research to the Bérenger Saunière story, and confronted the authors of *The Tomb of God* with questions to which they had no answers. As a television programme, it was a rare example of serious historical investigation.

When we first came across the story of Rennes-le-Château in 1996, we had no preconceived ideas as to the reliability or otherwise of the story as generally told. However, a visit to the village and a walk round the area quickly revealed to us that many of the statements that we had read had no foundation. Subsequent investigations drove us to our present conclusions. This book came about because we felt that with such a large amount of uncritical acceptance of the story, there ought to be in print a critical analysis of the claims that were being made.

We do not expect all our readers to agree with our conclusions. Whichever way one looks at it, the affair of Rennes-le-Château makes a very strange story, involving some unlikely events and some extraordinary people. Saunière was an unusual man, Plantard and de Chérisey were unusual in the extreme. The amount of effort that the latter two expended in inventing the puzzles, the genealogies and the fake history is immense. Our critics will say, as others have done,[13] that no one would have done this simply to mislead – financial gain does not appear to have been their motive – to which we reply, strange as it may seem, all the evidence indicates that they did

187

exactly that. Philippe de Chérisey died in 1985, before some of the wilder speculations reached the printing press, but Pierre Plantard, who died in 2000 aged eighty years, lived to see the amazing results of his fabrications. By intention or not, these two men carried out one of the most amazing historical deceptions that there has ever been.

Appendices

A The Latin Manuscripts

For a discussion of the coded messages introduced into these texts, see chapter 6 and Appendix B.

Manuscript 1

The Latin text is taken from the Vulgate translation of John, chapter 12: 1–11. There are a number of editions, which have been published at various times, all differing in small ways. For a full discussion of these see the prefaces to the 1991 edition of *Novum Testamentum Latine* by Kurt and Barbara Aland.

The five versions that come close enough to our Manuscript 1 to be considered as the text from which it was copied are:

Kurt and Barbara Aland (Westphalia Monastery, first edition 1983, second edition 1991)
S – Fischer, Gribomont et al (Stuttgart, first edition 1969, fourth edition 1994)
W – Wordsworth/White (Oxford, first edition 1889)
Wi – Wittemberg (1529)
V – (fifteenth- and sixteenth-century editions including G, Co, E, St, L, P, Si, and C)

Of these Aland and Fischer can be dismissed as the source since they were not published until after Gérard de Sède had seen the parchments in 1967 (in spite of the fact that Fischer is identical to our Manuscript 1). Wittemberg and the fifteenth- or sixteenth-century editions have significant differences from Manuscript 1 both in choice of words and order of words, and can be ruled out on this basis. This leaves Wordsworth/White as the clear source, in spite of one change of word order (*odore unguenti*), a mistake that could easily occur in copying. This edition was first published in 1889 and was widely available from that date. The correct Latin text is as follows:

Iesus ergo ante sex dies Paschae venit Bethaniam, ubi fuerat Lazarus mortuus, quem suscitavit Iesus. Fecerunt autem ei cenam ibi, et Martha ministrabat,

Lazarus vero unus erat ex discumbentibus cum eo. Maria ergo accepit libram unguenti nardi pistici, pretiosi et unxit pedes Iesu et extersit capillis suis pedes eius; et domus impleta est odore unguenti. Dicit ergo unus ex discipulis eius Iudas Scariotes, qui erat eum traditurus: 'Quare hoc unguentum non venit trecentis denariis et datum est egenis?' Dixit autem hoc, non quia de egenis pertinebat ad eum, sed quia fur erat et, loculos habens, ea, quae mittebantur, portabat. Dixit ergo Iesus 'Sine illam, ut in diem sepulturae meae servet illud. Pauperes enim semper habetis vobiscum, me autem non semper habetis.' Cognovit ergo turba multa ex Iudaeis quia illic est, et venerunt non propter Iesum tantum, sed ut Lazarum viderent, quem suscitavit a mortuis. Cogitaverunt autem principes sacerdotum, ut et Lazarum interficerent, quia multi propter illum abibant ex Iudaeis et credebant in Iesum.

This means:

Six days before the Passover Jesus came to Bethania, where Lazarus had died, whom Jesus raised from the dead. The people there provided supper for him, and Martha served, and Lazarus was among those sitting with him. Mary took a pound of ointment of spikenard, very expensive, and anointed Jesus' feet and wiped them with her hair and the house was filled with the scent of the ointment. One of the disciples, Judas Iscariot, who was to betray Jesus, said, 'Why was this ointment not sold for three hundred denarii and the money given to the poor?' He said this, not because he cared about the poor, but because he was a thief. He looked after the public purse, and kept what was put in it. Jesus said, 'Allow her to keep it until the day of my death. You have the poor always with you, but you will not always have me.' A large crowd of Jews heard that he was there and came, not so much for Jesus, but to see Lazarus whom he had raised from the dead. The chief priests then decided to kill Lazarus also, since many had left Judaism because of him, and believed in Jesus.

In Manuscript 1 this is arranged in twenty lines. In the following analysis: the original bible text is given in italics; the manuscript version in roman; the extra letters inserted in CAPITALS; errors in transcription are underlined; and biblical text that has been omitted is enclosed in square brackets [].

1. *jesusergoantesexdiespaschaevenitbethaniamubi*
    jesuseVrgoantCesexdiPespascShaevenJitbethQaniamuRai
2. *fueratlazarusmortuusquemsuscitavitjesusfecerunt*
    fueraOtlazarVusmortYuusqueMmsusciYtavitjYesusfeDcerunt

3. *autemeicoenamibietmarthaministrabatlazarus*
    LautemeTic<u>a</u>enaPmibietOmarthaHministRrabatlBazarusO

4. *verounuseratexdiscumbentibuscumeomariaergoaccep*
    verounXuseratTexdiscOum<u>l</u>entDi<u>l</u>uscuJm[eo]mariaLergoacBcep

5. *itlibramunguentinardipisticipretiosietunxitpe*
    itlKibramuNng[u]entiJnardipFisticiQpretioUsietunExitpe

6. *desjesuetextersitcapillissuispedeseiusetdomusim*
    dPesje<u>r</u>uAetexteJrsitcaYpil<u>ri</u>sNsuispePdese<u>rt</u>P<u>i</u>etdomB<u>e</u>sim

7. *pletaestexunguentiodoredixitergounusexdiscipul*
    plFitaestEexung[u]eIntiod<u>a</u>Eredix<u>a</u>LtergouRnu<u>m</u>exdGiscipuHl

8. *iseiusiudasiscariotesquierateumtraditurusquarehocun*
    iseiu<u>I</u>xiud<u>dx</u>[I]iscarioRt<u>i</u>squi YerateuBmtradiTturusqTuarehoCcun

9. *guentumnonvaeniittrecentisdenariisetdatumeste*
    <u>b</u>[u]enVtumnonIv[a]eniittGrecen<u>p</u>DisdenaAriisetdDatumesGte

10. *genisdixitautemhocnonquiadeegenispertinebat*
    geniEs?dixiN[ta]utemhoEcnonquSiadeegAenispeRrtinebEat

11. *adeumsedquiafureratetloculoshabenseaquaemitteba*
    adeuTmsedquHiafureLr[a]tetloUculoshCabenseCaquaemVitteba

12. *nturportabatdixitergojesussiniteillamutindiems*
    nMturpoT[r]<u>ra</u>b<u>et</u>EdixiteJrgojesHussin[it]ePillamuNti<u>x</u>diePms

13. *epulturaemeaeservetilludpauperesenimsemperha*
    epulGturaemSeaeserV<u>n</u>etillQudpaupJeresenHimsempGerha

14. *betisvobiscummeautemnonsemperhabetiscogno*
    beMtis<u>n</u>obL<u>t</u>iscumFmeauteTmnonseSmperhaVbetiscJogno

15. *vitergoturbamultaexjudaeisquiaillicestetvene*
    viLter[g]otZurbamuQltaexiMudaeisTquiailOlicestXetvene

16. *runtnonpropterjesumtantumsedutlazarumvider*
    AruntnoNnpro[p]tePriesumEtantumMsedutlU[a]zarumPvider

17. *entquemsuscitavitamortuuiscogitaveruntautemp*
    eHntquemKsusci[t]aOvitamoRrtu[u]iscPogitavKeruntaHutemp

18. *rincipessacerdotumutetlazaruminterficerentq*
    rVincipeJssacerCdotumuMtetlazCaruminAterficTerentq

19. *uiamultipropterillumabibantexjudaeisetcre*
    Luiamul VtipropQteril<u>h</u>XumababibG[a]ntex[j]uG<u>t</u>aeisNetcred

20. *debantinjesum*
    DebantiTniesum

At the bottom of the manuscript is the prayer *Jesu medela vulnerum, spes una poenitentium, per Magdalanae lacrymas peccata nostra diluas* (Jesus, healer of wounds, the one hope for repentance, through the tears of the Magdalene wash away our sins.') This was copied from the base of Saunière's new church altar (though it has now disappeared). There is also a device drawn upside down, which includes SION and A and N with a symbol of unknown meaning in between.

The production of the manuscript has been very carelessly done. Twenty-five letters have been wrongly copied, and twenty letters have been omitted. In several places the pattern of the extra letters coming every seventh letter is broken, and this suggests some other sort of muddle. It is difficult to say whether the text was accurately prepared and carelessly copied into the manuscript, or whether both processes were carelessly done. The nature of the errors suggest that neither operator knew Latin. It is of course possible that they had a poorly printed Vulgate text, but this cannot explain all of the errors. Even the name Jesus is misspelled in line 6.

The possibility that all this is deliberate to confuse the reader and suggest further mysteries cannot be excluded, but the present authors feel that they are simply what they appear to be – errors.

All occurrences of the letters d, q, h, b and a are in lower case. This may be because the scribe was not used to writing (also suggested by a backwards Z), or may be meant to suggest some other secret content. Eight letters are written in miniature, spelling *REXMUNDI*, 'King of the World'. Some of the extra inserted letters are displaced slightly from the line, but this is not regular and may not be intended. I and T are absolutely indistinguishable, but the identification can be got from the sense or from the letters required to make the coded message.

Whenever it occurs, ii is written as a v, and counts as one letter.

Manuscript 2

The Latin text is the story of Jesus and his disciples eating grains of wheat on the Sabbath. This occurs in three places in the New Testament, Luke 6:1–4, Matthew 12:1–4, and Mark 2:23–26. All of these are different from one another and from Manuscript 2, substantially so.

The version given in Manuscript 2 is:

> et factum est eum in
> sabbato secundo primo a
> bire per sccetes discipuli autem illiris coe
> perunt vellere spicas et fricantes manibus + mandu
> cabant quidam autem de farisaeis di
> cebant ei ecce quia faciunt discipuli tui sab
> batis + quod non licet respondens autem ins

se ixit ad eos numquam hoc
lecistis quod fecit david quando
esurut ipse et qui cum eo erai + introibit in domum
dei et panes propositionis
manducavit et dedit et qui
cum erant uxiio quibus no
n licebat manducare si non solis sacerdotibus

Allowing for errors in the copying of the manuscript, the passage means:

'And it came about that on the second Sabbath he walked through a cornfield. But his disciples began to pluck the ears and rubbing them in their hands ate them. Some of the Pharisees said to him 'Behold because your disciples are doing on the Sabbath that which is not lawful'. Replying he said to them 'Have you never read what David did when he was hungry? He and those who were with him entered into the house of God and ate the bread of the sacrament and gave it to those who were with him, for whom it was not lawful to eat, except only for priests.'

This does not match any of the Vulgate versions. However, recent research in Germany by Wieland Willker has identified the source as the *Codex Bezae*, a bilingual Greek and Latin manuscript originating in the sixth century AD from France or possibly Italy[1]. It is at present held by Cambridge University. Its version of Luke 6:1–4 is undoubtedly that of Manuscript 2, allowing for small errors in transcribing. It is not entirely clear how Philippe de Chérisey came to access this document. Pierre Jarnac (see chapter 9) suggested that he made use of the *Dictionnaire d'archéologie chrétienne et de liturgie*, edited by Dom Fernand Cabrol and Dom Henri Leclerc. However, a page by page search of this large work by the present authors has failed to find the passage concerned, or any but the briefest mention of the *Codex Bezae*.

A facsimile of the Codex does however appear in the *Dictionnaire de la Bible*, by F. Vigouroux, published in Paris in 1895. He was a priest at St Sulpice in Paris. Philippe de Chérisey was very familiar with this church, and could easily have worked in its library. The Vulgate would have been available for Manuscript 1, and the facsimile of the *Codex Bezae* would not only have provided him with the unusual version of the story, but also the uncial script, giving the manuscript a false appearance of antiquity.

Willker interestingly points out that the small crosses in the text of Manuscript 2 occur at the positions of the marginal verse numbers in the *Codex Bezae*, and this may be their origin. *Redis*, *bles* and *ps* are not present in the Codex.

In the following analysis the probably intended biblical text is given in italics, the actual text of the manuscript in roman, and the raised letters are raised in the manuscript:

1. *et factum est eum in*
    et factum est eum in

2. *sabbato secundo primo a-*
    sabb^{a}to secun^{d}o primo ^{a}

3. *bire per segetes discipuli autem illius coe-*
    bire per sccetes dis^{g}ipuli autem illiris c^{o}e

4. *perunt vellere spicas et fricantes manibus + mandu-*
    perunt vellere spicas et fricantes mani^{b}us + mandu

5. *cabant quidam autem de pharisaeis di-*
    cabant quidam aut^{e}m de fa^{r}isaeis d^{t}

6. *cebant ei ecce quia faciunt discipuli tui sab-*
    cebant e^{i} ecce qu^{i}a faciunt discipuli tui sab

7. *batis + quod non licet respondens autem ip-*
    batis + quod non licet ^{r}esp^{o}ndens autem ^{i}ns

8. *se dixit ad eos nunquam hoc*
    s^{e} ix^{i}t ad eos numqu^{a}m hoc

9. *legistis quod fecit david quando*
    leci^{s}t^{i}s qu^{o}d fecit david qua^{n}do

10. *esuruit ipse et qui cum eo erant + introibit in domum*
    ^{e}surut ip^{se} e^{t} qui ^{c}um ^{e}o erai + in^{tr}oibit in domum

11. *dei et panes propositionis*
    d^{e}i et pane^{s} propositi^{o}nis ^{r}edis

12. *manducavit et dedit et qui*
    manducavit ^{et} dedit et qu^{i} b^{les}

13. *cum eo erant ????? quibus no-*
    cum eran^{t} uxiio quibus no

14. *n licebat manducare si non   solis sacerdotibus*
    n ¹iceb^at ^manducare si n°n   solis sace^rdo¹ibus

15.   ps

The secret message actually written in roman, intended in italics, reads:

a dacoberi ii roi ei a sion est ce tresor et il est la mort
a Dagobert II roi et a Sion est ce tresor et il est la mort

Clearly the scribe was unfamiliar with Latin and has written nonsense where he could not read the manuscript he was copying (particularly lines 3 and 13, but also elsewhere.) He misread *g* for *c* in *discipuli*, and *t* for *i* in *dicebant*. (There was a *g* handy in *segetes*, had it not been miscopied.) He made a complete muddle of *ipse dixit*. The letters *uxiio* in line 13 do not seem to make any sense at all and do not appear in the Codex.

B The Solution to the Cipher in Manuscript 1

Decryption of the Manuscript

As explained in chapter 6, the normal method of encrypting with the Table of Vigenère is to replace each letter of the message in turn with the letter that occurs at the intersection of the column headed by the keyword and the row begun by the plain text letter that has to be encrypted. Decryption is by finding the row defined by the intersection of the diagonal of the encrypted message and the column headed by the keyword.

In the following solution, which is that given by Lincoln in *The Holy Place*, the normal procedure is not followed – we have to decrypt using the procedure for encryption. So each time the Table of Vigenère is used, we look at intersections of the column headed by the keyword and the row begun with the encrypted letter to arrive at the letter for the next stage.

We start with the correct sequence of letters, which is the set of 128 letters from Parchment 1, with changes in the 18th, 19th and 62nd letters (E for O, F for H and T for X, respectively), and put the keyword above the columns.

```
MORTEPEE   MORTEPEE   MORTEPEE   MORTEPEE

VCPSJQRO   VYMYYDLT   PEFRBOXT   ODJLBKNJ
FQUEPAJY   NPPBFEIE   LRGHIIRY   BTTCVTGD
LUCCVMTE   JHPNPGSV   QJHGMLFT   SVJLZQMT
OXANPEMU   PHKORPKH   VJCMCATL   VQXGGNDT
```

After using the procedure for encryption for the first time, using the keyword MORTEPEE, we get the following:

```
IQHMNGVS   IMERCSPY   CSXLFEBY   BRBFFARN
RFMYTPNC   AEHUJTMI   YGYBMYVC   NILVAJKH
YJTVACYI   VVHHTVXA   DYZAQBJY   FKBFDGQY
BLRHTTQZ   CVCIVFOL   IYTGGPYP   IFOAKDHY
```

We now advance one letter down the alphabet to get:

```
JRINOHXT   JNFSDTQZ   DTYMGFCZ   CSCGGBSO
SGNZUQOD   BFIVKUNJ   ZHZCNZXD   OJMXBKLI
ZKUXBDZJ   XXIIUXYB   EZABRCKZ   GLCGEHRZ
CMSIUURA   DXDJXGPM   JZUHHQZQ   JGPBLEIZ
```

The third stage makes use of the inscription on the tombstone of Marie de Nègre d'Ables, which was (including errors):

CT GIT NOBLE MARIE DE NEGRE DARLES DAME DHAUPOUL DE BLANCHEFORT AGEE DE SOIXANTE SEPT ANS DECEDEE LE XVII JANVIER MDCOLXXXI REQUIESCAT IN PACE

The letters PSPRAECUM were added to make up 128 and then the whole was reversed to give the second keyword.

```
MUCEARPS   PECAPNIT   ACSEIUQE   RIXXXLOC
DMREIVNA   JIIVXELE   EDECEDSN   ATPESETN
AXIOSEDE   EGATROFE   HCNALBED   LUOPUAHD
EMADSELR   ADERGENE   DEIRAMEL   BONTIGTC
```

When this is encrypted for a second time using the Table of Vigenère we arrive at:

```
VMKROZMM   ZRHSSHZS   DVQQOASD   TBZDDMHQ
VSFDDMCD   KNQRHZZN   DKDERCPQ   ODCBTOFV
ZHDLTHCN   BDICMLDF   LBNBDDOC   RGQVZHZC
GZSLNZDR   DAHBDKDQ   MDDZHDDC   KUDUTKCB
```

The fifth stage is again to advance the letters down the alphabet by one, giving:

```
XNLSPANN   ASITTIAT   EXRRPBTE   UCAEENIR
XTGEENDE   LORSIAAO   ELEFSDQR   PEDCUPGX
AIEMUIDO   CEJDNMEG   MCOCEEPD   SHRXAIAD
HATMOAES   EBICELER   NEEAIEED   LVEVULDC
```

To get the final, clear message the letters have to be rearranged. They are set out on two chessboards, the first 64 letters on one, the second 64 on another:

```
8  X  N  L  S  P  A  N  N        1  A  I  E  M  U  I  D  O
7  A  S  I  T  T  I  A  T        2  C  E  J  D  N  M  E  G
6  E  X  R  R  P  B  T  E        3  M  C  O  C  E  E  P  D
5  U  C  A  E  E  N  I  R        4  S  H  R  X  A  I  A  D
4  X  T  G  E  E  N  D  E        5  H  A  T  M  O  A  E  S
3  L  O  R  S  I  A  A  O        6  E  B  I  C  E  L  E  R
2  E  L  E  F  S  D  Q  R        7  N  E  E  A  I  E  E  D
1  P  E  D  C  U  P  G  X        8  L  V  E  V  U  L  D  C
   a  b  c  d  e  f  g  h           a  b  c  d  e  f  g  h
```

The letters are now read off from the first board in the following sequence of knight's moves . . .

```
f6  e4  d6  c4  e5  c6  d4  e6  c5  d3  c1  a2  b4  a6  b8  d7
f8  h7  g5  h3  f4  g2  e1  c2  a1  b3  a5  b7  d8  f7  h8  g6
h4  f5  e3  d5  c3  e2  g1  f3  h2  g4  h6  g8  e7  c8  a7  b5
a3  b1  d2  f1  g3  h1  f2  d1  b2  a4  b6  a8  c7  e8  g7  h5
```

. . . and from the second board in the same sequence, but note that the board is inverted compared with the first.

The final message, with spacing and punctuation added to improve intelligibility, is:

BERGERE, PAS DE TENTATION, QUE POUSSIN TENIERS GARDENT LA CLEF. PAX DCLXXXI. PAR LA CROIX ET CE CHEVAL DE DIEU, J'ACHEVE CE DAEMON DE GARDIEN A MIDI. POMMES BLEUES.

In chapter 6 we noted that there is not a unique method of solution and that the two stages of a single step down the alphabet could have been combined into one double step. One can go a lot further and combine all the stages, including the chessboard transposition into one keyword. If we do this the keyword is:

```
FCCNUBMB    EUQGVBCA    KPDXMCYK    BLLHRYAK
ZXNACSXC    ENOMOHRY    AMZIROLE    KDDUMVTO
AFAPSVDA    KUOORYDE    UTXXVSPP    HGYSXNPK
ODEZZJQJ    QSHOQODS    QZBVNOSB    ICEFYHBZ
```

This underlines the statement made in chapter 6, that when the parchments were supposedly submitted to experts for examination, there was no way that they could have come to the pronouncements that they were alleged to have made.

How it may have been encrypted

It is interesting to put ourselves in the place of whoever wrote the parchments in the first place and encrypt the message. Having rearranged the letters of the clear message they would have got XNLSPANN (quoting only the first eight letters in this illustration) and they finished with VCPSJQRO, which were inserted into the Latin text. If it was done using the Table of Vigenère, possibly the steps were:

1.	M	U	C	E	A	R	P	S	First keyword
2.	X	N	L	S	P	A	N	N	Rearranged letters of message
3.	K	S	J	O	P	I	Y	U	K found by dropping down the M-column as far as X: S by dropping down the U-column to N etc.
4.	M	O	R	T	E	P	E	E	Second keyword
5.	K	S	J	O	P	I	Y	U	From step 3
6.	Y	E	R	U	L	S	T	Q	Y found by dropping down the M-column as far as K etc.
7.	V	C	P	S	J	Q	R	O	Back 2 letters in the alphabet: inserted in Manuscript 1

It does not matter which of the keywords was used first, the same answer is obtained.

Going back two letters at the end seems rather artificial and leads us to think that the encryption was actually done as follows:

1.	M	U	C	E	A	R	P	S	First keyword
2.	X	N	L	S	P	A	N	N	Rearranged letter of message
3.	J	R	I	N	O	H	X	T	J found by taking the horizontal row headed by the keyletter M, reading across to X, then dropping down to the bottom line.
4.	M	O	R	T	E	P	E	E	Second keyword
5.	J	R	I	N	O	H	X	T	From step 3
6.	V	C	P	S	J	Q	R	O	V found by taking the horizontal row headed by M, reading across to J, then dropping down to V. These letters are inserted in Manuscript 1.

Note that, by going to the bottom of the table, instead of (as is conventionally done) going to the top, a shift of one letter occurs in stages 3 and 6 above.

Numerical encryption

In chapter 6 we touched on numerical encryption. In the Table of Vigenère, if A = 0, B = 1, C= 2, etc., the rule for encryption is simple. One adds the letter values of the message and the keyword, and then converts back to a letter. Thus if the keyword is BRAIN and the first word of the message is SAUNIERE (as in one example given in chapter 6 where we are using a 25-letter alphabet), we have:

```
B   1 R 17 A   0 I   8 N 13 B  1 R 17 A 0
S  18 A   0 U 20 N 13 I   8 E  4 R 17 E 4,   giving
T  19 R 17 U 20 V 21 V 21 F  5 J  9¹ E 4.
```

$$(^1\ 9 = 17 + 17 - 25)$$

If we apply the numerical method to the message in Manuscript 1, to get the correct result we have to make A = 1 and B = 2 etc.; this procedure introduces a shift of one letter per operation (since A encrypted with a keyletter A would give us 1 + 1 = 2, and 2 = B). The working is as follows:

```
  X 23 N 14 L 12 S 19 P 16 A   1 N 14 N 14    Message
     48    39    37    44    41    26    39    39     Add 25
- M 13 U 21 C  3 E  5 A   1 R 18 P 16 S 19    2nd keyword
- M 13 O 15 R 18 T 20 E   5 P 16 E   5 E  5    1st keyword
= V 22 C  3 P 16 S 19 J 10¹ Q 17² R 18 O 15    Manuscript
```

$$(^1\ 10 = 35 - 25;\ ^2\ 17 = -\ 8 + 25)$$

Whichever way the encryption was done, this was not the difficult part of the task: the real problem in the parchment was to get the message and the second keyword to be anagrams of each other and achieve a readable (if not very meaningful) text.

	0	1	2	3	4	5	6	7	8	9	10	11	12	13	14	15	16	17	18	19	20	21	22	23	24	0
0	A	B	C	D	E	F	G	H	I	J	K	L	M	N	O	P	Q	R	S	T	U	V	X	Y	Z	A
1	B	C	D	E	F	G	H	I	J	K	L	M	N	O	P	Q	R	S	T	U	V	X	Y	Z	A	B
2	C	D	E	F	G	H	I	J	K	L	M	N	O	P	Q	R	S	T	U	V	X	Y	Z	A	B	C
3	D	E	F	G	H	I	J	K	L	M	N	O	P	Q	R	S	T	U	V	X	Y	Z	A	B	C	D
4	E	F	G	H	I	J	K	L	M	N	O	P	Q	R	S	T	U	V	X	Y	Z	A	B	C	D	E
5	F	G	H	I	J	K	L	M	N	O	P	Q	R	S	T	U	V	X	Y	Z	A	B	C	D	E	F
6	G	H	I	J	K	L	M	N	O	P	Q	R	S	T	U	V	X	Y	Z	A	B	C	D	E	F	G
7	H	I	J	K	L	M	N	O	P	Q	R	S	T	U	V	X	Y	Z	A	B	C	D	E	F	G	H
8	I	J	K	L	M	N	O	P	Q	R	S	T	U	V	X	Y	Z	A	B	C	D	E	F	G	H	I
9	J	K	L	M	N	O	P	Q	R	S	T	U	V	X	Y	Z	A	B	C	D	E	F	G	H	I	J
10	K	L	M	N	O	P	Q	R	S	T	U	V	X	Y	Z	A	B	C	D	E	F	G	H	I	J	K
11	L	M	N	O	P	Q	R	S	T	U	V	X	Y	Z	A	B	C	D	E	F	G	H	I	J	K	L
12	M	N	O	P	Q	R	S	T	U	V	X	Y	Z	A	B	C	D	E	F	G	H	I	J	K	L	M
13	N	O	P	Q	R	S	T	U	V	X	Y	Z	A	B	C	D	E	F	G	H	I	J	K	L	M	N
14	O	P	Q	R	S	T	U	V	X	Y	Z	A	B	C	D	E	F	G	H	I	J	K	L	M	N	O
15	P	Q	R	S	T	U	V	X	Y	Z	A	B	C	D	E	F	G	H	I	J	K	L	M	N	O	P
16	Q	R	S	T	U	V	X	Y	Z	A	B	C	D	E	F	G	H	I	J	K	L	M	N	O	P	Q
17	R	S	T	U	V	X	Y	Z	A	B	C	D	E	F	G	H	I	J	K	L	M	N	O	P	Q	R
18	S	T	U	V	X	Y	Z	A	B	C	D	E	F	G	H	I	J	K	L	M	N	O	P	Q	R	S
19	T	U	V	X	Y	Z	A	B	C	D	E	F	G	H	I	J	K	L	M	N	O	P	Q	R	S	T
20	U	V	X	Y	Z	A	B	C	D	E	F	G	H	I	J	K	L	M	N	O	P	Q	R	S	T	U
21	V	X	Y	Z	A	B	C	D	E	F	G	H	I	J	K	L	M	N	O	P	Q	R	S	T	U	V
22	X	Y	Z	A	B	C	D	E	F	G	H	I	J	K	L	M	N	O	P	Q	R	S	T	U	V	X
23	Y	Z	A	B	C	D	E	F	G	H	I	J	K	L	M	N	O	P	Q	R	S	T	U	V	X	Y
24	Z	A	B	C	D	E	F	G	H	I	J	K	L	M	N	O	P	Q	R	S	T	U	V	X	Y	Z

Fig. B.1 Table of Vigenère for a 25-letter alphabet (omitting W)

C *Le Serpent Rouge*

Le Serpent Rouge (The Red Snake)[1] is one of the documents described in chapter 10. Its full title is *Le Serpent Rouge – Notes sur Saint-Germain-des-Prés et de Saint-Sulpice de Paris* and its contents include guides to the two churches as well as the thirteen prose poems and some other material. It seems to be the source of many of the ideas and allusions which have come via de Sède's books into the general mythology of Rennes-le-Château.

Saint-Germain-des-Prés

The two churches are situated quite close together on the south bank of the Seine in the 6th *arrondissement*, one on either side of the line of the Roman road from the Gallo-Roman settlement of Lutetia towards the south-west. To the north of the road is Saint-Germain-des-Prés (St Germain in the meadows). It was founded as a monastery in 542 by the Merovingian king Childebert I and was the burial place of several Merovingian kings, which is presumably the reason for its inclusion in *Le Serpent Rouge*. From the eighth century to the Revolution it was an important Benedictine abbey. The church, originally built as the monastery chapel, is the oldest in Paris, though the original church was destroyed by the Normans and the existing building dates from the eleventh century.

Saint-Sulpice

Saint-Sulpice, on the south side of the Roman road (and near a street called rue Lobineau), is reputedly built on the site of a temple to the Egyptian goddess Isis, but the official guide book does not confirm this.[2] There was a church on this site in the thirteenth century and its foundations are still visible in the crypt. The construction of the present church was begun in 1646, when Jean-Jacques Olier (1608–57) was parish priest. The church was completed in 1732, except for the facade at the west end, which was begun in 1776.

The church is a masterpiece of classical architecture, richly decorated and with numerous sculptures. Among the twenty or so painters who contributed to the interior decoration, the best known is Eugène Delacroix (1793–1863). Lesser known ones include Emile Signol (1804–90), who painted an early portrait of Hector Berlioz (1832) and who painted four pictures in the church in the 1870s.

Inside the church is a most unusual astronomical instrument, a gnomon, which was used for measuring the height of the sun at noon. On the floor of the church is marked out the local meridian, or north–south line, clearly indicated by a brass insert in the pavement. There is an opening in a window in the south transept through which the sun shines, its rays illuminating a circular patch on the floor. The disc of light crosses the meridian line at noon each day and the crossing position along the brass line indicates the day of the year. In winter, when the sun is low in the sky, the light falls on a white marble obelisk near the north transept. A line marked on the obelisk indicates the mid-winter solstice. An elliptical copper plate set in the floor by the altar rail indicates the equinoxes.

The gnomon was set up in 1727 by the English clock-maker and astronomer Henry Sully (1680–1728) at the request of the then priest Jean-Baptiste Languet de Gergy (1675–1750), so that he could fix the date of Easter.

Although the church of Saint-Sulpice began as a neighbourhood church in a poor parish, in the middle of the seventeenth century it became famous because of the work of Jean-Jacques Olier, who founded a community for the training of priests – the St Sulpicians, or Society of Priests of St Sulpice, which still exists today, working in many of the poorer countries of the world. Olier was greatly influenced by the work of St Vincent de Paul (1581–1660) who was founder of the Mission Vincentians for educating pastoral clergy.

The thirteen prose poems, which constitute a major part of the text of *Le Serpent Rouge,* are very obscure. There are allusions to the churches of Rennes-le-Château and Saint-Sulpice, to the countryside around Rennes, to Poussin and to the fairy story of the Sleeping Beauty. Having been unable to find a satisfactory English translation of the text, we give our own. Capital letters are as in the original. Footnotes are added to clarify some of the obscurities, but much remains impenetrable.

Aquarius

How strange are the manuscripts of this friend,[3] great traveller of the unknown. They came to me separately, yet they form a whole for him who knows that the colours of a rainbow give white light, or for the artist who, from six colours of his magic palette, makes black spring out from under his paintbrush.

Pisces

This friend, how can I introduce him to you? His name remained a mystery, but his number[4] is that of a famous seal. How can I describe him to you? Perhaps like the navigator[5] of the unsinkable ark, as impassive as a column on his white rock, gazing to the south, beyond the black rock.[6]

Aries

In my arduous pilgrimage I tried with a sword to clear a way for myself through the thick vegetation of the wood, I wanted to reach the house of the sleeping BEAUTY,[7] whom some poets see as the QUEEN of a lost kingdom. In despair of finding the way, the parchments of this friend were for me the thread of Ariadne.

Taurus

Thanks to him, henceforth with careful steps and a clear eye, I can find the sixty-four scattered stones of the perfect cube,[8] which the brothers of the BEAUTY of the dark wood, while escaping from the pursuit of the usurpers, had strewn on their way while they fled from the white fort.

Gemini

To put the scattered stones together again, using the set square and compass to put them back in regular order, look for the line of the meridian[9] while going from east to west, then looking from south to north, finally in all directions to obtain the desired solution, place yourself in front of the fourteen stones marked with a cross.[10] The circle is the ring and the crown, and the crown the tiara of the QUEEN of the castle.[11]

Cancer

The flagstones of the mosaic pavement of the holy place could be alternating black or white, and JESUS, like ASMODEUS sees their alignments;[12] my eyesight seemed unable to see the summit where the Sleeping Beauty remained hidden. Not being HERCULES with his magic power, how can I decipher the mysterious symbols engraved by the keepers of the past? In the sanctuary though, the stoup of holy water, the fountain of love for the faithful, brings back the memory of these words: BY THIS SIGN YOU WILL CONQUER him.[13]

Leo

From her whom I desired to free, the wafts of perfume which permeate the tomb rise towards me. Once they had called her Isis, queen of the healing springs,

COME TO ME ALL YE THAT LABOUR AND ARE HEAVY LADEN AND I WILL GIVE YOU REST.[14] To some others she was MAGDALENE, with the famous vase of healing balm.[15] The initiates know her true name, NOTRE DAME DES CROSS.

Virgo

I was like the shepherds of the famous painter Poussin, puzzled in front of the riddle '*Et in Arcadia Ego. . .*'[16] Was the voice of blood going to bring me the image of an ancestral past? Yes, a flash of inspiration crossed my mind. I could see again, I understood! I knew now this fabulous secret. And marvel at the leaps of the four horsemen, the hooves of one horse had left four prints in the rock;[17] there is the sign that DELACROIX had given in one of three paintings in the Chapel of the Angels.[18] There is the seventh sentence which a hand had traced out DELIVER ME OUT OF THE MIRE AND LET ME NOT SINK.[19] Twice IS, embalmer and embalmed, miraculous vase of the eternal White Lady of the Legends.[20]

Libra

Begun in the shadows, my journey could be finished only in the light. At the window of the ruined house, I was looking through the trees made leafless by the autumn towards the summit of the mountain. The cross on the ridge[21] stood out in the midday sun, it was the fourteenth[22] and the tallest of all with its 35 cm![23] Here am I on my knight's tour,[24] on the sacred steed crossing the chasm.[25]

Scorpio

There is a celestial vision for those who recall the four works of Em. SIGNOL round the line of the Meridian,[26] at the very choir of the sanctuary from where radiates this source of love, one for another; I turn around, passing from a look at the rose of the P to that of the S, then from the S to the P. . .[27] and the spiral in my mind becomes like a huge octopus[28] squirting out its ink, the shadows obscure the light, I am dizzy and I put my hand to my mouth, instinctively biting my palm, perhaps like OLIER[29] in his coffin. Curse it, I understand the truth, HE HAS GONE, but doing good to him also, as he did at the flowery tomb.[30] But how many have ransacked the HOUSE, leaving only embalmed corpses and a number of metal objects which they were not able to take away?[31] What strange mystery is concealed in the new temple of SOLOMON, built by the children of Saint VINCENT.[32]

Ophiuchus

Cursing the profaners in their ashes, and those who follow in their tracks, leaving the chasm into which I was thrown with a gesture of horror: 'Here is the proof that I knew the secret from the seal of SOLOMON, that I have been to the hidden dwellings of this QUEEN.' To this, Dear Reader, take care not to add or to take away an iota . . . think and think again, the base lead of my text may contain the purest gold.

Sagittarius

Returning then to the white hill, with the sky having opened its floodgates, I seemed to feel a presence near me, with feet in the water, as one who has just received the mark of baptism; turning round towards the east, in front of me I saw, his coils winding endlessly, the enormous RED SERPENT mentioned in the parchments, salty and bitter, the huge unleashed beast at the foot of this white mountain, scarlet with anger.[33]

Capricorn

My emotion was great, 'DELIVER ME OUT OF THE MIRE' I was saying and my awakening was immediate. I didn't tell you in fact that this was a dream I had this 17 January, Saint SULPICE's Day.[34] Afterwards, still embarrassed, I wished after the usual second thoughts I had told you a story by PERRAULT. Here then, Dear Reader, in the pages which follow is the result of a dream which has cradled me into the world from the strange to the unknown. It is to him who PASSES to DO GOOD.

D Translation of *Vaincre,* Issue No. 1, 21 September 1942

Below the masthead are the words 'For a young knighthood'. The address of the editor is given as 10 rue Lebouteux, Paris XVIIe. The badge to the left of the masthead shows a cockerel standing on a globe. Beneath are seven stars and the name of the organization 'Alpha Galetes'. The motto is *'Honneur, Patrie'* (Honour, Fatherland). The main article is *Vaincre* (To conquer) by 'Pierre de France', pen-name of Pierre Plantard, aged twenty-two, whose photograph appears in the text. Italics are as in the original.

Vaincre, a prestigious word which always had the power to summon the people, is today the title of this publication which is devoted to giving back to the country the power to live, with a knightly ideal and self-sacrifice.

The very best party, you see, is the collection of all men bending over their work, in workshops, in universities, in offices, coordinating their desires in the same ideal of mutual help and who sometimes lift their eyes, dreaming that they must conquer (*Vaincre*) to assure their future.

The future for them is neither a political intrigue nor a traitor's trap, it's neither hatred nor anarchy, it's not war, nor revolution with its bloody funeral processions, it is much simpler than that.

The future, it's to overcome (Vaincre) so as to live in safety, with the certainty that 'salary' will not be synonymous with 'unpleasant surprise', that work will have compensations the day after tomorrow.

Vaincre, it's coming back to one's home in the evening after work, to find someone waiting, and in a corner a cradle over which two heads are going to lean.

Vaincre, it's to build up, penny by penny, the little nest egg which will ensure an easy mind in times of hardship, and which will permit perhaps . . . even the purchase of the little house one dreams about, or a supplement to the daily allowance, it's also to build up a dowry, that the daughters or the sons, who when the time arrives, will have to set up in their turn.

Vaincre, it's to organize one's life as one ploughs a furrow, deep and straight.

Vaincre, it is the national mutual help and understanding of Peoples, united in a true socialism, banishing for ever quarrels created by capital interests.

I know a lot about the honest workers who doubt of tomorrow, who stagger from deception to deception, vigorously rejected by the riches of this world with its cosy selfishness, or quite sadly deceived by cynical leaders disguised as apostles.

Those men, what do they think then?

They dream with anxiety of their daily bread, of the immediate future, of their fate and the fate of their loved ones.

It is all this great family which I want to bring together irrespective of origin or party.

Age itself is not a limit, because there are false old men and false youths. There are men of an age for whom the number of years is only ever accumulated youth, and youths who have always had feeling for leadership.

Firstly we have to be united, to rally together, to be numerous, that is to form a Great Order of Chivalry, because if we are *numerous and disciplined, we will be strong, because if we are strong we will be feared and will be able to conquer, that is* to say, to impose on the crowd a doctrine and an ideal.

Also I want to open the list of workers' demands, centralize their grievances, their recriminations, to let loose their common aspirations, to change them to stand out from the crowd, leaders, persistent and enthusiastic. *I want to conquer with them, for them.*

That is why I want first to create a frame of mind, then call on men of action. It is to do with focussing desires.

It is to do with bringing together all men who have not been infected with the political germ in a coalition which will dominate the present and safeguard the future.

Let it be well known, to carry out this task I have no need for help from organized political parties, complacent volunteers or fanatical politicians.

SYNTHESIS OF FORCES

'. . . When a stream is polluted to find pure water it is necessary to go back to its source; it is the same for tradition, it is only as pure as its source.'

Paul Lecourt, Director of Atlantis.

'. . . The new structure of the west will draw its power from the old Celtic order, and Brittany which keeps the unspoilt store of sacred science, will most certainly be the cradle of the Order of Chivalry.'

G Trabieux d'Egmont, writer and poet.

'Speeches are very fine, but what use are they? Do you see that what our country needs is action, a chivalrous action, free from political intrigues, in which our eminences get entangled?'

19 Bérenger Saunière's temporary altar and first library in the grounds of the church, positioned over a water tank, now disused.

20 The ossuary in the churchyard at Rennes-le-Château in 1997.

21 The probable original altar table which Bérenger Saunière removed from the church, now acting as a step in front of the statue of the Virgin Mary.

22 The restored Calvary in the churchyard at Rennes-le-Château.

23 The original altar support as displayed in the Museum.

24 The *Dalle de Chevaliers*, the Knights' Stone, as displayed in the Museum.

25 Château d'Hautpoul in the village at Rennes-le-Château.

26 The *Villa Béthanie* at Rennes-le-Château, now part of the Bérenger Saunière Centre.

27 The living room in the *Villa Béthanie*, reconstructed in the style of the late nineteenth century, photographed in 1996.

28 Bérenger Saunière's altar in the *Villa Béthanie,* used when he had been forbidden to celebrate Mass in the church, photographed in 1996.

29 The belvedere at the *Villa Béthanie*.

30 The orangery at the east end of the belvedere at the *Villa Béthanie*.

31 *La Tour Magdala*, Bérenger
Saunière's extraordinary library.

32 Inside *La Tour Magdala*, Bérenger Saunière's library at the *Villa Béthanie*.

33 The baluster from the church at Rennes-le-Château, photographed in 1996.

34 The painting by Nicolas Poussin entitled *Les Bergers d'Arcadie*.

35 The skyline behind the site of the tomb at Arques, supposedly represented in *Les Bergers d'Arcadie.*

36 Site of Château Blanchefort, 4 km east of Rennes-le-Château.

37 The original grave of Bérenger Saunière in the churchyard at Rennes-le-Château.

38 The tablet commemorating Marie Dénarnaud, which used to be in the churchyard at Rennes-le-Château.

39 The Old Presbytery at Rennes-le-Château.

Henry Coston, Director of 'Free Speech'.

'. . . an Order of Chivalry, but that's the foundation stone of a nation, France is rightly dead for having replaced its knights by its cavaliers.'

Franchet d'Esperey, Marshal of France.

'. . . Certainly a knighthood is indispensable, for our country can be revived only by its knights.'

Genevieve Zapperat, Director, the 'National Arch'.

Our Order is not in search of men who are eager for titles or ribbons.

These lines are addressed only to the healthy forces in my country, to those who are capable of giving themselves over to a disinterested cause, to those who have pledged, like us, to conquer to save France.

E The Geometry of the Pentagon

The Regular Pentagon

The pentagon appeared first in the context of Rennes-le-Château in Lincoln's television film *The Priest, the Painter and the Devil*, where it was claimed that Poussin had based the composition of his painting *Les Bergers d'Arcadie* on this geometrical figure. In his next film he described how he found pentagonal geometry in the relative positions of mountain peaks in the area, (see chapter 5). Later writers have produced complex ramifications of this idea.

A pentagon is any five-sided figure, and clearly any five points can be connected to make a pentagon. The regular pentagon has all its sides of equal length and all its corners have an angle of 108°. The pentagram is formed by extending the sides of the pentagon to make a star and it becomes a pentacle when the whole is enclosed in a circle.

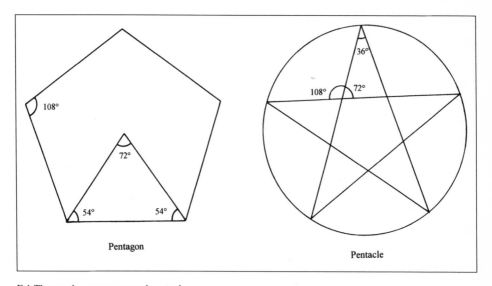

E.1 The regular pentagram and pentacle.

The Golden Section

Closely connected with the pentagon is the Golden Section, or Golden Mean, which is the division of a line in such a way that the ratio of the small section to the large section is the same as the large section to the whole line. Putting it mathematically: if we have a line AC divided at a point B, and B is positioned so that $AB/BC = AC/AB$, then AB/BC is the Golden Section, GS.

In the line above, $a/b = (a + b)/a = 1 + (b/a)$.
On multiplying both sides by (a/b), we get $(a/b)^2 = (a/b) + 1$.
The solution to this equation is that $(a/b) = \frac{1}{2}(1 + \sqrt{5}) = 1.618034$.
From two lines above one can see that adding 1 to the Golden Section gives its square:
$GS + 1 = 2.618034 = GS^2$.
Note that you can write $a/b = (a + b)/a$ as $a/b - 1 = b/a$.
So subtracting 1 from the Golden Section gives its reciprocal: $GS - 1 = 0.618034 = 1/GS$.

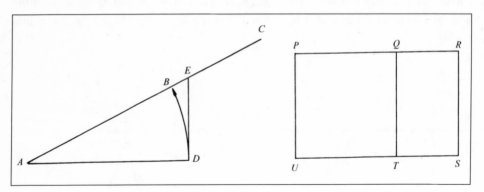

E.2 Golden section construction for a line and a rectangle.

It is easy to draw a line divided into the Golden Section. One method as shown in Fig. E.2 is to construct a right-angled triangle (ADE) with one side (AD) two units long and the other (DE) one unit. The hypotenuse (AE) will be $\sqrt{5}$ units long. Next extend the line of the hypotenuse by 1 unit to give a line AC equal to $1 + \sqrt{5}$ units. Measure off two units along the line AC to give a length AB. AC is now divided by B into the Golden Section.

A rectangle with sides in the ratio of the Golden Section has this interesting property: if it is divided into a square and a smaller rectangle, as shown in the above figure, the sides of the smaller rectangle are also in the ratio of the Golden Section.

The Golden Section in a Regular Pentagon

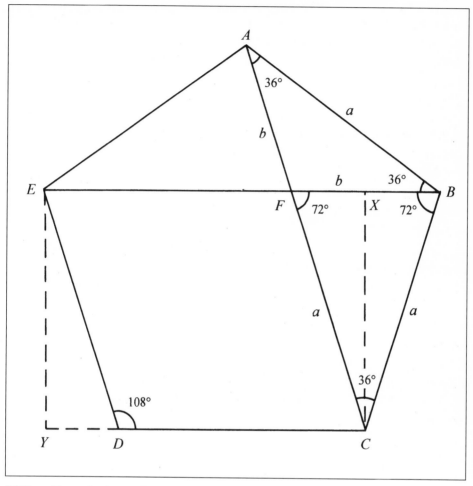

E.3 The golden section in a regular pentagon.

In the above pentagon, the triangle ABF is isosceles, with sides $AF = FB = b$. Also in the triangle BCF, $BC = FC = a$, and because it is a regular pentagon $AB = BC$. Therefore triangle ABC is similar to triangle BFA, and $AC/AB = AB/BF$, or $(a + b)/a = a/b$, which is what we had above. The point F therefore divides AB in the ratio of the Golden Section.

The Golden Section appears again in the pentagon as the ratio of a side to a chord, for example AB/AC, which, as is seen from the diagram is $a/(a + b)$.

The rectangle $EXCY$ has sometimes been chosen by painters (including Poussin) as the shape of their canvases. Its width is $(a + \frac{1}{2}b)$ and its height is $\sqrt{(a^2 - \frac{1}{4}b^2)}$. The ratio of width to height can be put in terms of the Golden Section as $\sqrt{\{(GS + \frac{1}{2})/(GS - \frac{1}{2})\}} = 1.3764$. Sometimes the distance DF is required. $DF = a\sqrt{(3 - GS)} = 1.1756a$.

Fibonacci Series

The Fibonacci Series is also intimately connected to the Golden Section. It was discovered by Leonardo Fibonacci (*c*.1170–*c*.1240), an Italian mathematician from Pisa. In this series, starting with 0, 1, each number is the sum of the two preceding numbers.

0 1 1 2 3 5 8 13 21 34 55 89 144 233 377 and so on.

Once beyond the first few numbers, dividing a number by the preceding one gives (approximately) the Golden Section. The larger the numbers, the closer the division approaches 1.618034. Thus 21/13 = 1.615385, and 377/233 = 1.618026.

The Golden Section in Art

The geometry of the pentagon and its connection with the Golden Section was known in antiquity and appears in Euclid's *Elements*. In 1509 Luca Pacioli (*c*.1445–*c*.1514), who was a friend of Leonardo da Vinci and Pierro della Francesca, wrote a thesis on the Golden Section, in which he claimed there was an aesthetic principle, to be found in architecture and in the proportions of the human body. Leonardo did a series of drawings of the body incorporating this ratio, and many painters, particularly in the Renaissance period, have since made use of the Golden Section, or proportions close to it, in their paintings. The Golden Section is generally regarded as pleasing to the eye, and it is not easy to be sure that when it turns up in a painting that it has been put there deliberately.[1]

The Pentagon and Venus

The pentagon has from the earliest times been linked with the planet Venus because of that planet's apparent movements in the sky. Venus is closer to the Sun than the Earth is, and it has a shorter orbital period. The Earth's period is one year, 365.26 days. That of Venus is 224.7 days. The ratio of the two orbital periods is 13.004/8. In other words, while the Earth is doing eight orbits round the sun, Venus does almost exactly thirteen orbits, which means that in eight years it overtakes the Earth fives times and comes back to the same point in the sky. So every eight years it seems to repeat the motions it did eight years previously.

The apparent cycle of motions is fairly simple. Starting when the planet is furthest away from the Earth, i.e. on the opposite side of the sun, it appears in the evening sky shortly after sunset. As the months pass, it appears further away from the sun, becoming very conspicuous – in fact it is the brightest object in the night sky apart from the moon. Then quite quickly, over a period of several evenings, Venus closes in towards the sun, disappears into the sunset, and a few days later can be seen in the sky before dawn, as bright as before. Venus has passed between the sun and the Earth, and this passing is called the 'inferior conjunction'. Venus then draws away from the sun rapidly for a while, and eventually turns back towards the sun and very slowly disappears into the twilight, to emerge later as an evening star again.

The inferior conjunction is a very noticeable movement to any one who looks often at the night sky, and its regularity must have been known from very ancient times. Dates of inferior conjunctions over a fifteen-year period are as follows:

21 August 1991; 31 March 1993; 2 November 1994; 10 June 1996; 15 January 1997;

20 August 1999; 30 March 2001; 31 October 2002; 7 June 2004; and 14 January 2006.

We can see that they do in fact repeat on very nearly the same day in the calendar every eight years. Successive inferior conjunctions are separated by 216° (3 x 72°) in the sky, and during the eight years the five inferior conjunctions which occur are spread around the sky almost exactly 72° apart. This is what is meant when astrologers say that the planet Venus describes a pentagram in the sky.

F Alignments

How many alignments to expect?

We give here in more detail a solution to the problem raised in chapter 13: how to estimate the number of alignments one could expect to find in an area containing randomly positioned points.

We define an alignment as follows: if we have three points which are very nearly lying on a straight line, we call it an alignment if the point in between the other two is within a predetermined miss-distance E from the line joining the other two. More generally, if we have N points within an area, the number of possible lines joining them in pairs is $\frac{1}{2}N(N-1)$, and we say that we have an M-point alignment with miss-distance E if $M-2$ of the remaining $N-2$ points lie closer to the line than the miss-distance E.

It is possible to find out how many alignments one would be likely to get using a computer simulation. One could make the computer randomly select the coordinates of a chosen number of points, pick out lines joining the points in pairs, then calculate the distance from the line of every other point to see if it lies closer to the line than the predetermined miss-distance. In fact we have done this, but the disadvantage of the method is that it is slow, and to get statistically acceptable results we have to repeat the whole calculation several times. To avoid a long computation we use the following different approach.

We begin with a rectangular area which we shall call A, with length Ln and breadth Br, containing N randomly selected points. On Fig. F.1, two of these points are shown as X and Y. As stated above, the number of possible lines joining such points in pairs is $\frac{1}{2}N(N-1)$. (The $\frac{1}{2}$ comes in because the line XY is the same as the line YX.) If the length of the line XY is L, and the miss-distance is E, the area of the small rectangle is $2EL$. The probability that *any one* of the $(N-2)$ remaining points is inside this rectangle is $2EL/A$, which for convenience we shall call p.

So the probability that a given point is *not* within the miss-distance of XY is $q = 1-p$, and the probabilities of exactly nought, one, two, three and so on points lying within the miss-distance are given by the well-known Binomial Probability Distribution defined by p and q, taking our $N-2$ as the n-value (i.e. the probability of having an $x+2$ point alignment is $_nC_x p^x q^{n-x}$). These probabilities can be derived by a

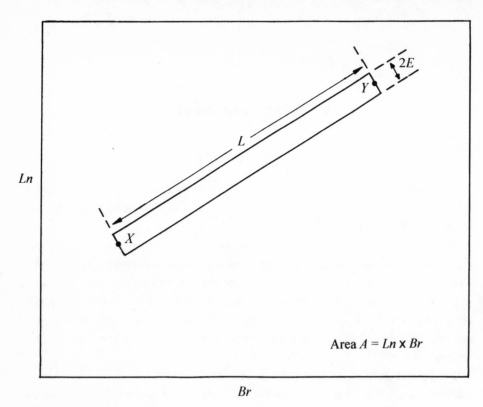

F.1 How many alignments to expect.

simple iterative procedure, and give us, respectively, the probability that the line XY represents a two-, three-, four- and so on point alignment.

The attached computer program, written in pseudo-code, will do the arithmetic. The program begins by generating the coordinates of the N random points. (A point is rejected if it lies within a distance $2E$ of another point, on the grounds that two points very close together would not be regarded as two separate sites.) The next step is to calculate the length of each line; the program then works out the probabilities of exactly nought, one, two, three, four, five, six or seven points lying within the miss-distance as described above, and adds them for all the $\frac{1}{2}N(N-1)$ lines. This gives us the *expected numbers* of two-, three-, four-, five-, six-, seven-, eight- or nine- point alignments. In order to get consistent results, the program repeats the calculations several times and takes the averages. (Ten repeats should be enough, but if there are more than 100 points the user may wish to make do with 5 to shorten the calculation time.)

Here is a typical output for a 5 km square with 100 points and miss-distance 10 m:

Length of rectangle   5,000 m
Breadth of rectangle   5,000 m
Total number of points   100
Miss-distance   10 m
Number of runs   5

Points =	2	3	4	5	6	7	8	9
Lines =	4,056	790	95	9	1	0	0	0

As a check one can note that the total of all the lines (4951) should be very nearly $\frac{1}{2} \times 100 \times 99 = 4950$.

Alignments of churches round Rennes-le-Château

As well as the above program for estimating the number of alignments in an area, we have written another program which checks the number of alignments of the observed sites over an actual area of land. The coordinates of all the points are listed in a data file; the computer then takes them all in pairs and checks whether the other points are within the pre-chosen miss-distance. This is a much quicker and more certain way of looking for alignments than poring over a map with a pencil and ruler, and the computer does not miss any.

We have prepared a data file of the sites of all the 40 churches in the area around Rennes-le-Château (but no châteaux, crosses or natural features). The area is defined by St Salveyre (north), Belviane (south), Valmigère (east) and Les Sauzils (west); a rectangle 18 km by 16 km. If we take a miss-distance of 50 m, the above program gives the following estimate of expected number of alignments:

Length of rectangle   18,000 m
Breadth of rectangle   16,000 m
Total number of points   40
Miss-distance   50 m
Number of runs   10

Points =	2	3	4	5	6	7	8	9
Lines =	694	80	6	0	0	0	0	0

Using the second program we got the results listed at the end of this appendix. There are seventy-seven three-point alignments and seven four-point alignments, with no five-point or higher number alignments. The miss-distance of the church or churches in the centre of the lines is given in metres (actually to the nearest metre, though the data is only accurate to 10 m). In summary, the number of alignments on the ground is very close to the number that would be expected by chance, and therefore, as far as the alignment of churches is concerned, there is nothing especially remarkable about this area.

Alignments of natural objects

In defence of the validity of his discovery of alignments in the area around Rennes-le--Château, Henry Lincoln[1] has remarked "I have been told that . . . an examination of any map will probably produce much the same results. Such an argument, of course, is easily refuted simply by making the attempt to find such alignments elsewhere. But the argument totally ignores the reasoning that were churches, castles and mountain tops placed in perfect alignment wherever one might choose to look for them, then such would be an even more remarkable fact. And is it not remarkable that no one has ever noticed it?"

It would seem that Lincoln is unaware of the vast number of claims for alignments made by those who devote time to searching for ley lines, but his point that one should look elsewhere to see if alignments exist is perfectly valid. Thus we have used our computer programs to search for alignments of natural objects, and lest it should be thought that we have picked points to achieve a desired result, we have used National Grid Coordinates of peaks of the English Lake District as selected by Alfred Wainwright in his famous series of books, *A Pictorial Guide to the Lakeland Fells*. We took 64 peaks which lie within an area 32 km by 29 km (i.e. the first ten listed in order of height in each of his seven books, except for six which were outside the area of the four Explorer Series Ordnance Survey Maps covering the Lake District). The miss distance was 50 metres. The results were

Points on each line	=	2	3	4	5	6	7
Observed number of lines	=	1737	255	24	0	0	0
Expected number of lines	=	1812	191	12	1	0	0

Again, the number of alignments is fairly close to the number one would expect by chance. In summary, if there is a sufficient number of points on the landscape, you can expect to find alignments, whether they mark features that are man-made or not.

Computer Program for calculating the expected number of alignments

List of Variables

N	Number of sites
R, S	Site numbers
X(R), Y(R)	Co-ordinates of site N R
L	Distance between a pair of sites
flag	Flag is set unless sites are too close
Ln	Length of working area
Br	Breadth of working area
E	Miss-distance
NR	Number of runs of simulation to obtain average
NRC	Simulation number
P	Probability of any one site lying within the miss-distance of a given line
Q	$1 - P$, i.e. probability of site *not* lying within the miss-distance of given line
T	Number of sites within miss-distance of given line (including end-points)
Pr(T)	Probability of exactly T sites within miss-distance (binomial distribution)
Tot(T)	Total of Pr(T) values over all point-pairs and all NR runs
Ex(T)	Expected no. of T-point alignments = average Pr(T) totalled over all point-pairs

Program

```
DECLARE as DOUBLE PRECISION ARRAY:      Pr(9)
DECLARE as DOUBLE PRECISION NUMBERS:    P, Q
DECLARE as FLOATING POINT ARRAYS:       X(200), Y(200), Tot(9), Ex(9)
DECLARE as FLOATING POINT NUMBERS:      L, Ln, Br, E
DECLARE as INTEGER:                     N, R, S, NR, NRC, T
DECLARE as BOOLEAN:                     Flag

INPUT Ln, Br, N, E, NR
```

(Initialise totals): FOR T = 2 to 9

                    SET Tot(T) = 0

                    END-FOR

FOR NRC = 1 TO NR

  FOR R = 1 TO N

    REPEAT

        ASSIGN X(R) a random value between 0 and Ln

        ASSIGN Y(R) a random value between 0 and Br

        SET Flag = TRUE

        (Re-plot if any other point is closer than 2E):

            FOR S = 1 TO R – 1

            (Is point R within distance 2E of point S?):

            IF $(X(R)–X(S))^2 + (Y(R)–Y(S))^2 < 4E^2$ THEN Flag = FALSE

            END-FOR

        UNTIL Flag = TRUE

    END-FOR

    FOR R = 1 TO N - 1

      FOR S = R + 1 TO N

        (Calculate distance between points R and S):

        SET L = $\sqrt{((X(R)–X(S))^2 + (Y(R)–Y(S))^2)}$

        SET P = 2EL / (Ln * Br)

        SET Q = 1 – P

        (Calculate first term of Binomial series): Pr(2) = $Q^{(N–2)}$

        (Calculate Pr(3) to Pr(9) iteratively):

            FOR T = 3 TO 9

                SET Pr(T) = Pr(T–1)*P*(N–T+1) / ((T–2)*Q)

            END-FOR

        (Add each Pr(T) to total):

        FOR T = 2 TO 9

            SET Tot(T) = Tot(T) + Pr(T)

        END-FOR

      END-FOR

    END-FOR

  END-FOR

END-FOR

(Calculate averages over the NR runs of program):
FOR T = 2 TO 9
   SET Ex(T) = Tot(T) / NR
END-FOR
Print Headings

(Print expected numbers of alignments):
FOR T = 2 TO 9
   PRINT Ex(T) correct to the nearest integer
END-FOR

END-OF-PROGRAM

Alignments of churches in the area around Rennes-le-Château

There are forty churches in the list. The maximum miss-distance is 50 m: the calculated miss-distance for a particular alignment is given in the column headed *E*.

3-point alignments

There are 77: the number expected due to chance is 80.

One end	middle	*E*	other end
Alet-les-Bains	Castel Nègre	26	St Louis-et-Parahou
Alet-les-Bains	Terroles	37	Valmigère
Antugnac	Couiza	20	Sougraigne
Antugnac	Coustaussa	6	Missègre
Belvianes	Cavirac	46	Arques
Belvianes	Cavirac	17	Cassaignes
Belvianes	Cavirac	38	Coustaussa
Belvianes	Cavirac	13	Granès
Belvianes	Cavirac	10	Serres
Belvianes	Cavirac	45	Rennes-le-Château
Belvianes	Cavirac	14	Valmigère
Belvianes	Cavirac	48	Véraza
Belvianes	Couiza	6	St Salveyre
Belvianes	St Julia-de-Bec	15	Missègre
Belvianes	St Just-et-le-Bézu	7	Le Bézu
Campagne-les-Bains	Luc-sur-Aude	40	Véraza
Campagne-les-Bains	Peyrolles	38	Valmigère

One end	middle	E	other end
Campagne-sur-Aude	Campagne-les-Bains	47	Terroles
Campagne-sur-Aude	Luc-sur-Aude	34	Véraza
Campagne-sur-Aude	St Just-et-le-Bézu	49	St Louis-et-Parahou
Campagne-sur-Aude	Rennes-le-Château	7	Arques
Castel Nègre	Castillou	23	Peyrolles
Cavirac	Campagne-les-Bains	16	Antugnac
Cavirac	Cassaignes	33	Terroles
Cavirac	Granès	8	Peyrolles
Cavirac	Laval	7	Luc-sur-Aude
Cavirac	St Ferriol	20	Couiza
Cavirac	St Just-et-le-Bézu	10	Le Bézu
Conilhac	Croux	16	Granès
Conilhac	Montazels	28	Bugarach
Conilhac	Rennes-les-Bains	17	Sougraigne
Conilhac	Véraza	32	Terroles
Couiza	Cassaignes	32	Serres
Croux	Antugnac	41	Cassaignes
Croux	Campagne-les-Bains	11	St Ferriol
Croux	Luc-sur-Aude	5	Peyrolles
Croux	Montazels	24	Couiza
Esperaza	Couiza	26	Peyrolles
Esperaza	Coustaussa	40	Arques
Esperaza	Luc-sur-Aude	19	Castillou
Esperaza	Montazels	36	Terroles
Esperaza	Rennes-le-Château	28	Missègre
Fa	Antugnac	12	Castel Nègre
Fa	Campagne-sur-Aude	10	St Ferriol
Fa	Couiza	27	Arques
Fa	Couiza	18	Cassaignes
Fa	Esperaza	40	Missègre
Fa	Esperaza	16	Rennes-le-Château
Fa	Esperaza	31	Rennes-les-Bains
Granès	Serres	46	Valmigère
La Serpent	Esperaza	22	St Louis-et-Parahou
La Serpent	Fa	41	Laval
La Serpent	Montazels	49	Couiza
Laval	Esperaza	25	Antugnac
Laval	Le Bézu	1	Sougraigne

One end	middle	E	other end
Laval	Esperaza	25	Antugnac
Laval	St Ferriol	39	Couiza
Laval	Serres	29	Valmigère
Le Bézu	Castillou	43	St Salveyre
Les Sauzils	Antugnac	34	St Salveyre
Les Sauzils	Coustaussa	11	Cassaignes
Les Sauzils	Esperaza	31	Montazels
Les Sauzils	Granès	45	Bugarach
Les Sauzils	Luc-sur-Aude	38	Castillou
Luc-sur-Aude	Coustaussa	8	St Louis-et-Parahou
Montazels	Couiza	37	Missègre
Peyrolles	Serres	36	Sougraine
Quillan	Castel Nègre	27	St Salveyre
Quillan	Castillou	9	Véraza
Quillan	Couiza	1	Luc-sur-Aude
Roquetaillade	Castel Nègre	50	Castillou
Roquetaillade	Castillou	7	Peyrolles
Roquetaillade	Croux	32	Campagne-les-Bains
Roquetaillade	Esperaza	50	St Julia-de-Bec
St Julia-de-Bec	Granès	18	Alet-les-Bains
St Ferriol	Cassaignes	30	Peyrolles
St Ferriol	Couiza	32	St Salveyre
Véraza	Peyrolles	42	Bugarach

4-point alignments

There are 7: the number expected due to chance is 6.

One end	middle	E	middle	E	other end
Belvianes	Cavirac	17	Cassaignes	28	Terroles
Belvianes	Cavirac	13	Granès	0	Peyrolles
Cavirac	St Ferriol	8	Couiza	27	St Salveyre
Fa	Couiza	47	Cassaignes	49	Serres
La Serpent	Montazels	9	Couiza	44	Rennes-les-Bains
Les Sauzils	Esperaza	15	Montazels	24	Terroles
Roquetaillade	Croux	34	Campagne-les-Bains	5	St Ferriol

G Units of Measurement

In chapter 13 we looked at the evidence for the use of the English mile in the layout of man-made structures near Rennes-le-Château and found it unconvincing. However this is not the only unit of length which, it is claimed, was used in prehistoric times in the area. There is another, based on the almost forgotten English pole (now more usually called a rod), of 5½ yards ($\frac{1}{320}$ of a mile, or 5.0292 m).

We have already discussed the circle of churches with a radius of 2.93 miles, discovered by David Wood (Fig. 13.3). Henry Lincoln found several other circles of churches passing through Coustaussa, all of the same radius, which he gives as 933.586 poles or about 2.92 miles. In passing, it has to be pointed out that by convention, if one gives a number to six significant figures, it implies that the number is accurate to one part in a million, in this case 0.001 pole, or ⅕ inch. This is a spurious accuracy when it is not possible to measure on the map to better than 1 pole, and pointless when the objects we are dealing with are as large as churches.

The pole turns up again in Lincoln's examination of the points of intersection of his fan of lines and the Paris Meridian, when he records that 'Each point is separated from the next by exactly one third of 933.586 poles'. As we have seen (Fig. 13.9), the separations are not equal and therefore cannot be exactly any unit of length, but one third of 933.586 poles is 1.565 km, which is certainly close to the mean distance between intersections (calculated to be 1.56 km).

Lincoln arrives at this unusual unit of length by reasoning as follows. He assumes that the east–west line of the pentacle, Rennes-le-Château to Point 3 on Fig. 13.4, was 1618 poles, i.e. one thousand times the Golden Section.[1] The line Rennes-le-Château to Point 3 is a chord of the circle of churches, and if it was actually one side of an equilateral triangle, as it appears to be on the map, the radius of the circle would be 0.577 (i.e. $1/\sqrt{3}$) of the length of the chord. So the radius works out at $0.577 \times 1618 = 933.586$ poles,[2] which gives him his unit.

Henry Lincoln lists eighteen pairs of places which he says are separated by 933.586 poles (2.92 miles). We have been able to check sixteen pairs and the results are given at the end of this appendix. The distances between paired points all fall between 2.86 and 3.16 miles. If we had 50 potential sites of churches, châteaux, calvaries, sinkholes and peaks (a gross underestimate) we would have a possibility of 1,225 pairs, randomly spaced at all distances up to say, 15 miles. The number expected to be in the range from 2.86 to 3.16 miles is 1225 × (3.16 − 2.86)/15 = 24. It would seem that Lincoln did not list all the pairs that could have been expected statistically. In fact the evidence for this unit is as unconvincing as the evidence presented for the use of the English mile.

In view of the lack of firm evidence for the use of either the pole or the English mile in the geometry of the landscape around Rennes-le-Château, one might think that Henry Lincoln's hypothesis on how the mile may have been established[3] requires only a brief mention. However, a quick reading of his theory can give an erroneous impression of its significance.

He supposes that the size of the Earth was known in prehistoric times and somehow the distance from the North Pole to the Equator had been accurately measured. In fact he is anticipating what was actually done in France in the eighteenth century, when the Earth was carefully surveyed, and the metre was officially defined as one ten millionth of the distance of a line from the Equator to the North Pole along the longitude of Paris. Lincoln supposes that the prehistoric surveyors took one ten-thousandth of the same distance (i.e. 1 km) which is 39,370 inches. He then:

1. Takes the square root of 39,370 to get 198.41874, which is rounded down to 198, and this gives him the number of inches in a pole.
2. Next he multiples 198 by the Golden Section, 1.618, to give 320.364, and rounds this down to 320, which becomes the number of poles in a mile.
3. Having fixed the number of inches in a pole (198) and the number of poles in a mile (320), he has fixed the number of inches in the mile (198 × 320 = 63,360).
4. He divides this number by 1.618 to get 39,159.456. This time he rounds up to 39,160, takes it from the number he began with, 39,370, leaving 210, which is 1 pole plus 12 inches spare to define the foot. Thus, according to Lincoln, were the units of length defined.

Let us see more closely what has been done. Step by step as above:

1. He defines the number of inches in a pole as $\sqrt{39,370}$.
2. He multiples this number by the Golden Section to get the number of poles to a mile. i.e. GS × $\sqrt{39,370}$.
3. Multiplying the two numbers above he gets the number of inches to a mile
   i.e. GS × $\sqrt{39,370}$ × $\sqrt{39,370}$ = GS × 39,370.
4. He now divides by GS; one would expect the answer to be 39,370, the number he started with, but his roundings up and down lead to 39,160 instead.
We have a numerical conjuring trick, nothing more.

All the evidence from studying archaeological sites, excavated artefacts, old inscriptions and some early documents supports the generally accepted view that our units of linear measurement were originally based on simple, natural techniques like measuring against some part of the human body (for small lengths) or counting the number of paces (for greater lengths). Admittedly there are some uncertainties in the details of the refining of standards, but the overall picture will not be made clearer by adopting bizarre theories for which there is no supporting evidence.

Evidence for the Measure of 933.586 Poles (2.92 miles)

From	To	km	miles
Rennes-les-Bains, church	Le Bézu, church	4.75	2.95
Rennes-les-Bains, church	Rennes-le-Château, château	4.68	2.91
Rennes-les-Bains, church	Aven, sinkhole	4.68	2.91
Laval, church	St Just, church	4.60	2.86
Sougraigne, church	La Pique, peak	4.73	2.94
Les Sauzils, church	Ginoles, church	5.08	3.16
Les Sauzils, church	St Ferriol, church	4.81	2.99
Croux, church	Bourière, church	4.69	2.91
Campagne-sur-Aude, church	Aven, sinkhole	4.68	2.91
St Julia-et-le-Bézu, church	Aven, sinkhole	4.77	2.96
Luc, church	Serres, church	4.63	2.88
Veraza, church	'Poussin' tomb	4.71	2.92
La Soulane, church	'Poussin' tomb	4.62	2.87
Castillou, church	'Poussin' tomb	4.70	2.92
Campaigne-sur-Aude, church	*Tour Magdala*	4.68	2.91
Antugnac Calvary	*Tour Magdala*	4.66	2.89

Sixteen distances are shown above, the smallest being 2.86 miles (915.2 poles) and the largest 3.16 miles (1,011.2 poles).

Grid Co-ordinates of locations listed

Aven, sinkhole	594.05, 3067.73	Luc, church	594.52, 3073.21
Bouriège, church	586.07, 3076.15	'Poussin' tomb	600.32, 3072.28
Campagne-sur-Aude,		Rennes-les-Bains,	
church	589.42, 3068.45	church	598.62, 3068.74
Castillou, church	596.05, 3074.25	Rennes-le-Château,	
		château	594.06, 3069.80
Calvary near Antugnac	590.50, 3072.96	*Tour Magdala*	593.91, 3069.78
Croux, church	589.58, 3073.04	St Ferriol, church	590.82, 3065.80
Ginoles, church	585.34, 3063.13	St Julia, church	597.53, 3063.21
La Pique, peak	600.09, 3067.67	St Just-et-le-Bézu	594.29, 3064.38
Laval, church	589.81, 3063.33	Serres, church	598.97, 3071.93
Le Bézu, church	595.60, 3065.08	Sougraigne, church	601.45, 3066.84
Les Sauzils, church	586.58, 3069.06	Veraza, church	597.54, 3076.08

H Henri Boudet and
La Vraie Langue celtique

Several writers have speculated that Henri Boudet, *abbé* of Rennes-les-Bains from 1872 to 1914, played some part in the affair of Rennes-le-Château. Gérard de Sède, as we have mentioned in chapter 4, put his name forward as a likely candidate for the authorship of the coded parchments. In chapter 6 we showed that this could not be the case, because the edition of the Bible from which Parchment 1 was taken was not published until 1889, only a few months before the alleged discovery of the parchments. It is inconceivable that Boudet, or for that matter anyone else, could have hidden them in the structure of the altar without Saunière's knowledge.

But having introduced Boudet to the story in *L'Or de Rennes*, de Sède deals with him at some length, not only giving us a short biography but also a description of the church at Rennes-les-Bains, with implications of mysteries and important alignments. Later authors have built on de Sède's speculations and Boudet's name is now linked, vaguely but frequently, with the Saunière affair. Hence we think it is necessary to set out a few facts about Boudet and his book.

Henri Boudet was born at Quillan in 1837, son of the director of the local ironworks. His brother Edmond, who became a notary in Axat, was born three years later. Henri studied in Carcassonne, first at the *Petit Seminaire* (secondary school), then at the *Grand Seminaire* (priest's training college). He was ordained priest in 1861 and appointed to the parish of Rennes-les-Bains in October 1872. He had been there for thirteen years when Saunière arrived at Rennes-le-Château.

While at Rennes-les-Bains Henri Boudet developed an interest in linguistics, history and archaeology. He wrote papers, which he submitted to the Aude Society for Scientific Studies. His major surviving work is his book *La Vraie Langue celtique et le Cromleck de Rennes-les-Bains* (The true Celtic language and the Cromlech of Rennes-les-Bains), which he had published at his own expense in 1886.

As we remarked in chapter 4, this is an extremely odd work, a mixture of history, legend, etymology and local archaeology. In the first five of the eight chapters Boudet puts forward the bizarre hypothesis that ancient languages, such as Basque, Celtic, Hebrew and Punic, are derived from an even more ancient language – identical to modern English. To substantiate this claim he gives numerous 'cod' derivations, most of which are clearly absurd.

In the seventh chapter of his book, Boudet describes the *cromleck*, by which he means a stone circle. (The word cromlech in English has been used for both stone circle and megalithic tomb.) He does not describe a stone circle such as are found in the British Isles: a well-defined ring of say 30 m or occasionally up to 100 m diameter. He leads us on a tour of the mountain ridges surrounding Rennes-les-Bains, beginning at the confluence of the rivers Sals and Rialsesse, then he traces the ridge southward through Blanchefort and Rocque Nègre, to the point where the Sals is fed by the Blanque. The circular tour is completed on the ridge to the east of Rennes-les-Bains, via Serbaïrou and the western slopes of Pech Cardou. On this route Boudet describes standing stones, natural outcrops and other features, all of which combine to make his *cromleck*. The area is illustrated by a map drawn by his brother Edmond.

On arriving at each natural feature, Boudet gives a derivation of the name. For example he writes: 'The Rialsès [i.e. Rialsesse] runs in a valley whose fertile earth enables the inhabitants to pay their taxes and where the Celts till their ground for easy produce.' He derives Rialsesse from two English words, real (i.e. effective) and cess (tax, now dialect).[1] A second of many examples is Cardou, which is a steeply sloping mountain and therefore one which it would be difficult to get a cart up. Hence his derivation from the English words cart (to travel in a cart) and how (in what way?). Thus he arrives at Carthow which has evolved to Cardou.[2] Other derivations are equally ridiculous.

According to Boudet, the *cromleck* marks out a *drunemeton*, or central meeting place of the Tectosages, a Celtic tribe known through the writings of Strabo.[3] With his usual ingenuity Boudet derives this word (*dru-neme-ton*) from the English trow (now obsolete, but meaning to think or believe) and name. This was therefore the place where the learned members of society gathered to think up names for the places they lived in, or as Boudet puts it 'to carry out their scientific functions and make up the particular or general nomenclature'.[4] In other words it was a special place where the tribal dignitaries came together to invent these incredible names based on words from a language that had not yet come into existence.

It is very difficult to know what to make of this book. Boudet had a reputation for being an intelligent and learned man, and throughout the book there is evidence of much study and a breadth of reading. How, therefore, could such a man write a book like this? Was he someone who had got a cranky idea that he was determined to push at all costs, or was he writing tongue in cheek for his own amusement? He published the book at his own expense in 1886 and the following year submitted it to the Toulouse Academy of Sciences for a prize. It was turned down. Did Boudet intend it as a serious work or was he playing an elaborate prank on the local intelligentsia?

The book would almost certainly have remained in obscurity if it had not been for de Sède's including a description of it in *L'Or de Rennes*. De Sède clearly shows the absurdity of the derivations, but puts forward the suggestion that Boudet is writing in a coded language. De Sède writes:[5]

> . . . the work is coded with a procedure beloved by hermetists: that of puns and playing on words. The pseudo-linguistic ramblings have no other role than to mislead the inattentive reader and alert the perspicacious one; they make up an 'assembly' which lets [Boudet] hide, in a work of three hundred and ten pages, some key passages which are decoded either purely phonetically like puns, or by guessing the proper meaning from the figurative one, as with plays on words.
>
> These passages are usually indicated with a preposterous introduction of a 'key' word. An example: 'Cayrolo', a place name often found in southern France, comes from *caire* which indicates a square stone, in Latin *quadrum*. But Boudet pretends that against all evidence that 'Cayrolo' comes from three English words key, ear of corn and hole. This howler is put there only to indicate to us the key passage which immediately follows [Boudet p. 295] 'The Cayrolo of the Redones, a silo or storage pit for the precious cereal, was located to the south of Montferrand, quite near a track leading to the Coume stream and to Artigues. There being very heavy production of corn, they had to involve strangers from outside this region in order to harvest it with more speed.' But as everyone knows corn in dialect is gold. The pit near Montferrand containing the precious cereal is none other than the ancient mine located at this place. . . . And in the foreign harvesters, the informed reader will recall without difficulty the German miners and smelters brought to these places in the twelfth century by the Knights Templar.

With this sort of analysis it is not surprising that readers of de Sède's book wanted to consult Boudet's book for themselves. Since very few of the original 500 copies had survived, there was a demand for a reprint. In fact it has been reprinted no fewer than five times; one edition with a preface by Gérard de Sède (1978), and another the same year published by Belfond with a preface by Pierre Plantard. The most recent edition, with an introduction by Philippe Schrauben, was in 1984.

Pierre Plantard's preface is particularly interesting because it puts a slant on the story quite different from any we have seen elsewhere. In the first part of the preface Plantard states that his grandfather Charles, after lunching with Bérenger Saunière on 6 June 1892 went back with Henri Boudet to Rennes-les-Bains. Charles Plantard spent the night there and the following day Boudet gave him a copy of *La Vraie Langue celtique et le Cromleck de Rennes-les-Bains*, from which the Belfond edition is said to be photocopied.

Plantard's preface is quite lengthy and contains some very obscure comments on the content of Boudet's book, ostensibly with the aim of making it easier to understand, but in fact only succeeding in making it even more impenetrable. He introduces numerology, tarot cards, the signs of the zodiac, the nautical mile, the tomb near Arques, the Paris Meridian and the Knights Templar. All this leads him to the conclusion that Boudet was Saunière's master and directed everything that he did, including all the refurbishment of the church at Rennes-le-Château.

Plantard contends that the aim of all the decoration of the church of Ste Marie Madeleine was to illustrate Boudet's book. He wrote:

> His failure with the academic world of the Toulouse Academy of Sciences had given him an idea of writing a supplement to his publication of 1886. He thought and resolved to leave an illustration of it. Just as the scale of his map appears in the book in an unexpected place,[6] the illustrations of the book were going to appear *ex libris*. We find them at Rennes-le-Château where the young priest Saunière was available; the account books of the *Abbé* Boudet confirm this deduction. For several years Marie Dénarnaud received considerable sums which allowed the *abbé*, Bérenger Saunière to build and live like a millionaire. But a day arrived when the gifts dried up. The Boudet plan was complete. The *Abbé* Saunière had nothing for himself, he was incapable of decoding the masterpiece and had to indulge in expedients in order to survive.
>
> These illustrations are to be found in the church of Rennes-le-Château. Henri Boudet was the architect.[7]

Plantard states that Boudet's account books were thrown out on his death and were found on a tip by 'someone from Axat', who rescued them on account of their fine binding. He claims that between 1887 and 1891 Boudet gave Marie Dénarnaud 3,679,431 francs and between 1894 and 1903 he gave her 837,260 francs. In the same period he gave the Bishop of Carcassonne, *Monseigneur* Billard, 7,655,250 francs which was spent partly on a religious foundation at Prouille and partly on a children's home founded by Saint Vincent-de-Paul.

Some authors accept Plantard's explanation for Saunière's source of money,[8] but there are very strong grounds for not doing so.

1. There is no evidence that *Abbé* Boudet had wealth to the extent of being able to make donations amounting to tens of millions of francs. Plantard himself states that Boudet came from a poor family.
2. The alleged account books have not been seen and Plantard does not disclose who is supposed to hold them.
3. There is no evidence in Saunière's papers, which we discussed at length in chapter 14, that Boudet was involved in any way with the refurbishment of the church.

4. Plantard was a main source of information for de Sède's first book on Rennes-le-Château, written eleven years before the preface was published. Why then does nothing about Boudet's financial involvement appear here?

5. If Saunière had received money from Boudet, there is no reason whatsoever for him to keep this secret from the bishop – who, according to Plantard, had also received contributions from Boudet.

The last point is the most telling of all: Saunière's conflict with the bishop resulted in his being relieved of his priestly duties.

Knowing Plantard's liking for secret documents and spurious papers full of invention, such as those he and de Chérisey placed in the Bibliothèque nationale, it is fair to assume that this preface was yet another in the long line of deliberately misleading documents to come from the pen of Pierre Plantard.

The introduction to the Belisane edition of 1984 was written by Philippe Schrauben who makes an observation about Boudet's book which we have not had the opportunity to verify, but which deserves a mention because he reveals that Boudet's work relied more heavily than normally realized on the works of other authors. Schrauben writes: '. . . we notice that *La Vraie Langue celtique* . . . is a huge mosaic of extracts of 19th-century works carefully chosen to make them more or less coherent. There are not only detailed quotations but whole pages transcribed word for word and put end to end.'

Although Boudet gives some references, these are not always precise and Schrauben considers that to understand the book one would have to research his sources and read them in the context of the time. Whether this would be worth the effort is quite another matter.

I Select Chronology of Rennes-le-Château

1732   5 November, marriage of Marie de Nègre d'Ables to François d'Hautpoul, first *marquis de* Blanchefort.

1781   17 January, death of Marie de Nègre d'Ables. Antoine Bigou priest at Rennes-le-Château.

1837   16 November, birth of Henri Boudet.

1852   11 April, birth of Bérenger Saunière.

1855   17 February, birth of Alfred Saunière.

1868   12 August, birth of Marie Dénarnaud.

1872   16 October, Henri Boudet appointed priest at Rennes-les-Bains.

1884   Alleged publication of Stüblein's *Pierres gravées du Languedoc*.

1885   1 June, Bérenger Saunière appointed priest at Rennes-le-Château, at the church of Ste Marie Madeleine.

1886   Publication of Boudet's *La Vraie Langue celtique et le Cromleck de Rennes-les-Bains*.
        Saunière temporarily transferred to the Seminary at Narbonne for delivering pro-monarchist sermons during the election.
        1 July, Saunière returns to Rennes-le-Château.

1888   Church renovations begin.

1890   4 May (to 12 June 1891) Saunière temporarily in charge of Antugnac as well as Rennes-le-Château.

1891   21 June, dedication of the statue of the Lourdes Virgin on the supposed Visigothic pillar.
        21 September, Saunière records 'Discovery of a tomb' in his diary.

1895   March, letters of complaint to the Prefect of the Aude about Saunière's activity in the churchyard.

1897   6 June, the renovated church consecrated by the Bishop of Carcassonne, *Monseigneur* Billard.

1902   *Monseigneur* Beauséjour appointed Bishop of Carcassonne.

1901   Building work starts on the *Villa Béthanie*, the *Tour Magdala*, the belvedere and the gardens.

1905   25 June, members of the Aude Society for Scientific Studies visit Rennes-le-

Château and see the tombstone of Marie de Nègre d'Ables.

9 September, death of Alfred Saunière.

1908   16 August, second visit of the Aude Society who see the Knights' Stone.

1909   22 January, Saunière transferred to Coustouge but refuses to go. Replaced by *Abbé* Marty.

1 February, Saunière resigns.

1911   1 February, the Bishop forbids Saunière to administer the Sacraments.

1915   30 March, death of Henri Boudet.

3 July, Bishop issues reminder to Saunière that he is forbidden to administer the Sacraments.

1917   22 January, death of Saunière. His housekeeper, Marie Dénarnaud, takes over the estate.

1920   Birth of Pierre Plantard.

1946   26 July, Noël Corbu buys Saunière's old estate from Marie Dénarnaud, allowing her to live there for her lifetime. Many of Saunière's possessions have been stolen by this time.

1953   29 January, death of Marie Dénarnaud.

1955   10 April, opening of *l'Hôtel de la Tour*.

1956   12, 13, 14 January first account of the supposed treasure in the local newspaper, *La Dépêche du Midi*.

7 May, Priory of Sion officially registered at St Julien-en-Genevois.

1960   Plantard and de Chérisey meet de Sède.

1961   May, l'ORTF films a television programme on Rennes-le-Château, *La roue tourne*.

1962   De Sède's *Les Templiers sont parmi nous* published, with Appendix by Pierre Plantard.

14 June, Corbu's *L'Histoire de Rennes-le-Château* deposited in the archives at Carcassonne.

3 December, Descadeillas's *Notice sur Rennes-le-Château* deposited in the archives at Carcassonne.

1964   Lobineau's *Genealogy of the Merovingian Kings* deposited in the Bibliothèque nationale.

1965   The Corbu family leave Rennes-le-Château.

1966   Henri Buthion buys *l'Hôtel de la Tour*.

March, De Sède visits Rennes-le-Château, meets Descadeillas and shows him copies of the parchments.

13 May, *A Merovingian Treasure at Rennes-le-Château* deposited in the Bibliothèque nationale.

20 June, Extracts from Stüblein's book deposited in the Bibliothèque nationale.

1967   20 March, *Le Serpent Rouge* deposited in the Bibliothèque nationale.

27 April, *Secret Papers of Henri Lobineau* deposited in the Bibliothèque nationale.

October, de Sède's *L'Or de Rennes* published.

1968 20 May, Noël Corbu killed in a car crash.

1970 December, Lincoln first meets de Sède.

1971 February, Lincoln's first visit to Rennes-le-Château.

March, de Sède gives Lincoln the solution and the key to the code for Parchment 1.

September, BBC films at Rennes-le-Château.

1972 12 February, *The Lost Treasure of Jerusalem?* broadcast.

1974 Descadeillas's *Mythologie du Trésor de Rennes* published.

30 October, *The Priest, the Painter and the Devil* broadcast.

1978 Republication of Boudet's *La Vraie Langue celtique et le Cromleck de Rennes-les-Bains*, with a preface by Pierre Plantard.

1979 March, Lincoln first meets Plantard and de Chérisey.

27 November, *The Shadow of the Templars* broadcast.

1982 Baigent, Leigh and Lincoln's *The Holy Blood and the Holy Grail* published.

1985 July, Death of de Chérisey.

1986 Baigent, Leigh and Lincoln's *The Messianic Legacy* published.

1988 The 'Poussin' tomb demolished.

1996 Andrews and Schellenberger's *The Tomb of God* published.

17 September, BBC's *Timewatch* programme on Rennes-le-Château.

1997 Lincoln's *Key to the Sacred Pattern* published.

2000 3 February, Death of Plantard.

2004 29 May, Death of de Gérard de Sède.

Notes

Chapter 2 – The First Account of the Treasure

1. See for example *Les Archives de l'Abbé Saunière*, 101 documents collected by Pierre Jarnac, Collection 'Coleur Ochre'.
2. The best account of the surviving documents belonging to Bérenger Saunière can be found in Corbu and Captier *L'Héritage de l'Abbé Saunière*.
3. A. Salamon, *La Dépêche du Midi*, 12, 13, 14 January 1956.
4. Charles Nungesser, a French wartime fighter pilot, and his navigator François Coli disappeared on 9 May 1927, during an attempted flight from Paris to the east coast of USA in a Levasseur PL8 aircraft called *L'Oiseau Blanc* (The White Bird) – *Chronicle of Aviation*, JL International Publishing, 1992, p. 240. Pierre Corbu died on 2 September 1927 in a Farman biplane. His co-pilot was called Givion, ibid., p. 247.
5. Markale, *Rennes-le-Château*, p. 213.
6. Descadeillas, *Mythologie*, p. 65.

Chapter 3 – The Archives at Carcassonne

1. Although known to be by Noël Corbu, since no author's name is on the document, it is listed in the Bibliography under Anonymous.
2. See Lobineau, *Dossiers secrets*. In this file there is a letter signed by Noël Corbu, postmarked 1962, in which he asks what documents Sauniéres (*sic*) showed to *Abbé* Hoffet. Irregularities in the typescript (e.g. the displacement of the letter 'A' in *Abbé*) are identical to those in the copy of *Histoire de Rennes-le-Château* deposited in the Archives at Carcassonne.
3. Marie de Nègre d'Ables had several titles. She became Countess of Hautpoul and Marchioness of Blanchefort on her marriage.
4. It is impossible to be precise about the value of money over a long period of time. We have noted that there were 25 French francs to the pound sterling in 1895 and that the 1895 pound was worth about £100 in today's money; thus 1 franc in 1895 would be equivalent to £4 in 2003. However, if one compares the prices that Saunière paid for objects for the refurbishment of his church, for example, or wages of workmen, which were typically 4.5 francs per day, it is clear that to find the equivalent purchasing power we have to multiply by a factor larger than 4. We have arbitrarily chosen a factor of 7.
5. Descadeillas, *Notice*, p. 2.
6. Ibid.
7. Ibid.
8. Ibid.
9. Ibid., p. 4.
10. Ibid., p. 5.
11. Ibid., p. 6.

12. Ibid.
13. Ibid., p. 11.
14. Ibid., p. 12.
15. Ibid.
16. Ibid., p. 13.

Chapter 4 – The Gold of Rennes

1. The texts of the two books are very similar but not quite identical. We have taken extracts from *L'Or de Rennes*. Amazingly, there was no English translation of this book available for over thirty years, until *The Accursed Treasure of Rennes-le-Château* was published in 2001. The translations in chapter 4 are our own.
2. De Sède, *L'Or de Rennes*, p. 22
3. Ibid., p. 23. Having said on the previous page that there were three tubes, he now says four parchments. Descadeillas described them as two or three scrolls.
4. Ibid., p. 26.
5. Ibid., p. 29.
6. Tesseyre, *Excursion à Rennes-le-Château*.
7. De Sède, *L'Or de Rennes*, p. 46.
8. Ibid., p. 89.
9. Ibid., p. 91. The name Blancasall is clearly an invention (a version of Blanchefort), as is Celse-Nazaire. The church at Rennes-les-Bains is dedicated to Saints Celse and Nazaire.
10. Another discrepancy in the dates. De Sède has the visit to the bishop in 1893 and the trip to Paris after that. We give the full text of this passage in chapter 10.
11. De Sède, *L'Or de Rennes*, p. 108.
12. Ibid., p. 150. In a later book on the affair of Rennes-le-Château, *Signé:Rose+Croix*, p. 149, de Sède gives us the following solution to this puzzle: 'The soldier holds his shield up high (*haut bouclier*), you see a tower half-hidden (*demi tour*) and a dome (*dôme*); Veronica washes God (*Véronica lave le Dieu*); Simon looks on (*Simon regarde*).'
    Stringing the French together we have: *Haut bouclier; demi tour; dôme; Véronica lave le dieu; Simon regarde* which has the same sound in French as *Au bouclier, demi-tour d'homme vers haut nid qu'à Laval-Dieu six monts regardent* – 'Towards the boucliers (a mining term), a half turn of a man towards the high nest so that six mountains look out on Laval-Dieu (a place).' This is supposed to be a clue for finding the treasure.
13. Rosicrucian, a member of a world-wide brotherhood claiming to possess esoteric wisdom handed down from ancient times. The name derives from the order's symbol, a combination of a rose and a cross. The teachings of Rosicrucianism combine elements reminiscent of a variety of religious beliefs and practices. *Encyclopaedia Britannica CD*, Standard Edition, 1999, *Rosicrucian*. See also chapter 12. In the later version of his book, *Signé:Rose+Croix*, de Sède expands on the subject of the supposed Rosicrucian connection.

Chapter 5 – The Chronicle Programmes

1. Baigent, Leigh and Lincoln, *The Holy Blood*, p. xiii. The edition he read was *Le Trésor Maudit de Rennes-le-Château*.
2. The Knights' Stone, or *Dalle des Chevaliers*, see chapter 9.

3. Lincoln, *Key to the Sacred Pattern*, pp.7–12. We give details of this message in chapter 6.
4. Ibid., p. 15.
5. Ibid., p. 40.
6. Ibid., p. 44.
7. Ibid., p. 62.
8. Ibid., p. 34.
9. Ibid., p. 66. The broken stone and its significance are described in chapter 9.
10. For the geometry of the pentagon and an explanation of the Golden Section, see Appendix E.
11. Lincoln, *Key to the Sacred Pattern*, p. 120.
12. For an analysis of the geometry of the area around Rennes-le-Château, see chapter 13.
13. Lincoln, *Key to the Sacred Pattern*, p. 146.
14. Plantard's statements, as recorded on film, are given verbatim in chapter 11.

Chapter 6 – The Parchments

1. Wordsworth/White, Oxford 1889.
2. If the message had been written in lower case with punctuation and accents, it could have been either *à Dagobert II, roi, et à Sion est ce trésor, et il est là, mort* (this treasure belongs to King Dagobert II and to Sion and he is there dead) or *à Dagobert II, roi, et à Sion est ce trésor et il est la mort* (this treasure belongs to King Dagobert II and to Sion and it [the treasure] is death). The first translation leads to the question 'Where is Dagobert dead?' At Sion? Dagobert is in fact buried in Stenay in northern France. The second translation, which gives a warning that to have anything to do with the treasure is dangerous, seems the more plausible.
3. De Sède, *Signé:Rose+Croix*.
4. Andrews and Schellenberger, *The Tomb of God*, p. 41.
5. Ibid., p. 85.
6. Baigent, Leigh and Lincoln, *The Holy Blood*, Introduction, p. xiv.
7. De Sède, *Signé:Rose+Croix*, Annexe II.
8. Lincoln, *The Holy Place*, Appendix One.
9. Encyclopaedia Britannica, 1991, vol. 16, p. 80.
10. De Sède, *L'Or de Rennes*, p. 111.

Chapter 7 – Stones and Inscriptions

1. Marie, *Rennes-le-Château, Etude Critique*, p. 27.
2. De Monts, *Bérenger Saunière curé à Rennes-le-Château*, p. 9.
3. Descadeillas, *Mythologie*, p. 71.
4. De Sède, *L'Or de Rennes*, pp. 28, 29.
5. Descadeillas, *Mythologie*, p. 22.
6. De Sède, *L'Or de Rennes*, p. 31.
7. Some authors describe it as a spider and deduce from the French word for spider, *araignée*, that it really indicates *à Rennes*, but its appendages are sinuous like tentacles and not straight like spiders' legs. There is a carving of an octopus in the church of Saint-Sulpice in Paris, which may have been its inspiration.

8. de Sède, *L'Or de Rennes*, p. 29 (quoted already in chapter 4, but repeated here because of its importance). De Sède gives the reference as: Stüblein, Eugène, *Pierres gravées du Languedoc*, Limoux, 1884. We have not included this work in the bibliography.

9. Fages, *De Campagne-les-Bains à Rennes-le-Château*.

10. Descadeillas, *Mythologie*, p. 67.

11. Stüblein, *Description d'un voyage aux Etablissements Thermaux de l'arrondissement de Limoux*. The importance of this book is that it provides an authentic example of Stüblein's signature.

12. Descadeillas, *Mythologie*, p. 68.

13. Ibid., p. 76.

14. Ibid., p. 72.

15. Ibid., p. 73.

16. Saul and Glaholm, *A Bibliography*, p. 13.

17. De Sède, *L'Or de Rennes*, p. 101.

Chapter 8 – Evidence from History

1. For the history of the Merovingian kings, see Pfister, *Cambridge Medieval History*, vol. II, chapter IV.

2. Wallace-Hadrill, *The Long-haired Kings*, pp. 234–8.

3. Costen, *The Cathars and the Albigensian Crusade*, p. 11.

4. The Knights Hospitaller (the Sovereign Military and Hospitaller Order of St John of Jerusalem, Rhodes and Malta) originated at a hospital in Jerusalem founded in the eleventh century and were formally recognized by the Pope in 1115. They are mostly remembered for their famous defence during the siege of Malta in 1565. The order exists to this day.

   The Templars (the Knights of the Order of the Temple of Solomon) were founded in the early twelfth century. They supported the crusades through their banking and financial activities. They held castles and extensive lands in France, Spain and elsewhere. Their consequent wealth and the failure of the crusades eventually led to their downfall at the hands of Philip IV of France in 1312. Much of their wealth was transferred to the Hospitallers. For an account of their extraordinary story see Helen Nicholson, *The Knights Templar – A New History*, Sutton 2001.

5. Josephus, *The Jewish War*, book vii, p. 148: 'a lamp stand, likewise made of gold, but constructed on a different pattern from those which we use in ordinary life. Affixed to a pedestal was a central shaft, from which there extended slender branches, arranged trident fashion, a wrought lamp being attached to the extremity of each branch; of these there were seven, indicating the honour paid to that number among the Jews.'

6. Pernoud, *Blanche of Castile*, p. 140.

7. Encyclopaedia Britannica CD, Standard Edition, 1999, *Blanche of Castile*.

Chapter 9 – Evidence on the Ground

1. Pliny, *Naturalis Historia*, 3, 4, 5: 37.

2. Items are on display in the Bérenger Saunière Centre Museum.

3. Costen, *The Cathars*, p. 82.

4. Fourié, *Histoire de Rennes-le-Château antérieure à 1789*, p. 99.

5. Baigent, Leigh and Lincoln, *The Holy Blood*, p. 46.

6. Fourié, *Histoire de Rennes-le-Château antérieure à 1789*.

7. By the St Jean Knights of Jerusalem.

8. A similar though not identical devil, in bronze, appeared on the BBC's programme, *Antiques Roadshow*, in November 1997. It was made in Paris in the 1870s or 1880s and was valued at £6,000.

9. The source for the text is the Roman historian Eusebius, who relates that, during his campaign against Maxentius, the Emperor Constantine had a vision of the Christian chi-rho monogram together with the words 'By this sign you will conquer'. He had the monogram painted on the shields of his troops and subsequently defeated Maxentius at the Battle of the Milvian Bridge, AD 312. But note the addition of the word 'him'.

10. De Sède, *Rennes-le-Château: le Dossier*, p. 190.

11. Corbu and Captier, *L'Héritage de l'Abbé Saunière*, p. 99.

12. Fages, *Bulletin de la Société d'Etudes scientifiques de l'Aude*, vol. 20, p. 128.

13. Guy, *Bulletin de la Société d'Etudes scientifiques de l'Aude*, vol. 31, p. 197.

14. Fages, *Bulletin de la Société d'Etudes scientifiques de l'Aude*, vol. 20, p. 128.

15. Ibid., p. 76.

16. Ibid., p. 84.

17 . Tisseyre, *Bulletin de la Société d'Etudes scientifiques de l'Aude*, vol. 17, p. 98.

18. Boumendil, *Les Cahiers de Rennes-le-Château*, vol. 11, p. 31.

19. Tisseyre, *Bulletin de la Société d'Etudes scientifiques de l'Aude*, vol 17, p. 98.

20. Baigent, Leigh and Lincoln, *The Holy Blood*, fig. 6. Lincoln made errors in the case endings and actually suggested *Christus Antiquus Ordo Mysticusque Prioratus Sionis Defendit*.

21. Bedu, *Rennes-le-Château, Autopsie d'un Mythe*, p. 64.

22. Fanthorpe, *Rennes-le-Château, its Mysteries and Secrets*, among plates following p. 120.

23. Baigent, Leigh and Lincoln, *The Holy Blood*, plate 18.

24. Andrew Baker (http://smithpp0.tripod.com/psp/id35.html), *Shugborough and Rennes-le-Château*, states that the first documentary evidence for the memorial dates from 1758. He suggests that it was originally intended to be mounted over the fireplace in the dining room, after extensions to the hall in 1748/9. It has been suggested that the inscription refers to lines written by an eighteenth-century poetess, Anna Seward (1747–1809):

> Out Your Own Sweet Vale, Alicia, Vanisheth Vanity
> Twixt Deity and Man thou shepherdest the way.

As she would have only been a small child at the time of its construction this seems very improbable. Baker thinks that the lines were composed to fit the inscription, rather than the other way round.

In 2004 cryptographers who had worked at Bletchley Park (the United Kingdom's wartime centre for code-breaking) were asked to apply their expertise to solving the inscription. Among the many solutions offered the one favoured by the staff at Shugborough Hall was *Dis Manibus Optimae Uxoris Optimae Sororis Viduus Amantissimus Vovit Virtutibus*. 'To the Gods and Spirits. A loving widower dedicated [this memorial] to the virtues of a noble wife and noble sister.' While such a meaning is possible, we should point out that it is not a familiar Latin dedicatory text, and it is unlikely that anyone except the author and those in whom he confided would know what it meant.

Chapter 10 – Secret Papers

1. Descadeillas, *Mythologie*, p. 83.

2. The Bulletin is untraceable because no details are given.

3. Descadeillas, *Mythologie*, p. 81.

4. Baigent, Leigh and Lincoln, *The Holy Blood*, p. 70.

5. A *curé* of Rennes-les-Bains was called Jean Vié (1808–72).

6. The myth about the Merovingian kings being descended from the tribe of Benjamin (Table 4 in the Genealogies) finishes with the following lines: 'At the great enigma of Arcadia, Virgil, who was in the secret of the Gods, lifted the veil to the Bucolics,' Eclogue X, lines 46–9:

> Tu procul a patria (nec sit mihi credere tantum)
>
> Alpinas a! dura, nives et frigora Rheni
>
> Me sine sola vides. A! te ne frigora laedant!
>
> A! tibi ne teneras glacies secet aspera plantas!

'You are far from your homeland (I can hardly believe it). Unfeeling one you gaze on the Alpine snows and the cold water of the Rhine, all alone without me. May the frosts not harm you! May the sharp ice not cut your tender feet!'

The passage relates to two lovers in Arcady: Gallus is dying for hopeless love of his absent mistress Lycoris. Here the words are given a different slant – that the Merovingian line, in Austrasie, near the Rhine, is far from its origins. The name of the spurious publishing house, Alpina, was taken from this passage.

7. There is another and later version of the discovery, according to which a glass phial containing a roll of paper was found in an old baluster. See Captier, Captier and Marrot.

8. Altar stone now in the Museum at Toulouse. The inscription is as follows (lines divided by /):

MATRI DEUM/CN POMP/PROBVS/CVRATOR TEM/PLI V S L M

'To the mother of gods, Cnaeus Pompeius Probus, the curator of the Temple, willingly and deservedly paid his vow.'

9. Altar stone now in the Museum at Perpignan:

C POMPEIVS QVARTVS/A M/SVO

'Caius Pompeius Quartus (dedicated this) to his friend.'

10. Fragments of a tombstone, possibly in private hands at Alet:

DIS MANIBUS/L CALPARIS/ VOL SENI ASSARI/DE SUA PECVNIA OTIOS/C

'To the gods and spirits of the dead, and the spirit of Lucuis Calparis Assuarius Senior, of the Voltinian tribe, erected from his own private money.'

11. Guy, *Reproduction d'une pierre tombale*.

12. The signatures are compared at the following website:
http://www.multimania.com/insolite/rennes/chevaliers.htm

13. Picknett and Prince, *The Templar Revelation*, p. 56. The deposit slip was dated 15 February, i.e. before the deaths, but Pickett and Prince write: 'However, subsequent research has shown that the work was deposited among the dossiers on 20 March – after they were all found dead – and the deposit slip was deliberately falsified to bear the February date.'

14. Marie, *Etude Critique*, p. 194.

15. Picknett and Prince, *The Templar Revelation*, p. 58

Chapter 11 – Plantard and de Chérisey

1. Baigent, Leigh and Lincoln, *The Holy Blood*, p.67.
2. De Sède, *Les Templiers sont parmi nous*, Annexe 1, pp.273–291.
3. Baigent, Leigh and Lincoln, *The Holy Blood*, p.192–193.
4. Paul Smith has an interesting web site: http://priory-of-Sion.com/, on which there are the texts of documents, letters and articles relating to Pierre Plantard and his associates and also to the Priory of Sion. We have, with his permission, used some of that material in revising Chapters 11 and 12.
5. Baigent, Leigh and Lincoln, *The Messianic Legacy*, pp.361–366.
6. There were other publications with the same title during the occupation.
7. Baigent, Leigh and Lincoln, *The Holy Blood*, Note 27 to Chapter 8.
8. Baigent, Leigh and Lincoln, *The Holy Blood*, p.231.
9. Baigent, Leigh and Lincoln, *The Messianic Legacy*, chapter 23.
10. Hisler, *Rois et gouvernants de la France*. Ann-Léa Hisler died in 1970 and in the following year Plantard married Anne-Marie Cavaille.
11. Plantard, *Deux Curés* in Preface to Belfond Edition of Boudet's *La Vrai Langue celtique*.
12. Rivière, *Le Fabuleux Trésor*, pp.159–163.
13. Plantard, *Souvenirs reconstitués* in Preface to Belfond Edition of Boudet's *La Vrai Langue celtique*. . .
14. Descadeillas, *Mythologie*, p.76.
15. Markale, *Rennes-le-Château*, pp.224, 225.
16. Baigent, Leigh and Lincoln, *The Holy Blood*, p.188.
17. Markale, *Rennes-le-Château* . . ., p.218.
18. Ibid, p.218.
19. Ibid, p.225.
20. Chaumeil, *Le Trésor du Triangle d'Or*, p.80.
21. Markale, *Rennes-le-Château*, p.225.
22. Descadeillas, *Mythologie*, p.67.
23. Pierre Jarnac (real name Michel Vallet) has written on Rennes-le-Château.
24. We wrote two letters and made two telephone calls to Jean-Luc Chaumeil requesting a meeting. Unfortunately he declined to see us.
25. We think de Sède's judgment on Plantard is rather harsh. He could not have compiled the *Dossiers secrets* without a huge amount of research and considerable knowledge.
26. Dagobert was assassinated in 679, as is correctly stated in Plantard's genealogies.

Chapter 12 – The Priory of Sion

1. Since Sion is usually translated as Zion in English, it should perhaps be known as the Priory of Zion. We have however followed the practice of other authors by calling it the Priory of Sion.
2. We have not come across the constitution book and it may not exist.
3. Encyclopedia Britannica CD, Standard Edition, 1999, *Rosicrucian*.
4. Baigent, Leigh and Lincoln, *The Holy Blood*, p. 92.
5. Ibid., p. 142.
6. *Dictionary of National Biography*, vol. 7, p. 348.
7. We consulted Michael White, author of a recent biography of Isaac Newton, who told us that he was aware of the claims made about the Priory of Sion and added: 'Sadly I have nothing on Newton and the Priory. I wish I had, as I would have loved to have included it in my biography. But I could find no evidence and could not therefore speculate.'

8. Barrett, *Secret Societies*, p. 99.

9. Baigent, Leigh and Lincoln, *The Holy Blood*, p. 200.

10. Three points to note about this hypothesis are:

    a. Baigent, Leigh and Lincoln were not the first authors to question if Jesus was married. See for example Phipps, *Was Jesus Married?*, published twelve years earlier.

    b. There is a tradition in Provence that Mary Magdalene, Mary Jacoby (sister of the Virgin Mary), Mary Salome (mother of the saints John and James), Sara their servant and others reached France in a boat and landed at Saintes Maries-de-la-Mer. Their arrival is commemorated annually in the town.

    c. In none of the secret papers is it claimed that the Merovingians were descended from Christ. On Table 4 of the genealogies it is stated that the Merovingian kings were from a tribe called the Sicambriani who had come from Israel via Greece and had then crossed the Rhine.

11. Baigent, Leigh and Lincoln, *The Messianic Legacy*, pp. 288–90.

12. Ibid., p. 329.

Chapter 13 – Lines on the Landscape

1. Institut Géographique National, Sheet 3615, Paris 1994.

2. Lincoln, *The Holy Place*, p. 67. Fig. 13.1 and other figures in this chapter have been drawn using grid coordinates from the map published by IGN.

3. Ibid., p. 70.

4. The azimuth, A, of a sunrise can be found from the formula:

$$CosA = (Sin\delta - Sin\phi\ sinh)/(cos\phi\ cosh),$$

   where δ is the declination (i.e. angle above the celestial equator) of the sun on the particular date, h is the angle of elevation of the horizon and ϕ is the latitude of the place. The latitude of Rennes-le-Château is 42.9°. In the direction of Château de Blanchefort from Rennes-le-Château, the distant horizon has an elevation of + 0.7°. On 22 July, the declination of the sun is about 20.5°. Putting δ = 20.5°, h = 0.7 and ϕ = 42.9° into the above equation we find that azimuth of sunrise is 62.2°, which is about 12.6° north of the line from Rennes-le-Château to Château de Blanchefort.

5. Wood, *Genisis*, p. 56.

6. Ibid., p. 243.

7. Lincoln, *The Holy Place*, p. 94.

8. Ibid., p. 96.

9. Ibid., p. 155. We have examined the grotto and are sure it is an entirely natural feature.

10. BBC *Timewatch*, *The History of a Mystery*, In-Vision Productions, produced by Bill Cran. Broadcast 17 September 1996.

11. Andrews and Schellenberger, *The Tomb of God*, p. 255.

12. Ibid., p. 295.

13. Wood, *Genisis*, p. 54.

14. Lincoln, *The Holy Place*, p. 146.

15. Book covers, *The Holy Place, Genesis, The Tomb of God*, respectively.

Chapter 14 – Bérenger Saunière

1. Bedu, *Rennes-le-Château*, p. 18.

2. They also had two children, Antoine and Jean, who had died in infancy. De Monts, *Bérenger Saunière*, p. 26.

3. Bedu, *Rennes-le-Château*, p. 10.

4. Ibid., p. 18.

5. Corbu and Captier, *L'Héritage*, p. 233.

6. Preserved by Claire Corbu and partly published in Corbu and Captier, *L'Héritage*.

7. Corbu and Captier, *L'Héritage*, p. 71.

8. Bedu, *Rennes-le-Château*, p. 26; also Rivière, *Le Fabuleux Trésor*, p. 76.

9. Bedu, *Rennes-le-Château*, p. 26; also Rivière, *Le Fabuleux Trésor*, p. 68.

10. Corbu and Captier, *L'Héritage*, p. 74.

11. Ibid., p. 75.

12. Ibid., p. 77.

13. Ibid., p. 78.

14. Rivière, *Le Fabuleux Trésor*, p. 88.

15. Corbu and Captier, *L'Héritage*, p. 85.

16. Descadeillas, *Mythologie du Trésor de Rennes*, p. 22.

17. Rivière, *Le Fabuleux Trésor*, p. 93.

18. Corbu and Captier, *L'Héritage*, p. 87.

19. Rivière, *Le Fabuleux Trésor*, Appendix, p. II, Bill No 6.

20. Reproduced in Corbu and Captier, *L'Héritage*, pp. 105–10.

21. Corbu and Captier, *L'Héritage*, p. 114.

22. Ibid., p. 140.

23. Ibid., p. 140.

24. Ibid., p. 140.

25. Ibid., p. 151.

26. Stated by Guy Patton in a lecture to the Saunière Society, Bournemouth University, 10 July 2004.

27. Draft in Corbu and Captier, *L'Héritage*, p. 165.

28. Reproduced in Corbu and Captier, *L'Héritage*, p. 193ff.

29. Discussed in detail in Bedu, *Rennes-le-Château*, p. 107ff.

30. Corbu and Captier, *L'Héritage*, p. 179.

31. Féral, *Deux Abbés Saunières à Rennes-le-Château*, Association Terre de Rhedae No. 8, October 1994, p. 34.

32. Corbu and Captier, *L'Héritage*, p. 253.

33. Ibid., p. 216.

34. Ibid., p. 180.

35. Ibid., p. 182.

36. Bedu, *Rennes-le-Château*, p. 123ff.

37. Ibid., p. 134.

38. Ibid., p. 135.

39. Ibid., p. 135.

40. Plantard, *Conclusions* in Preface to the Belfond Edition of Boudet's *La Vraie Langue celtique*, 1978.

Chapter 15 – History and Pseudo-history

1. Flem-Ath and Wilson, *The Atlantis Blueprint*, pp. 216–20.

2. Kit Williams, *Masquerade*, Jonathan Cape, 1979. This is an illustrated story, and hidden within it was a riddle, which when solved led the reader to the location of a 22 carat gold hare buried somewhere in the British Isles. The puzzle was solved in 1981.

3. BBC *Timewatch* programme, broadcast 17 September 1996.

4. Picknett and Prince in *Turin Shroud: In Whose Image?* are aware of the problem of distortion of the image of the face and contend that it is actually a picture of Leonardo da Vinci, taken by himself, using a primitive photographic technique.

5. De Sède, *L'Or de Rennes*, p. 22.

6. Ibid., p. 23.

7. Ibid., p. 30.

8. Andrews and Schellenberger, *The Tomb of God*, p. 50.

9. Ibid., p. 69.

10. De Sède, *Signé:Rose+Croix*, p. 160.

11. Andrews and Schellenberger, *The Tomb of God*, p. 118.

12. For example, Markale, *Rennes-le-Château et l'égnime de l'or Maudit*.

13. Picknett and Prince, *The Templar Revelation* (chapter 10, p. 58), write:

    It is a mistake to dismiss the *Dossiers secrets* simply because their overt message is demonstrably implausible. The sheer scale of the work behind them argues in favour of their having something to offer.

Appendix A – The Latin Manuscripts

1. For a full discussion of the topic see Wieland Willker's website http://www-user.uni-bremen.de/~wie/Rennes/index.html

Appendix C – Le Serpent Rouge

1. The red snake is the winding River Sals, which flows to the east of Château de Blanchefort and at times of heavy rain runs red due to suspended particles of clay.

2. Picknett and Prince, *The Templar Revelation*, p. 150. According to de Carbonnières, *Lutèce, Paris Ville Romaine*, a statuette of Isis has been found in Paris, but the site of the temple is unknown.

3. Addressed to Pierre Plantard by Philippe de Chérisey.

4. Presumably the famous seal is the seal of Solomon, which is mentioned in Ophiuchus. This is the seal of David, the six-pointed star, which also figures on the Plantard coat of arms as depicted in *Les Dossiers secrets*.

5. In the French *Nautonnier*, the name given to the Grand Masters of the Priory of Sion, confirms that the poems are referring to Plantard.

6. Plantard owned the mountain of Blanchefort (*The Holy Blood and The Holy Grail*, p. 188). If you stand on Blanchefort, the white rock, and look south you see the black rock, Roque Nègre.

7. Fairy story by Charles Perrault (1628–1703) first published in 1695 as *La Belle au Bois Dormant*. (His brother, Claude Perrault designed the building for the Paris Observatory, through which the Paris Meridian passes.) The first mention of Perrault (spelled Pérault) in the Rennes-le-Château story was by Noël Corbu, in the interview with Albert Salamon published on 14 January 1956 (see chapter 2). This may have been the inspiration for his inclusion in *Le Serpent Rouge*.

8. The chequered floor in the church at Rennes-le-Château, which in Saunière's day had sixty-four black and white squares.

9. This refers to the meridian line in Saint-Sulpice, not (as some authors have supposed) the Paris Meridian to the east of Rennes-le-Château.

10. If you stand on the meridian line in Saint-Sulpice and look to the north and south you see the rose windows of the north and south transepts with the letters P and S incorporated into their designs. The fourteen stones marked with a cross are the stations of the cross, in Saint-Sulpice marked very simply with a bronze cross and a text.

11. This is very obscure – it may be referring to the statue of the Virgin Mary at the east end of the church.

12. A clear reference to the church at Rennes-le-Château, with its black and white floor tiles, the statue of Asmodeus (or the Devil) beside the door and the statue of Jesus being baptised by St John the Baptist. Possibly the chequer-board pattern in the church gave de Chérisey the idea of using a knight's move in the encryption of Manuscript 1.

13. As we have noted in chapter 9, these words are inscribed above the statue of the Devil in the church at Rennes-le-Château.

14. In the church at Rennes-le-Château, below the painting on the west wall, Mark 11: 28.

15. Mary Magdalene had a vase of healing ointment, Luke 7: 7. She carries this vase on the painting in the church at Rennes-le-Château.

16. The Poussin tomb, which features prominently in the Rennes-le-Château saga, but note that there are three dots after 'EGO', as in the motto on the Plantard coat of arms.

17. The four horses represented the classical elements, fire, air, water, earth. Only the heaviest horse, earth, could leave an imprint in the rock.

18. Delacroix painted three pictures in the Chapel of the Holy Angels in Saint-Sulpice between 1855 and 1861. They are: on the ceiling, *St Michael overcoming the Dragon* (Revelations 12: 7–9); on the east wall, *Jacob wrestling with the Angel* (Genesis 32: 24–9); on the west wall, *Heliodorus being driven out of the Temple* (2 Maccabees 3: 22–8). In the last painting a horseman clad in gold armour rushes at Heliodorus and the horse strikes him with its hooves.

19. Reference to the seventh station of the cross in the Church of Saint-Sulpice, where the text is engraved in stone on the wall – 'Deliver me from the mire and let me not sink' – comes from Psalm 69, verse 14. (On the wall in the church this verse is attributed to Psalm 68, the number used in the Catholic liturgy.)

20. Isis, whose divine properties, such as virgin birth, some claim to be incorporated by Christianity into the image of the Virgin Mary.

21. In the French *La croix de crète* (the cross from Crete), instead of *La croix de crête* (the cross of the crest). Deliberate or an accidental error? See note 23.

22. There are fourteen stations of the cross in both churches.

23. Boudet in *La Vraie Langue celtique*, p. 235, writes, 'At the left of this menhir looking towards the thermal spa and the parish church, one discovers on the nearby rocks Greek crosses deeply carved with a chisel, measuring from twenty to thirty and thirty-five centimetres.'

24. The knight's tour is the sequence of moves on a chessboard by which the knight can land on all squares in turn – as used in the decryption of Manuscript 1.

25. By connecting the cross and the divine horse, de Chérisey is possibly making reference to the cross and the horse of God in the clear text of Manuscript 1.

26. Emile Signol painted four pictures in the Church of Saint-Sulpice: in the south transept the *Resurrection* and the *Ascension*; in the north transept the *Crucifixion* and *Christ Being Arrested in the Garden*. (The latter two are now popularly known as *Mort* and *Epée*!) The meridian line passes between the paintings.

27. The rose window in the north transept incorporates the letter P (for Saint Peter) and the one in the south transept has the letter S (for Saint Sulpice). Statues of the two saints stand nearby.

28. In Saint-Sulpice there is an octopus carved on the pedestal of the basin for holy water. This is possibly the inspiration for the octopus on the drawing of stone Marie II.

29. Olier died in the nearby seminary of Saint-Sulpice, which he himself had founded.

30. Possibly a reference to the tomb of Paul Urban de Fleury, who died in 1836 and was buried at Rennes-les-Bains.

31. The crypt of Saint-Sulpice was the burial place of several thousand people. During the French Revolution the church was pillaged, the tombs desecrated and the bones of the buried scattered.

32. The Church of Saint-Sulpice was known as the New Temple of Solomon, and referred to as such by de Sède in *L'Or de Rennes*, p. 24.
33. A description of the River Sals in flood.
34. Saint Sulpice's Day is 17 January: it is also a day that figures frequently in the Rennes-le-Château story.

Appendix E – The Geometry of the Pentagon

1. *Oxford Companion to Art*, OUP, 1979, p. 489.

Appendix F – Alignments

1. Lincoln, *The Holy Place* pp. 107–108

Appendix G – Units of Measurement

1. Our calculation based on grid coordinates gives 8.11 km = 5.04 miles = 1,613 poles.
2. Lincoln, *The Holy Place*, pp. 118–20.
3. Lincoln, *Key to the Sacred Pattern*, p. 211.

Appendix H – Henri boudet and La Vrai Langue celtique

1. Boudet, *La Vraie Langue celtique*, p. 227.
2. Ibid., p. 228.
3. Strabo, *Geography*, book 12. In this book, written about 7 BC, Strabo describes the *drunemeton* as a sacred meeting place of the Tectosages, though he is referring to the Tectosages of Asia Minor, not those of southern France. The word *drunemeton* is found nowhere else in ancient literature. It is not Latin or Greek and is therefore almost certainly Celtic. From linguistic parallels it seems likely that *nemeton* meant grove and *dru* meant oak. This derivation accords well with other descriptions of tribal government and worship in sacred groves, such as those given by Caesar, Tacitus and others.
4. Boudet, *La Vraie Langue celtique*, p. 226.
5. De Sède, *L'Or de Rennes*, p. 117.
6. There is no scale on the map. The following guide to find the scale of the map has been extracted from Plantard, *L'effect Boudet*, in Preface to the Belfond Edition of Boudet's *La Vraie Langue celtique*: Take the initial letters of the key at the bottom of the map, i.e. M(enhirs debout), M(enhirs couchés), D(olmens), C(roix grecques), giving MMDC or 2,600 in Roman numerals. The number 2,600 is said to be a multiple of the ell, which Plantard defines as 2.60 m (though in fact the ell is usually taken to be 45 inches or 1.143 m). He now multiplies 2.60 m by the date of publication of the book, 1886, to get 4.90 km, which is approximately the north–south extent covered by the map, hence the scale! This reasoning alone convinces us that Plantard did not expect his preface to be taken seriously.
7. Plantard, *La Canne de l'Ermite* in preface to the Belfond Edition of Boudet's *La Vraie Langue celtique*.
8. See for example, Andrews and Schellenberger, *The Tomb of God*, p. 176.

Bibliography

Andrews, Richard and Schellenberger, Paul, *The Tomb of God*, Warner Books, 1997.

Anonymous (but written by Noël Corbu), *Histoire de Rennes-le-Château*, Carcassonne. Archives Départmentales, 2J248, deposited 14 June 1962.

Baigent, Michael, Leigh, Richard and Lincoln, Henry, *The Holy Blood and the Holy Grail*, Book Club Associates/Jonathan Cape, 1982.

Baigent, Michael, Leigh, Richard and Lincoln, Henry, *The Messianic Legacy*, Corgi Edition, 1994.

Barrett, David V., *Secret Societies*, Blandford, 1977.

Bedu, Jean-Jacques, *Rennes-le-Château, Autopsie d'un Mythe*, Editions Loubatières 1990.

Blancasall, Madeleine, *Les Descendants mérovingiens ou l'enigme du Razès Wisigothe*, Geneva, 1965. Bibliothèque nationale, 16⁰Lk⁷50224.

Boudet, Henri, *La Vraie Langue celtique et le Cromleck de Rennes-les-Bains*, Carcassonne, 1886.

——, *La Vraie Langue celtique et le Cromleck de Rennes-les-Bains*, with a preface by Gérard de Sède, Editions de la Demeure Philosophale, Paris, 1978.

——, *La Vraie Langue celtique et le Cromleck de Rennes-les-Bains*, with a preface by Pierre Plantard, Pierre Belfond, Paris, 1978.

——, *La Vraie Langue celtique et le Cromleck de Rennes-les-Bains*, with introduction by Philippe Shrauben, reprinted by Editions Bélisane, Nice, 1984.

Boumendil, Claude and Tappa, Gilbert (Eds), *Les Cahiers de Rennes-le-Château*, Editions Bélisane, Nice, 1984.

Calvé, Emma, *My Life*, Arno Press, New York, 1977. (Originally published by D. Appleton, New York, 1922.)

Captier Antoine, Captier, Marcel and Marrot, Michel, *Rennes-le-Château, Le Secret de l'Abbé Saunière*, Editions Bélisane, 11570 Cazilhac, 1995.

Charroux, Robert, *Trésors du Monde, enterrés, emmurés, engloutis*, J'ai Lu, Paris 1962.

Chaumeil, Jean-Luc, *Le Trésor du Triangle d'Or*, Alain Lefeuvre: Collection 'Connaissance de l'Etrange', Nice, 1974.

Corbu, Claire and Captier, Antoine, *L'Héritage de l'Abbé Saunière*, Editions Bélisane, Cazilhac, 1995.

Corbu, Noël, *Recherches de Mons. L'Ingenieur en Chef Ernest Cros*, 1964. Displayed on the wall of the Berénger Saunière Centre Museum.

Costen, Michael, *The Cathars and the Albigensian Crusade*, Manchester University Press, 1997.

Courtauly, Joseph (Ed), *Pierres gravées du Languedoc*, Villarzel-du-Razès, 1962. Bibliothèque nationale, 8⁰Lj⁶849, Deposited on 20 June 1966, by Antoine L'Ermite.

de Carbonnières, Philippe, *Lutèce, Ville Romaine*, Paris-Musées, 1997.

de Monts, Abbé Bruno, *Bérenger Saunière Curé à Rennes-le-Château*, Editions Bélisane, 1989.

Descadeillas, René, *Notice sur Rennes-le-Château et l'Abbé Saunière*, Carcassonne, 3 December 1962. Archives Départmentales, 2J249.

——, *Mythologie du Trésor de Rennes*, Editions Collot, 1991. This edition is a reprint: the book was originally published at Carcassonne in 1974.

de Sède, Gérard, *Les Templiers sont parmi nous, ou l'Enigme de Gisors*, Editions Juillard, 1962.

——, *L'Or de Rennes, ou la Vie Insolite de Bérenger Saunière*, Editions Juillard, 1967.

——, *Le Trésor Maudit de Rennes-le-Château*, J'ai Lu, Paris, 1967 (a version of *L'Or de Rennes*).

——, *The Accursed Treasure of Rennes-le-Château* (translation of the above book by Bill Kersey), DEK Publishing, 2001.

——, *Signé:Rose+Croix*, Librairie Plon, 1977.

——, *Rennes-le-Château: le Dossier, les Impostures, les Phantasmes, les Hypothèses*, Robert Lafont, Paris, 1988.

l'Ermite, Antoine, *Un Trésor mérovingien à Rennes-le-Château*, Vié, Anvers, 1961. Bibliothèque nationale, 8⁰Li⁹9537, deposited 13 May 1966.

Fages, A., *De Campagne-les-Bains à Rennes-le-Château*, Bulletin de la Société d'Etudes scientifiques de l'Aude, vol. 20, pp. 128–33, Carcassonne, 1909.

Fanthorpe, Lionel and Patricia, *Rennes-le-Château: Its Mysteries and Secrets*, Bellevue Books, Ashford, 1991.

Fédié, Louis, *'Rhedae' La Cité des Chariots*, Association Terre de Rhedae, 1994.

Féral, Alain, *Deux Abbés Saunières à Rennes-le-Château*, Association Terre de Rhedae, No. 8, October 1994, p. 34.

Flem-Ath, R. and Wilson, Colin, *The Atlantis Blueprint*, Warner Books, 2001.

Fougère, Pierre, Saint-Maxent, Louis and de Koker, Gaston, *Le Serpent Rouge – Notes sur Saint-Germain-des-Pres et de Saint-Sulpice de Paris*, Pontoise, dated 17 January 1967. Bibliothèque nationale, 4⁰Lk⁷50490, deposited 20 March 1967.

Fourié, Jean, *Histoire de Rennes-le-Château antérieure à 1789*, Editions Bardou, Espéraza, 1984.

Guy, Henri, *Reproduction d'une Pierre Tombale Carolingienne Découverte à Rennes-le-Château*, Bulletin de la Société d'Etudes scientifiques de l'Aude, vol. 31, p. 197, Carcassonne, 1927.

Hisler, Anne-Léa, *Rois et Gouvernants de la France*, Paris, 1964. Bibliothèque nationale, 4⁰Lc³796.

Jarnac, Pierre (Ed.), *Les Archives de l'Abbé Saunière*, Collection 'Coleur Ochre', Saleilles, 1984.

Josephus, *The Jewish War*.

Lincoln, Henry, *The Holy Place*, Corgi Books, 1991.

——, *Key to the Sacred Pattern*, Windrush Press, 1997.

Lobineau, Henri, *Généalogie des Rois mérovingiens et origine des diverses familles françaises et étrangères de souche mérovingienne, d'après l'Abbé Pichon, le Docteur Hervé et les parchemins de l'Abbé Saunière de Rennes-le-Château (Aude)*, Geneva 1956. Bibliothèque nationale, Lm³4122 deposited in 1964.

——, *Dossiers secrets*, 1967. Publisher given as Philippe Toscan du Plantier, 17 quai de Montebello, Paris Ve. Bibliothèque nationale, 4⁰LM¹249, deposited 27 April 1967.

Marie, Franck, *Rennes-le-Château, Etude Critique*, S.R.E.S. Vérités Anciennes, 1978.

Markale, Jean, *Rennes-le-Château et l'enigme de l'or Maudit*, Pygmalion, Gérard Watelet, Paris, 1989.

Nicholson, Helen, *The Knights Templar, A New History*, Sutton Publishing, 2001.

Pernoud, Régine, *Blanche of Castile*, Collins, London, 1975.

Pfister, Christian, *Gaul under the Merovingian Kings*, Cambridge Medieval History, vol. 2, chapter IV, 1976.

Phipps, William E., *Was Jesus Married?*, Harper and Row, New York, 1970.

Picknett Lynn and Prince, Clive, *The Turin Shroud: In Whose Image?*, Bloomsbury, London, 1994.

——, *The Templar Revelation*, Corgi Edition, 1997.

Plantard, Pierre (Ed.), *Vaincre*, 21 September 1942. Bibliothèque nationale, 4⁰Lc²7335.

Plantard, Pierre, *Gisors et son secret*, Bibliothèque nationale, 4⁰L⁷k 56747, 1961.

Plantard, Pierre, *Deux Curés*, Preface to the Belfond Edition of Boudet's book, 1978.

Pliny, *Naturalis Historia*.

Rivière, Jacques, *Le Fabuleux Trésor de Rennes-le-Château*, Editions Bélisane, Cazilhac, 1995.

Sacaze, Julien, *Inscriptions Antiques des Pyrénées*, Edouard Privat, Toulouse, 1892.

Salamon, Albert, *La Fabuleuse Découverte du Curé aux Milliards*, La Dépêche du Midi, 12, 13, 14 January 1956.

Saul, John M. and Glaholm, Janice A., *Rennes-le-Château, A Bibliography*, Mercurius Press, London, 1985.

Stüblein, Eugène, *Description d'un Voyage aux Etablissements Thermaux de l'arrondissement de Limoux, avec une Carte Routière*, Limoux, 1877. Bibliothèque nationale, $8^0 Lk^5 267$.

Tisseyre, Elie, *Excursion à Rennes-le-Château*, Bulletin de la Société d'Etudes scientifiques de l'Aude, vol. 17, pp. 98–103, Carcassonne, 1906.

Vigouroux, F. *Dictionnaire de la Bible*, Letouzey et Ané, Paris 1895.

Wallace-Hadrill, J.M., *The Long-haired Kings*, London, 1962.

Watkins, Alfred, *The Old Straight Track*, Abacus Books, 1974.

White, Michael, *Isaac Newton, The Last Sorcerer*, Fourth Estate, 1997.

Wilson, A.N., *Jesus*, Sinclair-Stevenson, London, 1992.

Williams, Kit, *Masquerade*, Jonathan Cape, 1979.

Wood, David, *Genisis, the First Book of Revelations*, The Baton Press, Tunbridge Wells, 1985.

Index